A Danger to Himself or Others

A Danger to Himself or Others

A STORY OF CHALLENGING MEMORIES
AND ABSOLVING FAMILY SILENCE

Sarah Measwell

Epigraph Books
Rhinebeck, New York

A Danger to Himself or Others: A Story of Challenging Memories and Absolving Family Silence Copyright © 2025 by Sarah Measwell

All rights reserved. No part of this book may be used or reproduced in any manner without the consent of the author except for in critical articles or reviews. Contact the publisher for information.

Paperback ISBN 978-1-966293-02-6

Library of Congress Control Number 2025901608

"What God Might Say" (self-published, 1994) courtesy of Jim Standish
Richard Cory by Edwin Arlington Robinson published in the collection *The Children of the Night* (1897)
The Hippopotamus by Ogden Nash copyright 1938
Silently Seduced copyright 2011

Cover art by Jean Herzel
Book design by Colin Rolfe

Epigraph Books
22 East Market Street, Suite 304
Rhinebeck, New York 12572
(845) 876-4861
epigraphpublishing.com

Trudy's Prequel

While the events described here are broadly what I remember, many of the details are entirely fictional to me. While I am not happy about Sarah going public, I am enormously grateful to her for doing her work. She figured out a story that deserves to be shared. When I heard the story, it was like the lens at the optometrist's office snapping in place, and I could see clearly for the first time in my life.

I have no desire to lay out my private life for display to the public. Sarah and I have lived in the same small town for thirty-five years, so I ask our mutual acquaintances, if you must read this, to bear in mind that she is telling her story not mine.

What God Might Say
Jim Standish

I.
You're always asking why,
why are you here, why
am I. I'd tell you
if I knew. You can wonder
and wonder how this is this way
  and that
is that, but the real wonder is how
This and that can be
any way at all.

II.
There is no god: I'm just you
  talking to yourself.
There is no god: I am
  the One God.
There are two gods, which are
    the One God and the
      opposite God: I am each
        and both of the two gods.
There are three gods, which are
    the two opposite gods and
      their Resolution: I am each
        and all of the three gods.
There are four gods, which are
    the three gods, which are
      the three gods and their
        Completion: I am each
          and all of the four gods.
There are five gods, which are
    the complete four and the
      One Left Out: I am each
        and all of the five gods.
There are numberless gods:
  For every One
there is an Opposite:
  for every two
there is a Resolution:
  for every three
there is a Completion:
  for every four
there is One Left Out.
    You and I are each and all
of the numberless gods.

III.
Why did I make you? I think
there is something I need, and you
are to get it for me. I don't know
what it is; you won't know
when you've got it. Please, just
  gather up
everything you can
        and bring it all.

Prologue

Who's Trudy?

"Well, back to work," Trudy says, kissing Dad, pushing herself away from the passenger side window, straightening one elbow and then the other. As she turns and walks away, I watch her—the way she holds herself as if she were in constant pain. Why? I don't know who she is anymore. She looks straight ahead, and I feel trapped beyond her perception. My heart beats faster, bringing me back to the driver's seat. I haven't heard what Trudy was saying. Hadn't heard what I am saying either, lost in my own head, a place it would seem too small to get lost in.

It is the Fourth of July in the first year of a new century, and Dad and I are out eating hotdogs.

"Who was that?" Dad asks, taking a bite. He is watching carefully so that he won't drop any of his lunch in his lap, but some escapes anyway.

—

"What?" I'm not surprised, but I am not expecting it. He'd finally been diagnosed with Alzheimer's, though I had suspected it ever since he and Mom had traveled nearly across the entire country to attend my wedding to Guy.

"Who was that?" he repeats.

"Trudy," I say.

Trudy said that he'd once called her by our mother's name before he kissed her. But she'd corrected him, and he'd recognized the mistake. Or seemed to. He didn't always recognize Guy, but he had never spent any time with Guy and had only met him that once at the wedding. I continue swimming in recent memories.

After he swallows another bite of his hotdog, and still looking straight ahead as if he doesn't see me, he says,

"Who's Trudy?"

—

I was introduced to my sister Trudy on the back seat of a car. My mom's dad had bought this car new that same year, then traded it to Dad. I was only two and a half that summer, but I remember the trade. Do I really remember it? Or do I remember a story I'd heard?

"I'm afraid you're losing your shirt on this one, Gary," said Dad. "I've got the wool pulled over your eyes just this once." I didn't understand about the shirt and the wool, but I did get it that Dad was happy and getting something he wanted.

With the grin of an eagle, cigar stuck in the side of his mouth, Grandpa said, "You know what I think of these Chryslers." He meant, "You know how much I love my daughter." I got that too. Dad had always driven Fords. After the trade, he drove only Chryslers.

So Trudy came home from the hospital on the back seat. Dad opened the back door, then went around to the passenger door to help Mom out. Nearly three, the top of my head the seat was level with the seat. I climbed and pulled myself over the edge of the seat to find only a pile of blankets with one wisp of hair running out the top. What was under it? I didn't know, but it was going to stay with us, in fact was ours forever.

At first, I only understood her green eyes were like mine—her brown hair, wavy like mine but darker than my dirty blonde. We had the same name: Sister.

Now I am here living in the same town as Trudy. I had hit a rough spot in my forties—divorced, with a failing business, in a bit of debt. Trudy had invited me to come and live with her and her husband. I'm guessing that it wasn't all that easy for Trudy to share a home with a wayward sister, but

one thing was clear. Sitting on her front steps with a bottle of champagne, I found my sister and my feet.

—

I look over at Dad examining the last bite of hotdog, looking at it sideways as he turns it in his fingers, then speaks, "Who's Trudy?"

—

My daydream swiftly recedes. My brain stalls instead of shifting. I need a deep breath, but I don't take it. "Trudy's your daughter," I say at last. "The first-third one." I try his joke from when we were growing up. Dad had tired of our bickering about who was "first." My brother Chuck was the oldest, so Dad told me that I was the "first second one" and Trudy was "first third." It made me feel special enough, though not perfect—as I thought my brother was. But I knew it was no different to be the first second one than to be the second one. It was a math joke with words that didn't mean anything, told by an engineer.

"Oh." He shrugs, turning back to finish his hot dog.

—

The implications lie scattered on the floor of my imagination like a dropped pack of cards, the cards Dad used to dump at my feet when we played 52 Pickup. My hands burn as if they are juggling hot lead. My thoughts leap and spin in the air, falling—and I scoop them up and throw them higher, watching to see whether they will land in a pattern, any pattern.

I put my hotdog down on the seat between us and look at Dad. I find myself struggling for breath as a question asks itself while I am still in the moment before, taking in Dad's shrug.

"Do you know who *I* am?" I hear myself whisper hoarsely.

"Huhn uh," he answers right away and off-handedly, as if I have asked him whether he wants another hot dog. "Nope."

—

The sky is falling, and I duck my head and close my eyes, feeling nothing in my body and a little dizzy. Then my head tips back as if to take a drowning breath, my arms straighten and lock against the steering wheel. The day is clear. It's sunny, it's summertime with hot dogs. A day to celebrate freedom.

Then I push on. "I'm Sarah. The first-second one. Sarah Smile," I say, using his old nickname for me.

"Okay." he agrees to my latest suggestion. There is no recognition in the green eyes that used to look at me sometimes with pride or irritation. Everyone knows it will happen, but maybe it won't happen to me, you think, he knows me too well—like, yeah, maybe I will be the first one who doesn't die. Like the time I saw a moose and thought "horse." Then "No, it's too big to be a horse"; then "Oh, a moose!" And noticed that my body had left the vicinity before I had decided to go.

—

Then another question occurs to me. I look back at him. "Are you afraid to be out with me in the car?"

"No." There is no mischief in the way he keeps his eyes looking straight ahead. "But you're cute."

—

A friend of mine walks by, catching my eye. She nods, raised eyebrows tentative. I nod back, not quite able to bring myself to smile. She doesn't know what Dad meant to me—she'd met him only after we moved him here. She just keeps walking at the same pace in the same direction. I feel a little snubbed.

I looked at myself sitting there in the red jeep, seeing from the outside in some oddly objective way. My father just forgot who I was, and the strangest thing happened. My memories of who I am came into question too. There is something authenticating, even freeing, about not being recognized and not being judged by your own father—as well as something traumatic. I wanted to be his daughter. Was I? I didn't consider the question long. Yes.

That wasn't so bad, I thought, managing not to cry. Was it the first time he had forgotten me? Who could know? Not even he could know, in his Alzheimer's.

I had read other stories of daughters not recognized. It wasn't so bad. If I could handle this, I could handle anything coming at me. Because by that day in July the Big Trouble was well under way. I had already started to think that the whole family had Alzheimer's, not just Dad. We didn't recognize each other anymore. And there would be days when I didn't recognize myself.

Part I

If, upon completion of the hearing and consideration of the record, the court finds by clear and convincing evidence that the proposed patient: (1) is mentally ill; and (2) is, because of such condition, likely to injure himself or others, or is gravely disabled due to mental illness; the court shall order the proposed patient committed to the custody of the department director for an indeterminate period of time not to exceed one (1) year.

State code

Chapter One

MEMORIES

Sometimes I wonder why
I spend the lonely nights
Dreaming of a song
Hoagie Carmichael

I had moved out of Trudy's house by the time Mom called. A new world started to turn—in the fall of the very last year of the very last century. It was hot, too hot, and I was in the garden trying to revive some of the third-planting, cold crops that were burning up or bolting, especially the spinach. I thought that the sun and the air and the water, all the things my garden loves, can kill it when they go too far. I have lost vegetables and flowers to bad soil, bad water, bad weather. When there wasn't too much sun, there was too much rain. The wind that fertilized the corn had been known to take out some of the less sturdy stalks; one year we'd lost the whole crop, ironed flat against the ground.

But the garden surprised me with its resilience too. I planted carrots year after year and never got much, so that spring I had thrown the packet of seeds into one end of a garden box without any attention to how deep and what the spacing was. They thrived and I scrampled to thin them. Things don't necessarily (or even usually) grow where I want to put them. Maybe when I am not growing, I will need to move. That's what I've mostly done in the past.

The "cherry bush" had survived the gorging deer to produce cherries but would grow no taller than me, a child tree with the fruit of a healthy adult. When you cut things, they grow better. Nature makes no value judgements, unlike us. Or religion. Jesus got it right. He loved everything. (And he could perform miracles to make things come out right.) Evolution loves everything too, but does it with blinders on, and sometimes it turns out in your favor.

Summer was over, and I could let go and fall back. With a sigh and an unpromising bunch of spinach, I went inside and dilly-dallied about the dining room, straightening chairs around the table, rearranging candlesticks, and blowing dust off the sideboard in the twilit calm. The thick, silent air that stuffed the room put things out of focus, just as it muffled footsteps. Thoughts swam by like fish, looking at me with only one eye.

"Partly menopause," I said to myself, just as the phone rang in the old, recognizable, nonjangling way that phones did back then; everyone's phone rang in the same way and you didn't know who it was until you answered it. It was a greeting, not a demand to be heard like they ring now. I picked it up.

"Hi, Honey."

"Hi, Mom."

"Well, we're here!" she chirped, like the birds she loved to watch, but there was a note of danger in her song, a note that a daughter was sure to hear.

"Where?"—my voice unsteady. The fact that it was a Monday and that I didn't know where "here" was, made my hair stand on end. Mom had only ever phoned me long-distance once before on a weekday: Dad had had a heart attack and was under observation at the hospital. She had waited to call until the danger had passed. She wouldn't have told me at all, except that she knew Dad liked to see me, and that I would come. That's one thing I learned from my family: Don't communicate about stress. Wait until it's over and you have good news. If it's not good news, say as little as possible. Don't ask for help. Overcome it yourself.

"We went to the doctor, and she recommended we look at this place—it's called, uh, I can't remember the name, but it's very nice. Then Dad got sick, so we just decided to stay here. We're on our way in to dinner. Dad wants to say hi."

Sick? Going in to dinner? I still didn't know where they were. I hear the phone fumbled into Dad's hands.

"Hi!" Dad's voice was as cheer-ridden as Mom's.

"How's it going?"

"Fine. Well, 'bye."

"Wait! I love you!"

"I love you too."

Click.

Mom didn't call back and I didn't have the number. They still lived without a cell phone, and she had called me on my land-line. It was all she could do to manage the complicated phone system Dad had installed with autodialing and group talk, and to keep within the strictures of calling only after nine at night to take advantage of the lowest rates. And make it short! I had a cell only because we were building a house out of town that summer where there was no land-line. Easy to forget those disconnected times now.

We all had known something was wrong, ever since two summers before, when Trudy and I had gone back for their fiftieth anniversary party. Mom hadn't vacuumed in months. And for the past year she had been calling more often, telling us stories of Dad falling, of his anger and foul swearing. I'd never heard him swear at all—snafu was as close as he got to that, and when I asked him what it meant, he told me, "Situation Normal All Fouled Up." Maybe he used it when he was thinking something else. So I wasn't surprised. She didn't ask for help on that call, but of course I knew she needed it. It was obvious that Dad was dangerous to himself. Now he had become dangerous to Mom, too.

Trudy called a few hours later in a hurry. Mom had called her too. "I've got reservations to go back Tuesday. He wouldn't get out of the taxi when they got to the assisted living place. It took the director of the assisted living two hours to talk him into getting out of the car. He ended up in the hospital. I'll rent a car and come pick you up when you can get there."

"I'll be there by Thursday," I told her.

"Okay. 'Bye."

Though the smoke of fear and worry was choking me, I didn't try to keep on her on the phone. "Just the facts, Ma'am," was what she wanted to hear. It was troubling, though I appreciated that her missions were always competently completed and on time to boot.

We had shared a bedroom as children for nigh on a decade, but until we left home, I sometimes felt as though we weren't like other sisters. It was gratifying that she chose to follow me to the same university our grandfather had attended. And although we kept regular touch, we led our own separate lives. Then, ending up in Trudy's small town deepened our connection. She and her husband helped me build a little cabin, and supported me until I got a small computer business started. Sharing meals and movies and music gave me a more adult—and sisterly—relationship with a strong, funny, generous, and kind sister.

I shook my head trying to concentrate. Repeating the name of the place, Classic Knolls, an image surfaces of my large father crammed in the back seat of a taxi, parked under a carport in front of a blurry building at night, resisting the blandishments of a strange woman who wants him to leave my mother, sitting next to him. I picture my mother, much smaller than he, usually so bright and optimistic, trying not to look scared and forlorn, nevertheless relieved. Funny that he wouldn't listen to Mom. But maybe the stranger had to convince Mom too.

—

After the call, we moved fast. Trudy made arrangements to leave town quickly, while I visited the three places that described themselves as "assisted living" in the town we now called home. I picked up brochures and newsletters. I also visited nursing homes—with Alzheimer's Units. One place (with birdcage in foyer) had a website. I emailed information to our distant brother, Chuck. I brought with me a manila envelope containing a scrap heap of info, and letters—from my new husband's mother, two of my stepsons, and the pastor of the First Presbyterian Church—asking Mom to make the decision to give up her life, move thousands of miles, and live close to her daughters. Up in the air, I tried to reassure myself that everything would be all right, wondering if it would convince Mom to move out with us. I pondered the timing of the request on the plane, and decided it would be best to wait a few days until the right moment.

Trudy had agreed to pick me up at the smallish airport for the long drive to the assisted living. It was already dark out. We wandered the luggage claim anxiously looking for each other, though I had only one carry-on, and we were probably within a hundred feet of each other most of that time. Looking back, it seems perfectly possible that we were so apprehensive that we walked right past and didn't recognize each other. Finally, as Trudy drove, we pondered what was ahead for us, but I don't remember whether we came up with any kind of plan. Nothing was predictable.

Classic Knolls was a large brick building with pillars at the entrance rising to the top of the second story. A set of double, automatic doors opened in front of a reception desk on the left that was ensconced in dark, wood paneling and faced an oversized living room area on the right with faux fireplace and large screen TV. The color scheme "utilized" ivory along with two other muted, just-off-primary colors that were heathered and gentle. On expansive walls hung larger-then-life paintings of anonymous, romantic, straw-hatted children with puppies in bucolic settings circa anytime except now; or hunters and game birds (I knew no one whose parents hunted pheasants, quail, or anything of the sort). These works of art were interspersed with enormously oversized dried wreaths, some brown with tea roses and feathers, others made of straw—all deliberately balanced in color, shape, and size. No one sat on the overstuffed sofa in front of the large-screen TV that was showing clips of some football game. I went over and turned it off while Trudy headed for the front desk to explain who we were.

The building was designed and constructed recently and on purpose to serve as an "assisted living" structure. But something bothered me. I felt uncomfortable in my mother's room, which was too much like a motel room, since Mom had not had the time or power to move any furniture or decorate there yet. But more than that: the ceilings were too high, as high as the ceilings in a public school, which positioned the fluorescent lights way too high as well. During those shortest days before Christmas, I was thirsty for light. I kept opening the too-big, long, stiff drapes that fell most of the way from the ceiling down to wide Formica sills. Mom kept closing them.

One 40-watt lamp stood on the dresser, a suitcase lay open on the closet floor, and undersized white towels of scant thickness lay stacked over the racks in the bathroom in standard-issue packets: one bath, one hand, one face. An odor that I was barely aware of clung unevenly to my skin. It made me itch and wriggle my shoulders.

We've got to get out of this place, my head sang, and we did. Dad was removed to the Sunny Hills, the nursing home behind Classic Knolls. I took Mom home. Settled in Dad's red jeep, we felt too short for the vehicle Dad had brought for himself as a gift to Mom because it was big enough to hold his six-foot-two frame. As Trudy focused on driving through the brown twilight, Mom had difficulty remembering the name of the place.

"What was it called? Can't get it."

"Classic Knolls," I remembered for her. "It means 'as old as the hills.'" She giggled.

She and I had not only done crosswords together. She sang songs to me, and we sent each other punning postcards from our travels. So my mnemonic not only made sense, it was a careful but relaxed acknowledgment that her forgetfulness was acceptable, even enjoyable—the source of a puzzle and a joke.

We all sat silently for a moment. "What're we going to do now?" Mom wondered.

"How would you feel about moving out with us?" I asked, tentatively and softly, looking out the window away over the winter-brown fields of stubble.

"When can we leave?" Mom chortled with relief and a smile of hot love and pride. "Give me a slug of that lemonade." When she says "slug," it's as if she is a gangster or a cowboy tough, ready for action, getting down to business, nonsense-be-damned. She tilts her head, squinting, straightens her shoulders, holds out her demanding hand, takes charge. Uncompromising. Over lemonade, at any rate. She was still all there.

"We'll have to get packed and sell the house." I sat silently for a moment then said, "I'd like to have Dad's Jeep if nobody else wants it." Where did that come from? It was so not the right moment. I had trouble taking a breath.

"It's a little early for that," Trudy said flatly. I blushed and looked out the window again, not seeing anything. I told myself that it had just been bad timing and would be resolved later on. But I burned with dislike for myself. I was glad to be in the back seat and that Trudy had her eyes on the road. *Was that the beginning of the Big Trouble?* I think to myself now. Surely something we quickly forgot.

The move was decided then, with no further discussion.

—

Mom and I spent each of the following days going to visit Dad. The place was forty miles away, so we didn't stay long, or not long enough for me. The hallway was dark, linoleumed, but wide enough to navigate, even in a wheelchair. The rooms were dark too. Here it was not "sunny." He shared a room in a basement, and his roommate who had the window side kept the curtains drawn. My father was usually dazed or dozing in a wheelchair in front of the nurses' station. When he was awake, he pestered the nurses. He wanted to see what they were doing, look in their notebooks, help them. He was still there, doing what he liked best, poring over data—and he still knew who we were. Or I thought he did.

We ate meals with him occasionally in a room with closed window curtains, the overheated and humid cafeteria. The air was so close and oppressive that it took away everyone's appetite. Most often, Mom and I simply sat by until he was finished eating, then kissed him and left for a local eatery. Already on the second day the waiter knew what drinks to bring us and remembered what we had eaten before. He made no small talk, asked no questions, just wanted to do his part. We ate the same lunch there for twenty-seven days in a row, except once when it was closed. On Christmas day we went to a truck stop, Dad's favorite place.

Driving there and back, Mom seemed lost in thought. Dad was still a handsome man starting the second half of his seventies, standing over six feet tall with silvery white hair and green eyes, and charming, even with Alzheimer's. Though she always gave out that her legs were too heavy and her glasses too thick, Mom was beautiful, funny, and smarter than the average bear. They married, Dad freshly back from witnessing the A-bomb test at Bikini Island. He eagerly settled into a career with the premier US engineering firm, which lasted almost four decades. During that time, Mom bore him three healthy boomers; they bought comfortable houses commuting distance from his work; income increased every year; he was eligible for stock options retirement and health insurance as well. Part of the "greatest generation" but on a different scale they were part of the silent one. And glad to settle into their life's challenges: minor surgeries for themselves and the kids, diseases requiring short bed rest and a mother's touch. He built cabinets and laid linoleum, when he wasn't engrossed in stamp and coin collecting or photography. She sewed everything from pajamas to prom dresses, learned to type braille, water colored, shopped, taught us to swim. They both spent most of their time with us. After Trudy graduated from high school, Mom went to work as a school nurse and happily acquitted herself through a decade of service to the school district that had prepared her children for what was expected to be a bright future.

During the time Dad was treasurer of the church, he had us count the offering to see who could count the fastest. Accuracy had to be a hundred percent. He taught me that I could do anything and be anything I wanted. He brought home plenty of money for everyone and saved enough to leave hefty sums to each of us when he died. "Sell everything and divide it in thirds," said his will. We all wore good clothes; ate good food; went to dentists, doctors, entertainment (not to go overboard or anything). A favorite memory was about one of the few times he spanked one of us. It was a ritual spanking, more shame than pain, and had only happened once or twice. He looked up at me standing and watching. I said, "Aren't you going to say, 'and that goes for you, too'?" That was the last of the spanking.

Later on, I found out that Chuck and Trudy had left our childhood far behind. For me, taking care of them gave me the chance to return to it.

—

Trudy did not accompany us very often. She entwined herself in a telephone cord, and did a thorough job of researching every possible airline route and fare from here to there. I listened to her mix and match, day after day, her voice sounding too responsible, weighted as she was with the terror of a parent's death. At first, I bristled. Why was my sister spending six hours a day talking to everybody and *their* sister? Why not just decide, and come along to visit Dad and help with the packing? But now I realize she was doing the thing I was worst at and didn't want to do. I envied her the safety and her competence on the phone, scheduling and calculating, choosing times and planning plane changes and wheelchairs. I sensed vaguely that she was keeping busy, focusing herself in one area and painstakingly building a fence along its border so as not to be aware of the unlighted and unlimited space beyond the fence. I sensed unclarity and some fear, but later I questioned whether this unclarity and fear was my own. How could I know what she was thinking? She was just on a mission. I see now how judgmental I was.

Our also over-competent brother phoned, not often enough for me, but enough to make me believe he cared. One night the sister and I were on princess phone extensions in separate bedrooms, each at the far end of the long house, when Chuck revealed that he wasn't convinced that Dad had deteriorated so far that he could never come home.

We both told him. "It's clear. He can't even manage the assisted living. Mom is worn out and wants to sell *everything* (not just the house) and move. She needs someone to cook and clean for *her*."

But the brother wouldn't hear it. I leaned back on the pillow at the head of the guest room bed, and tried to listen. It was too hard to follow what he was saying when his premise was that our parents needed no help. Finally, exhausted by the effort to keep a reasonable tone, a great sob rose out of me, and a husky voice said angrily into the phone, "Well, if you want to make the determination yourself, get on a plane and come. You can't sit so far away, taking no part in the emergency, and tell us what to do. Your opinion just doesn't count if you're not here."

I don't know how my brother responded, or maybe he didn't respond at all. Blind anger is bad enough, but mine is also deaf and numb. I don't remember that it had ever happened between us up until then. It may have been genetic: Mom fell asleep on a couple of occasions when we were disagreeing and things warmed up, especially when Dad was involved in the disagreeing. And Mom's brother had clashed big-time with Grandpa, who disowned him. It was something Mom never got over, trying to reconcile the two before Grandpa's death. But neither one of them would relent.

We persuaded Chuck to call an RN, an old friend of Mom's from her nursing-school days, for her opinion. We all trusted her. He called, and later she told us that it took her two hours to convince him that Dad would never return home. Well, I supposed, two hours is not that long a time. My anger would last well beyond that.

The minute we were off the phone, Trudy came striding the length of the house and stopped abruptly, looking down at me. "I'm glad you said what you did," she announced, "But I wish you could keep your emotions out of it." I picked up an image of clenched fists. And she left.

I thought, *how could I keep my emotions out of that? And, besides, is this a choice for me?* These turned out to be very good questions, especially the one about choice. At the time, they slipped away from me as more urgent business lay dead ahead.

—

Mom was as uninvolved in moving decisions as she had been before and accepted that whatever we decided was the thing to do, no questions asked. She wasn't one to process much; she just had her own answers, which she told me gently and left me to ponder. When, once before, I had called home once to talk to her about divorcing my first husband, she didn't help much. "Oh, honey, I'm so sorry to hear that." She kept any judgment out of her voice, though she had made clear to me this was not something she would ever, ever choose for herself. She wasn't apologizing to me, not asking for forgiveness, she was reporting on her compassion. And she didn't ask for any details, as if what she didn't understand on the surface of things would not be clarified by knowing more. When I went for a visit after the divorce, she said only "I'm glad to have my Sarah back. You are yourself again." Later on, when I brought another man I was interested in home to meet her, her question had startled me, even though it was delivered in a nonjudgmental tone. "What is it like to have sex with more than one man? You'd have to compare them. It must be awful." She only looked at how things hurt her children, and seemed helpless to pass judgment on what they, or other people, did. I hadn't actually thought of comparing my partners until she said that. I shrugged, and said nothing, thinking it would be *really* awful to have had sex with only one person in your whole life!

So I wasn't surprised when she didn't want to make the decisions about moving or not moving. She did not want to take sides in an argument between her three children. So the morning after Chuck's phone call, I woke up to find a note on the counterpane, struck by what she said as completely Mom:

> My daughter, my friend,
> Trust in the Lord with all thine heart and lean not unto thine own understanding. In all thy ways acknowledge him and he shall direct thy paths.

Mom's religion came to her not so much from institutions so much as naturally. I found the same proclivity in my own heart, even when I did not find it in the Bible.

—

Once I was reading the Bible and I was worried. I'd just gotten into trouble in English class for quoting Mark Twain's criticism making fun of James Fenimore Cooper. I was worried about whether God has a sense of humor, and when I told Mom, she quoted Proverbs 26:4–5: "Do not answer a fool according to his folly, or you will be like him yourself. Answer a fool according to his folly, or he will be wise in his own eyes." She laughed. "Of course! God made us! Where else do you think we got laughter from?"

She did take strong positions sometimes too. While on the school board she promoted building a round school with the library and all the bathrooms in the center, immediately accessible to all the classrooms. One man in the audience stood up and took a rectangular piece of paper out and cut a circle out of it. "It's too expensive—look how much space we lose." She held out her hand for the circle and asked for the scissors and cut a rectangle out of it and handed it back. Later in the year, she invited the man to run for school board and supported his campaign, knowing that he would not oppose decisions he helped to make.

One of my favorite stories was about Mom's mother. They were traveling along with Mom's brother, on a train through Canada.

"Where was Grandpa?" I wanted to know.

"He wasn't with us." Later I found out that Grandpa had been in Oregon where he knew a woman who needed some help that summer. "Mom wanted to take a vacation and travel by train. At one stop your Uncle Ted was off down the platform somewhere, we couldn't see him. The conductor yelled, 'All aboard!' and Mom sent me to find him, but I couldn't.

"'Final call, all aboard!' yelled the conductor.

"My mother put one foot up on the high boarding step. He reached down to give her a hand up, but she shook her head. 'Not leaving without my son.'

"The conductor was startled, and pulled back his hand. 'But ma'am. We've got to keep our schedule. It's time.'

"'Well, then, keep your schedule, but you will knock me off my feet first. I'm not leaving without my son.'

"So the conductor himself got down off the train and went to find Teddy, pulling him back by his ear. When we were back on the train, I asked her,

'What if the train left on time without me?' She said 'You've got a mouth on you, don't you?' Her eyes flashed as she said it. And that was the answer to that question which never had to be answered again. I never forgot it."

Many times during my life when I saw Mom's flashing eyes, I was nervous about opening my own mouth.

—

Mom relaxed a little more each day as we made calls, packed, laughed. And she whistled an old tune:

> When the red, red, robin comes bob, bob, bobbin' along, along,
> There'll be no more sobbin', when he starts throbbin' his old sweet song!
> I'm just a kid again, doin' what I did again singing a song,
> When the red, red, robin comes bob, bob, bobbin' along.

In that moment, I felt like Mom. Brave and happy. I was like her, and had followed her footsteps. She went to two schools and earned a masters, I went to two schools and earned a PhD. She supported me, encouraged me, took care of me—probably in ways I didn't even know.

But there were other ways I failed myself. I married unhappily, divorced, lived alone until I was forty-three. Left the next guy, a hermit, at forty-seven and married into a step-family at forty-nine. Mom was there for me all through everything, cheering me on. Only once, when I was living with the hermit, she sent me the poem *Richard Cory* that ends:

> And he was rich—yes, richer than a king—
> And admirably schooled in every grace:
> In fine, we thought that he was everything
> To make us wish that we were in his place.
>
> So on we worked, and waited for the light,

And went without the meat, and cursed the bread;
And Richard Cory, one calm summer night,
Went home and put a bullet through his head.

What was that? A statement that I was doing the right thing? A warning about what I was doing? Of the danger of wanting too much or too little? I couldn't tell.

At that moment packing, I wanted to be her—falling in love with a soldier during WWII; sailing, fencing, learning to sew—with a great love of reading, travel, and adventure but safe: family, health, laughing, unafraid. She could remember her songs but was starting to lose vocabulary, although able to beat that danger with crossword puzzle-type clues. "The thing Dad rolls around on," said Mom, not letting a small thing like a word just out of reach of her tongue stand in the way of her mouth.

"Wheelchair," said I, and we moved on in the conversation.

Mom left her knitted gloves behind her everywhere we went, finally losing them for good. "You lost your mittens, you naughty kittens," I sang, and Mom finished the ditty for me, "And they began to cry." We both laughed and went out to buy a new pair.

She cried only a few times—once when we were talking about mundane facts surrounding selling the house. Another time, we were sitting at the counter in the kitchen where we ate breakfast—a narrow, red Formica shelf that ran under the window facing west, away from the rising sun. She sat with one elbow on the counter, her hand holding her coffee cup. She didn't exactly slump in her chair, but for a woman who seemed to stand up straight effortlessly most of the time like the nurse that she was—to me, she looked like she was slumping.

I suddenly wanted to comfort her, and putting my cup aside, said softly, "It'll be all right, Mom." In an instant, she aged quicker than the picture of Dorian Gray; her face drooped and her eyes, normally small sparkling stars, dulled. I saw in her face all the pain she had suffered over the years of her marriage to Dad, and that losing him now would be a final straw. What secrets moldered in the muscles of her cheeks and chin, her real self so tired and wrinkled? She had put a good face on her life—and helped me to do it too. A brief lapse before her face came back to the fore, the skin filling out those momentary wrinkles, the eyes brightening again. And I got the smile I was after too. She was back for the morning.

—

After a long day of washing and packing, everything suddenly smelled to me like fabric softener, made me itch. Mom was already in her matching, pastel blue, cotton nightgown and duster, sitting in bed with a book in her lap. If Dad were here, the TV at the foot of the bed would have been on, but Mom, left to her own devices, had always been a reader.

Thinking she might miss Dad sleeping next to her after practically every night for more than fifty years, I asked her if she wanted me to sleep with her. She said yes.

I quickly showered remembering all the stories she had read to me before bed. So on my way back, I pulled one off the bookshelf still in my room. It was the one about the pushme-pullus: an animal with no tail but a head on each end. I flopped down next to her and sneezed—and she started to cry!

As I closed the book and dropped it beside the bed, she asked me to tell her again one of the stories I had made up for her—the one about the little girl. She snuggled down on her side of the bed, and I puffed up the pillows on my side and sat up straight, looking into my past, and narrated the scenes as if I were seeing them on the cold TV at my feet.

> Guy and I had spent a long, slow afternoon pulling the hydraulic pump off the bulldozer. Henry, our neighbor, had invited us to dinner; his son and daughter-in-law and their two children were visiting. We got to Henry's and peeled off our overalls. We were greasy-grimy, dirty hands and faces looking out of long underwear and bathrobes. Henry showed me to the bath. Just as I finishing, I heard small footsteps coming up the stairs and down

the hall. "Little girl? Little girl?" the four-year-old lilted. "Will you play with me, little girl?"

Mom giggled, turned over and went right to sleep. I looked over at her, now just a little girl I had played with all day long. The next morning, she was next to the bed singing, "Lazy Mary will you get up, will you get up, will you get up..." followed by, "can't you hear me callin' Caroline..." just as she had always done, when I was late getting up for school.

There had been lots of tunes she sang or whistled to tell us how she felt or to make a point. I asked her to sing them now as we packed her doll collection. When she was happy, it was:

When I asked her to sing my very favorite, she sat down on the edge of the bed and began,

> We went to the Animal Fair
> The birds and the beasts were there
> The old baboon by the light if the moon
> Was combing his auburn hair.
> The monkey he got drunk
> And sat on the elephant's trunk.
> The elephant sneezed
> Went down on his knees
> And what became of the monk, the monk?

Unlike her usual songs, this one scared me. Did the ugly baboon think he was beautiful? Why was he combing his hair at night? Where did the monkey get the alcohol? And what did become of him? I loved the tune and the rhythm that lumbered like the elephant when it wasn't sneezing, and enjoyed a shudder when she sang it.

—

"Little girl?" I called to Mom. I had a pot of vegetable soup roiling and bubbling on the stove. I had left her in the guest bedroom, packing up her massive doll collection. We had been carefully wrapping each one individually all morning while telling each other its story: where it was bought or who gave it to us, what its life was like in a different time or place. The bedroom was hung with posters and photographs of the many places Mom and Dad had traveled in five continents.

"Will you play with me, little girl?" she lilted now.

I walked into the room and immediately wanted to tell her how much she meant to me, how I loved her, what a wonderful mother and friend she had been. Was.

The moving men had put a pile of off-white packing paper on the bed. I picked up a sheet in one hand and a Barbie doll dressed at Queen Elizabeth I in the other, and turned to Mom. "Look, Mom, remember?" I said holding it up. She smiled over her shoulder. "Yes," she said in a way you could not doubt. "How old were you when we did that?"

—

A sophomore in high school, so maybe sixteen. The assignment from the history teacher, whom I had wrangled with before, was to make an art project based on something we had learned in his class. Most everyone (or was it just the boys?) was drawing, or building something out of clay or sticks. Dioramas. Boring! I tried to draw but didn't know how—and that made me irritable. When I got home, I told Mom about it.

"I just don't think it's fun!" I groused.

"I have an idea," she said eagerly. Didn't you tell me that story about Elizabeth the Queen from this class? Let's dress a doll as she would've been dressed." We found and undressed a Barbie doll quickly enough, and then started to plan the costume, but she stopped me. "Let's go to the library and find out what she really wore."

The trip was not just to the local library. Our local library was too small—only one room—to have books on Elizabeth, so she took me to the bigger one at the county seat. I had never been there before and was a little overwhelmed, but she knew how to navigate and we found a book and were out of there before I had time to get lost, and on our way to the sewing store, where we bought pieces of velvet and silk, and ribbons and beads resembling pearls. A piece of rabbit fur that we painted with little black tails as if it were ermine. I was fascinated to read in the book from the library that Elizabeth had dressed as a peasant sometimes and had gone out to visit her subjects to see how they were living and what they needed. So I learned how the peasants dressed too. And that Elizabeth never married, and had had small pox and a whole other kind of life that filled my imagination.

When I turned in the doll that Monday morning, the teacher would not accept it. He told me to write an essay to accompany it that explained where the fabric came from and what we could learn from that. Instead, I compared her costume to what the peasants wore, and mentioned that I learned the word "farthingale" and got an A for that. (I also had made a farthingale.) The boy who drew a car (a car?) didn't have to write anything.

—

I looked down at Elizabeth, wrapped her up in the white paper, and put her into the moving barrel, glad to have Mom and the queen coming home with me.

We started out toward the kitchen to eat our supper, and she started to sing an old popular song:

> Through all kinds of trouble
> What if the sky should fall?
> Just as long as we're together
> It doesn't matter at all.
> Though we've all had our troubles and parted,
> We'll be the same as we started,
> Just travelin' along, singin' a song
> Side-by-side.

She had stopped feeling that the sky was falling. She was telling me to do the same, and as long as we were still at home, I could.

"And if our room is on the second floor of this place," Mom said out of the blue, "Is there a place to eat?" I got out the building schematic and showed her again the hall, the elevator, the dining room.

We were packing up two entire lives (!), and I felt compelled to go through everything. Trudy wasn't that interested in the packing and spent her time taking care of the logistics. It's a good thing one of us was so practical.

There were old moving boxes I had left there when I moved out to Trudy's. Mom talked me into not looking in most of them before we gave them away. But I found some things that I wanted to take with me anyway—like my collection of small boxes. I picked up a jewelry box my dad had bought for me when I was quite little. When I opened it a ballerina popped up and the music box inside played Stardust. It made me think of the garbly lyrics I made up to sing along which had nothing to do with the real words. They started "Mrs. Fletcher's dot a detcher." Don't ask.

We all had our own collections of things: Dad had stamps and coins, Chuck had a hundred model airplanes hanging from his bedroom ceiling, Trudy had dozens of china horses. I tried to collect only one thing but failed time after time. Seduced by the beauty of almost everything I saw, I wanted to own more of it.

I didn't see any of the collected things of my siblings while packing, but there were even some of my clothes from the sixties still hanging in the guest room closet. For a while I held on to an old shirt that has not worn out for forty years, but I threw it away later. I kept lots of things from forty years ago, and I also kept too much that belonged to Mom and Dad. Bolo ties, which I gave away. Belts. Mom's furniture, lots of it: a sofa, a desk with inlaid ivory. (Dad hated this piece in particular; he hated the old stuff and was always buying new furniture—plastic when he could get it. "But it's so easy to clean and doesn't break," he would say.)

"What should we bring?" I asked myself. "What the hey," I decided and put the boxes into the mix. "I'll go through it later. Might miss something from my past, or forget it unless I keep a clue." We gave all the radios but one in Dad's collection to the auction but kept all of his notebooks and all the books, photos, and old letters from both of them. What was I thinking? Where was Trudy—to tell me not to do this? Hundreds of slides from their trips around the world would sit in my garage for another twenty years. I couldn't let go of anything.

Especially the papers. I had been interested in family history, making a photographic family tree in my twenties, collecting photos, interviewing family members, thinking about my family almost every day of my life. I felt comfortable in that past, and I wanted to understand their personal lives. Trudy seemed to have no interest, and Chuck not so much in their personal lives as how they reflected their historical times—from a distance with a larger, objective view. When he had children, he didn't promote the idea of a family history among the three, even when his daughter was assigned to do a family history for a high-school class. She investigated only her mother Julie's side of the family, never asking a thing of me. I can't remember how I knew that, but it's a memory as clear as any. Maybe I read my brother's mind.

—

When we visited Dad, he seemed to read Mom's mind. Once, when for days we couldn't get to the bank in time to transfer money, we found him talking about putting a check in the bank. "It's simple!" he told us.

Dad apologized to Mom for sleeping with two women in his bed at Sunny Hills. "I'm sorry."

"That's all right," she said putting a hand on his shoulder.

"But I shouldn't have done it." He looked confused, as if he'd forgotten what we are talking about.

She turned to me, "I know he wants to, but he never does it, so that's okay. They're all like that."

How come you never told me that when I needed to know? Whoever had this idea that there is reality and we talk about it was nuts, at least as far as emotions are concerned. They are totally created by our talking.

At home our conversation roiled and bubbled like vegetable soup. "Little girl?" we called out to each other and giggled. "Little girl?"

I found a charge for a dirty movie on the satellite dish bill. Mom told me, "He wanted me to watch one with him. Is he crazy?"

I was shocked. "It's better than sports," I dodged her question.

"He'd be so proud to hear you say that. You're your father's daughter. I told him I could get to like sports if he would let me watch 'em. He wouldn't." They were both State U. grads, but Dad would get angry when the neighbors talked about sports. He was not a fan and did not even come to see my brother play on high-school teams. That night I dreamt of a sports coach abusing his team.

Dad made fun of sports, giving Chuck little encouragement. And though I do remember going to the little league games and hanging under the shade of other peoples' backsides, there is no Dad there, nor at any of the high-school games, where my brother sat at the end of basketball and baseball benches—an enthusiastic supporter of his team, prevented from contributing not much more than his excited cheers. Somebody must've taken us to the little-league games; it must've been Mom.

Mom told me many times how much he loved us, how he held us in one large hand to bathe us. I heard Trudy say to me in an old, old conversation we must have had in our thirties, "He didn't like children."

He was a funny kind of Dad. I have no memory of him reading a newspaper. We subscribed to one, but it was my brother who sat in a chair leaning over the paper laid out on the living room floor, elbows on his knees, fingers in his ears, reading from front to back, the whole thing, saving the sports and the comics for last. He taught me to read the comics, but I didn't get any farther than that, being my father's daughter. Dad didn't trust the newspaper, as he didn't trust anything that he hadn't observed himself and written down in the voluminous records he kept in carefully labeled notebooks. After all, he was a reliability engineer, and he married a reliable nurse and mother. He got an award for working on an antiballistic missile system.

Dad wasn't racist or paternalistic, or at least not more than the average bear. He paid for a young Black man who worked in the mail room at his company to go to a college engineering program—and paid for both my sister and me to go to expensive schools. I suppose he must've succumbed somewhat to institutionalized attitudes toward women and Blacks, as too many do, but it wasn't apparent at home with the family. I was surprised when at the end of his life Dad finally found a home for the news with Rush Limbaugh.

As far as I know, Dad never drank a sip of alcohol, at least after he married Mom. He told a story about waiting for a bus in the middle of the night when he was on leave from the army during World War II. It was New Year's Eve, and he had been out with his high-school friends while he was on leave, and was drunk, standing at a bus stop below a second-floor apartment with a record-player in an open window. The 45-rpm arm of the contraption was in a position where, when the record was finished, it lifted itself and went back to the beginning and played over again. Over and over. And over. For who knows how long. It played Bing Crosby's *White Christmas*, a song banned in my house when I was growing up. And alcohol wasn't exactly banned. We just never discussed it. Mom had a story about drinking champagne once at a wedding and taught us that drinking was not a pleasant experience. That didn't stop me from drinking too much into my seventies.

—

By the time I came out of my reverie, Mom and I had finished with the bedroom and we started on the office. She had found an uncashed check in Dad's filing cabinets, and we both started to look carefully for more. I found the checks he wrote to pay the mortgage on the house where we grew up. He told me a story several times about how a banker tried to get him to refinance at a higher rate of interest when the interest rates started to rise. Back then, mortgages didn't have variable rates. He was proud of laughing at the banker: "Why would I do that?" It gave me the idea that many people, especially bankers, couldn't be trusted.

We found all the checks, slides, certificates, photos, documentation of their entire lives. We threw them out, it didn't matter to her now, and Mom didn't seem to want them. I took almost all of it out of the trash surreptitiously, thinking that they will be good to have when I have time for the family tree.

I noticed one unlabeled notebook, not his characteristic practice. It was a notebook where he tracked his health. I had kept notes about my health for years, following unknowingly in his footsteps. Though my notebooks are all unlabeled, I still feel OCD-compelled to take down my weight, each exercise I do; I have every mammogram report and blood test for a few decades past. He was an engineer—he needed to observe, he needed to write things down to see them for what they were, he needed more data and time to think. I also followed in his footsteps by not looking back at the records I kept.

Once, when I was in sixth grade, my teacher said he'd pay five dollars to anyone who could find a triangle that had interior angles of more than 180 degrees. I took the problem home to Dad, and he drew a triangle on the pink ball I liked to bounce against the front porch wall. It had 90-degree angles at every apex, so 270 degrees. I proudly showed the triangle to the class the next day, but the teacher said it didn't fit the rule, because triangles had to be in a plane.

"You didn't tell us that rule," I challenged. "You changed the rules." The class laughed and he had to agree—but he didn't give me the five dollars.

No doctor ever looked at Dad's notebooks, just as no doctor ever looked at mine. I stood there gawking at the columns and rows of numbers on the pages, feeling as if I had invaded his privacy, judging him, feeling sorry for him, missing that faith in him that I missed in myself, that the truth would set us free.

I recognized another notebook I held in my hand as the one where he had tracked the exercises he did after his back surgery the year before. He had shown it to me proudly at the time: every box in every spreadsheet cell had a check in it. But ... when I looked at the dates, I found that he had deleted the columns for the days when he hadn't exercised. I challenged him.

"Well, didn't you do your exercises on these days?! That's bad."

His chin went up, and he stuck out his bottom lip, overplaying the part. "It's only a record of what I did," he pouted. "Not of what I didn't do."

"They are *both* important. When you leave out anything you leave out important information."

"I can tell what I left out."

"Well, I can't. And I'm the one making you do this!" I grinned.

He grinned too. He was irresistible.

Still, I still asked myself how had my mother lived with this man? How lucky was I not to have to?

—

Chuck called again to discuss more mundane details. I asked him what sorts of things he wanted me to pack up for him, what to sell. "Well, I assume you'll bring the piece of the deck of the Saratoga."

"What's that?" I didn't know what it looked like, didn't remember ever having seen it or heard of it before.

"He was on the Saratoga at the end of the war. It was an aircraft carrier, and the deck was made of teak: a hard surface for the planes to land on. When they dismantled it, they cut the deck up and gave the pieces away for souvenirs."

I found it immediately, right on the first shelf above his desk. He had never talked about it to me. I had an appetite now to learn about this new past, to learn a lot more about how I grew up. It made me feel special. But it also caught my attention that my memory had big gaps in it. Things of critical importance had happened that I did not know about. So, as we started to take charge of Mom and Dad's situation, I decided to keep notes. To learn as much as I could about them, and later, about what was happening in my life. To find out more about who I was.

So a lot of this memoir is based on notes I took at the time of the Big Trouble and later. More of it is based on memory alone. And when it came time for me to write a coherent story, to put down what actually happened, I was blinded. My notes sometimes corroborated each other and sometimes did not, often enough outright contradicting my memories or even other notes.

Sometimes I didn't even *witness* what happened before my eyes or it didn't make it into my memory, or got changed there. The process was much more fraught than I ever imagined, as you will see with your own eyes.

Chapter Two — ALZHAMMERED

A dysfunctional family is a family in which conflict, misbehavior, and often child neglect or abuse on the part of individual parents occur continuously and regularly, leading other members to accommodate such actions. Children sometimes grow up in such families with the understanding that such a situation is normal.
Wikipedia

Snafus, which in ordinary time were only irritating, seemed life-threatening when we moved Mom and Dad. Trudy was so fried already at the first airport, that she offered the first-class travelers hundreds of dollars to buy their seats, so that we wouldn't have to squeeze into rows in second class. But the passengers didn't even raise their heads to look at us, almost psychotic in the lack of response. When they ignored her, I was outraged but said nothing. It didn't always work, what Grandma had said, using your mouth to tell people what you need. But when I asked to have the wheelchair returned by the taxi driver, we left the gel cushion by accident. Later it was shipped back to us. We never lost anything that belonged to Dad through all the moves and changes and strangers. This meant a lot to me.

During the change at the second airport, Dad made his trip to the bathroom on the ground with my stepson and Trudy's boyfriend doing the honors. I wondered whether Dad knew where he was when he found himself alone with strangers invading his personal space in that airport bathroom. By the time they got back, we had bought ice cream cones for everyone, and it was my turn to pee.

"Hey, Dad," hold this for me—will you?" I said holding out my cone.

"Sure."

Even though I was quick, both cones were gone when I got back, and Dad seemed to hide his eyes from me when I returned. Or maybe he just forgot or didn't even know he'd had two cones. But it wasn't out of character for him either.

Mom, too, stayed in character for the entire trip, alternately whistling and humming "Leaving on a jet plane, don't know when I'll be back again," under her breath.

We'd decided to carry Dad's coin collection in several gym bags; at the check-in counter where they still held the plane for us, the officials would not let us carry on the bags that held the coins, so we sent them off tra-lee tra-la unlocked into baggage, thinking we were sure to lose thousands of dollars. Nevertheless, I forgot to worry about the coins when we were all on the plane. Instead, I settled back and let go for the first time in six weeks and thought about how much we had gone through to get to this point. Our difficulties were starting to resolve themselves: We had worked together around our disagreements and were finally off. When the coins came through untouched, I told myself the worst was over.

—

It was raining, and of course dark, dark, dark in deep winter. Guy was there to pick up his stepson and wanted me to go with them. I acquiesced, not able to argue, as tired as I was. Nobody rode with Dad in the wheelchair ambulance sent by the WholeCare nursing home for a ride where he couldn't see where he was going for over an hour. He must've been at the least, confused—or at most, terrified.

Trudy took Mom safely to her room at the assisted living across the parking lot from the nursing home, where she could look out and see Dad's wing, with its sign that blared out a blue *Alzheimer's Unit* to the uninterested ski mountain. Only later did I feel a guilty stab. How could we have left Dad alone in the ambulance? Mom alone that night? I should have stayed with her. Both of them were physically safe, sure, but I'm also sure they were scared and felt abandoned.

The very first entry in the nursing notes says Dad had tried to hit one of CNAs when he was admitted. So right off the bat they treated him as a concept, "the dangerous patient."

Later, a friend of mine who had nursed in Alzheimer's units described the procedures for new patients. Dad was most likely brought in and put in a gown. It was way after dark, and there probably were only a couple of CNAs on the swing shift. The other patients were already in bed. Most on the unit were very ill, physically and mentally. The nurses on duty probably took away everything he had: clothes, shoes, his glasses, and his wedding ring—the only piece of jewelry I ever saw him wear (excepting his watch or a bolo tie), and which he never took off. Everything had to be listed on an inventory list. I have to give them this. His possessions were watched with the eyes of Americans. They never lost a single thing, except one of his teeth, which fell out or got swallowed when they were not looking.

He lay in a gown while they looked in his mouth and ears and in his crotch. If he had been a woman, they would have looked under his breasts. They categorized his level of mental alertness: comatose, semi-comatose, stuporous, combative, sleepy.

By this time, he was combative. Who wouldn't be? When he resisted being put to bed, they forced him. He took a swing at one of the aides and half-way connected. They didn't take into account that he had started the long journey at 5 a.m. and finished it at 10 p.m., with a Texas catheter and two ice cream cones.

I'm not sure exactly what happened. I could go back and look these details up in his nursing notes. They are all sitting right behind me on a shelf. I don't want to. I don't want to know. I didn't want to know that night either. Guy pressured me to stop and visit his son's family on our way home from the airport. We had a fight.

Back at the office, boxes on forms were being checked and filled. How many visitors? How often? Physical therapy? Meals? Baths? Time is a factor. Food can't stay out forever. It must be eaten, according to regulations, before it has to be thrown out. There are butts to be wiped. Order must be kept.

"Between time x and time y certain things have to happen," my nurse-friend explained. "There's a schedule you have to stick to." She also reminded me, "It's a hard job. There is no respect. Shit detail, literally and figuratively."

—

Dad was in a wheelchair when he arrived, so all they had to do was step back. It was the "swing-shift" after all! I was never clear exactly what "a danger to himself or others" meant for my dad. I knew he couldn't take care of himself, but he didn't seem dangerous to others. We moved him because my mother was in danger from some of his outbursts, but not really physically that I ever knew about. She never said he hit her, but once she said he swore at her at a gas station, in public, something so completely out of character that it must have been a symptom of Alzheimer's. She was embarrassed but scared enough to ask the gas station attendant for help. She was crying when she told me; I had not often seen her cry. She looked uncomfortably vulnerable to me, but he didn't hurt her. When I was at home with Guy that night, I took a verbal swing at him. Who wouldn't have?

The morning after Dad arrived, he had an appointment with a local doctor. Trudy was a friend of the doctor's wife, and he had accepted both of our parents as patients, even though his roster was full and there was a waiting list. Hurray for small towns, and sisters with connections. A doctor who was our friend came right to the Alz Unit, where all his patients were assembled—warm, dry, and well-fed. Whether the cost was charged to anyone, or how much was charged, I did not know. I left that to Trudy.

I burst into tears, happy at the thought that the hardest parts were over. We could handle this now that they were close by and safe. I was so happy!

And mistaken. Maybe the hardest parts were over for Dad, but not for the rest of the family. We had not been diagnosed with anything yet, and never would be. Right under the doctors' noses, and they never suspected a thing.

—

A normal day in an Alzheimer's unit is not like one in a regular unit, except that it has the same speckle-flecked linoleum that paves the rest of the building, the same food prepared the same way, and the same housekeeping and maintenance staff. It is a clean, well-lighted place, where no one is ever left alone, and they are locked in tight.

The patients require considerably more attention than inhabitants of the regular unit do: they cry, they fall, they aren't able to tell anyone when they have to pee, and those who can are usually unable to do more than make a face when it is too late. There are wanderers who peek in and out of all the rooms, lifting and moving things that must be found and returned to their rightful place. Sometimes it feels like Halloween.

The unit was bedlam crying out for dictatorship, but there were some who sat, calmly fascinated by the small things, like the lady who used to lean forward in her chair for hours, trying to pick up the speckles in the tiled floor. Was she happy to be cleaning up? Or frustrated by the dirt that fell back to the floor? A CNA told her to stop, explaining that she was mistaking the speckles for dirt.

"The floor isn't dirty, see?" the nurse said, sliding her rubber sole over the floor. The lady looked curiously at her fingers, as if to say, "what's she talking about?" then shrugged and bent to try again.

Visitors appeared from time-to-time, beelining toward their family member who has forgotten their name but often still recognized them. Unlike in the "regular" ward, most visitors did not engage with patients who were not their own family. Visitors looked at each other with eyes bereft, not even searching for comfort—just the acknowledgment that "all our families are in the same boat, even if mine is sinking faster than yours." Some talked to the nurses and CNAs, not knowing what to ask or say.

The CNAs that I knew responded quickly to everybody, patient and visitor alike. Their faces showed me that they were *worried* about my father and me and wanted to console or distract us, like we were their own brothers and sisters. They were overworked. I wanted to help them too.

After a week or so, I got the hang of it and was fitting in pretty well. It was when I started trying to help Dad that I got into trouble. I began to see that the unit was not about helping Dad, or our family, but was about some other outcome that wasn't clear to me for a while. In my eyes, there was conflict, misbehavior, and regular neglect, perhaps abuse, of the patients. Other visitors seemed not to notice, even if it was something occurring to their own family member.

I only heard one lady complain once. Her husband was near death, and I went to see them in a private room out in the regular wards. She was near hysterical because the doctors would not give him morphine for his pain. They told her they didn't want him to get addicted to it.

"Why?" she was crying, sitting in the chair next to his bed, where he was constantly moving and making noises of pain. "He's dying!"

When a nurse came in to check on him, I asked the nurse what the story was.

"I'm sorry, doctor's orders. You are just making things worse for her," the nurse told me and motioned for me to leave.

—

Dad had been smart and conservative with money, so we had enough to make him more than comfortable. We bought him a recliner that could help lift him when it was time to transfer to the wheelchair. I came and accompanied him to his physical therapy. When it became apparent that he would not improve, Medicare and his supplementary insurance refused to pay for more. They will only pay for therapies when the patient will recover, a hard line to take on the dying, and not that compassionate to the CNAs either, who are required to lift and maneuver these bodies with failing muscles that might keep a little strength if they were exercised.

Our family decided (or was it just me?) that we would hire a private therapist to keep Dad minimally limber and with strength enough to help us move him into a wheelchair or into his Red Jeep Cherokee for a ride. But, no, I was not allowed to bring in a physical therapist to the unit. It wasn't fair to the other patients that Dad could afford physical therapy and they couldn't, so the nursing home didn't allow anyone to have private visits. Silly me. I thought we lived in a free market, and that people who had money could spend it on anything they wanted. No one said it was unfair that other patients didn't have a family member to visit them every day. When I remonstrated, they finally allowed that the therapist could see him in his room with the door closed, and I would be allowed to help him walk a little up and down the hallways each day if I bought, and took lessons on how to use, a transfer belt.

—

Trudy was more interested in Mom than in Dad, so it was left to me to concentrate on the situation in the nursing home. In that mysterious process of assimilation that changes nothing, I moved and Reality didn't. The past changed and the future changed, though my guts still ached off and on as they always had done in their amorphous, somehow friendly, way.

The winter we moved them out was mild enough that I could bundle up and ride my bike along the town's flat, straight streets. But my mind rode through my childhood, floating through the town, seeing almost nothing of the side streets and alleys.

—

I grew up at the far end of a straight, level road, where it fell off in a steep drop to a left-hand turn at the bottom. The hill was so difficult to climb that I used to get off the school bus at the stop before on the level part, even though it was dozens of times farther away from home. It was too hard walking up the hill, making my legs ache. I saw only the sloping road in front of me and heard only my own breath which, hung out in front of my mouth, impossible to catch. There was one house between us and the top of the hill, and none on the hill itself. The hill seemed to me to be as dangerous as a cliff, and since the cars coming up it couldn't see us playing, there was a yellow and black sign that said SLOW CHILDREN just before the crest. Dad was fond of pointing out that the town had put up a sign because they thought we were slow, though all three of us were at the top of our classes in school, especially math classes. Our mother was the one who liked to read, and she explained with a tilt of her head that our father was correct. The sign should have a comma after "slow."

We all knew our father was kidding. He only said something like that because he knew who we were and liked to tease. Oddly, I understood that the drivers knew what the sign meant, comma or no comma. That constituted my introduction to the ghostliness of things we say, which haunts me still. I'm not even sure everything I have to say is exactly true, or that I truly understand what it means when I say it. Often, later on, things will clear up for me when other people respond to what I've said. Still, talking, giving voice to my own experience, usually gives me the sensation of moving forward, or at least a sense that I more or less understand who I am and what I want.

The house the slow children lived in was a low ranch house, built sometime or other before we moved into it when my brother, sister, and I were seven, almost three, and five years old. The house was not in a development as we picture it now. A farmer who owned the land over the gray split-rail fence in our backyard, had built two houses, each on about one-third of an acre. His name was Weed, and I thought it strange. He was mean, I judged just from his name, though I don't remember ever meeting him, only his cows grazing on the other side of the fence with their soft noses and big teeth slipping slowly sideways as they chewed the nasty grass sticking out the sides.

Unlike most houses built in that era, we had full-grown trees—a maple and two others on the edge of the front lawn by the side of the road. There was a garage which the family painted barn-red one summer, Trudy painting herself more than the garage, and then we hung an old plow on it, signaling our farming heritage. The driveway where I learned to ride a bike was gravel, not paved. No training wheels because then you'd never really learn to balance, according to my older brother. I lost much of the skin off my knees, but I loved the band-aids.

There were three immature blue spruce on the far side of the driveway next to the road. One year right before Christmas someone cut one of them down and stole it in the middle of the night. It was one of the only times I saw my mother cry. I remember thinking it odd that someone would care so much about a tree. But then, we had five other trees at the front, and there were a dozen or more along the border with our neighbor. And you can't climb a blue spruce—it's too prickly. Dad wanted to cut the other two down—he said they looked funny without all three.

One year, or perhaps for a few years, we had a giant garden in the backyard near a fence. I don't remember eating any produce, though, so I imagine it was a failure, and my mother gave up on it after a few years. Still, she tended the ageratums along the front walk, and pruned the forsythia and roses. Dad was never interested in growing things except the lawn, but after they retired to the top of a hill, he planted tomatoes in the middle Mom's flower border. He cared for them well enough to get a good crop and kept them all for himself and Mom. He loved tomatoes, and "cake hots" with lots of syrup. Besides those two foods and ice cream and pie, he never exclaimed over food, which was a good thing, since Mom kept a placard on the refrigerator which read, "My favorite thing to make for dinner—reservations." When they retired, Mom retired from cooking, and they ate out at every meal in the small local cafes or the large motel built for buses of tourists who came to eat local specialties. Or, at MacDonald's, always Dad's first choice, and Mom-the-nutritionist's last.

It was a good life, and not boring for a kid like me who lived mostly in my head. Dad taught me to add and subtract, how to sort things into kinds, how to use the tools in his workshop, ride a bike. He taught me about love once, and that judgements are relative: "It's all in the mind," he used to say. Mom taught me how to sew and cook and laugh. I had school and a lawn. There were three trees in the front yard to serve as bases for the softball games we played after dinner with Mom and Dad in the summer twilight, until we fell to fighting and were put to bed.

Mom was a nurse who had given it up to raise us and had gone back to work when we were all through high school. Dad was an engineer who did not give it up, but left for work every morning before I got up and returned after I got home from school. He took a nap every day before dinner and then watched television with us afterward.

We had good food and lots of toys and games—blocks; trucks; balls; hula hoops; monopoly; caroms; roller skates; plentiful decks of cards to play go fish, poker, and solitaire; and a badminton set. When the nets frayed, we repaired them with household string from the junk drawer in the kitchen, tying miniscule knots with our huge fingers. It was like repairing a spider web with your bare hands.

And we had the doll collection, I have it still. Mom's aunt had bought her a Lenci doll—an Italian doll with a shaped felt face and hands and legs—her first doll, when she was five years old. By the time we moved them out to deal with the Alzheimer's, she had over six hundred dolls, half of them American and half from foreign countries. She was proud that each of the dolls had been made and dressed in the country it was from. From her I learned the word "authentic." We didn't have tea parties with them. (We didn't have tea parties at all, come to think of it.) I never made mud pies, because you can't eat them. I didn't dress up like ballerinas or what I saw in movies, although I did like to try on my mother's jewelry and shoes. I didn't like to pretend.

Dad taught us math and teased us about being slow, when we knew we weren't. We had contests counting the Sunday church collection (Dad was the treasurer). We liked to tease each other, too, and I became a Monopoly monster by distracting Chuck and Trudy or making fun of their choices, pretending I wanted the blue ones and fooling them into letting me get the green monopoly. I also cheated by stealing money from the bank and hiding it under the board until I needed it. I don't remember anybody teaching me how to cheat, it must've been innate.

It was a happy childhood, especially because Dad had high standards which we all could meet, more or less, while it went unsaid that other people and other families could not. All we had to do was be perfect. We siblings were always trying to be better than each other. Dad tried too, but

Mom didn't, she probably was better than all of us put together, but she was never in the game. We were smarter "than the average bear" as Mom used to say, parroting the cartoon on TV. There are documents to prove it: our report cards and Iowa test scores; our SATs and the huge bills that arrived for college. Dad was a great one for saving documents. When he got Alzheimer's and we sifted through the contents of the house, we found every bank statement he had received from the time he opened his first account when he was thirteen until he was seventy-seven years old.

We watched Walt Disney and when the caterpillar asked, "Who are you?" caring more for his smoke rings than for Alice, I cringed. Pretty scary to be facing a fat, green caterpillar three times as big as you are. We watched You Are There on TV and saw history reported "live." And Detective Friday on Dragnet (who, by the way, never said, "Just the facts, Ma'am"—but might as well have said it). At the beginning of the show, a darkly authoritative voice intoned, "What you are about to see is true. The names have been changed to protect the innocent." Detective Friday would take a file out of the high top-drawer of a filing cabinet, and slam it shut, and then the story started. Or was that The FBI? My memory fails.

Once when Trudy was arguing with Dad she said, "It's true—it's in the files." And that became a family mantra. I later learned that Dragnet was a cover up of the crimes committed by the Los Angeles police force, one of the many realities that shattered the idyll of the childhood I remembered.

And there were scary shows that we loved to watch, too, like Twilight Zone. Remember the one where a little girl's doll came alive and tried to kill her when her parents weren't looking? I knew the difference between stories that were made up and factual ones, so I could enjoy the shivers and giggle at the monster doll and still go to sleep at night. Our dolls didn't do that.

For the most part, Dad hid his feelings. Trudy told me once that Dad never said he loved her. She had a therapist in college who told her to ask him for money to go on a vacation "because he loves you." She asked and he paid, but it didn't convince Trudy.

My own relationship with Dad was fraught. In my thirties, I'd once gone shopping with Mom and left Dad at home with my brother, where we had all come to help decorate his new house. Dad complained so loudly when Mom and I left, that Mom stopped to call him in the middle of the trip. When she came back from the pay phone, she said she was ready to go home. She didn't look that happy about it, and I didn't argue. Later in the same trip, I chastised Dad for making her come home.

"She didn't have to come home," he said confidently. "She wanted to."

We both knew that wasn't true. "I didn't want her to," I said.

"My marriage is none of your business."

What? I didn't want to talk about his marriage. So I just said, "True."

Suddenly we were talking about me. I admitted that sometimes I thought he didn't like me. I never thought he didn't love me, but I did think he judged me pretty harshly sometimes.

"Not like you?" His eyes went wide and he exhaled loudly-- it sounded like I had accused him of not liking chocolate ice cream or something. I felt bad for doubting him.

But what about how he treated Trudy if she thought he didn't love her? He'd only told me that a few times on the phone, once when I called home, and a couple of times later in my life, but I knew he loved me. At an important time in my life, he almost said it. I had taken a break when going through my divorce and fled home to relax for the weekend. I spent it mostly with Mom, shopping and sewing. Sunday morning, when I went to the kitchen to eat something before I left, I found a note on the fridge from Dad that said, "Can you stay an extra day?" This meant I would miss a day of work! Unheard of in our family. But I stayed. It was acting like love, but Trudy was right, it wasn't saying it.

For all his emotional rigidity, I have a clear memory of the time he instructed me about love. I must have been just over five, because I was in the car, and my knees were too far back to bend my knees at the edge of the seat. It was a Saturday, because Dad wasn't at work and had me in the back seat while he did errands at hardware stores and lumber yards. I was surrounded by things I didn't understand, but I was safe with Dad because he understood everything and I liked having him all to myself.

Dad had just quickly run into a store and had left me locked in the car. The radio was playing a song. A boy was going to see a girl but when he got to the street where she lived, he didn't go in. He just thought about how he felt. I sat looking at the crack between the top of the open window and the roof of the car as I banged the toes of my red oxfords together in front of me. The man flew up towards the sky. He was in love so he could fly! Was that like fairy dust? Did he know Peter Pan? Did he want to fly? Why didn't he go inside the building to see the girl he loved? Why did he stand around on the sidewalk thinking about her when she didn't even know he was there?

Just then, Dad came back when the little man was launching into another verse, and slid in behind the wheel, throwing a small bag on the passenger seat.

"Why can that man fly?" I asked.

"What man?"

"The one singing."

He listened for a moment.

"Well," he said, "He's not really flying. He just has a feeling that makes him feel like he's flying. He's in love."

"Oh." I tried to think about that. How could you have a feeling that makes you feel like you are flying when you are not really flying? What would that be like? I didn't know. Would it feel all right or would it be scary?

"Do you feel like that when you think about Mom?"

"It's a good feeling," said my dad. He had read my mind. "You can feel good without having to take a chance of really falling."

Still, I just had to take his word for it. I couldn't imagine what the song was about.

Another time, when I was readying myself to marry my first husband, I sensed Dad did not like him. He kept scowling at my fiancé for ordinary things like using the telephone for long-distance calls. Dad fled to the basement and was gone for quite some time. I finally found him behind the furnace, which was surrounded closely on all sides by cement block walls.

"What are you doing?"

"Cleaning the furnace."

Hmmm. I forged ahead.

"What's wrong?

He hesitated, then asked me, "Are you happy?"

As my body turned away quickly, the tears were already hitting the floor, and I left him there, covered in soot. I felt dirty too.

Mom, on the other hand, comforted me when I was upset and hurt. She encouraged me to be the artist, the teacher, the rebel, even when Dad was looking at me doubtfully for bucking the system. She encouraged me to speak my mind, use my talents, trust my own judgment, be myself.

Dad was big on following directions. But after I had installed several zippers with the help of Mom and a zipper foot, I decided to invent a better method, one that made it easier to make the zipper come out even at the neckline and at the bottom, so the dress would a hang straight. Mom started using it immediately, though the zipper foot was not designed to do that job.

Dad did not so much encourage as bribe me. I painted the whole house one high-school summer, dreaming of using the money to buy a stereo. Every day, listening to the local rock and roll radio station play the top hits on "WABC-e-e-e-e" radio. A whole house by myself. At the end of the summer, Dad insisted that I buy contact lenses instead of paying me. That was horrible, I did want contact lenses, but I wanted to make the decision myself with the first large amount of money that was mine—and he could have afforded contacts for me anyway.

When my brother got to be a teenager, he started to call Dad "sir" when he was in trouble, and sometimes when he was not.

Chuck was the first to bring home the music of our generation: Chad Mitchell Trio, Jefferson Airplane. Trudy and I fought over our living quarters and what to watch on TV. It seems to me she always sided with Chuck, who wanted to watch Victory at Sea when I wanted to watch Sky King and his flying daughter. But that couldn't be right. I also remember her sitting totally absorbed with Timmy and Lassie. We all discovered Bill Cosby together: "Who made you sheriff of the Jello?"

Chuck banged the car up by leaving it without emergency brakes on a hill and asked me to be the one to tell Dad. Once Trudy cut short the hair that had fallen out of her ponytail and had sideburns until they grew out. Once she spilled a bottle of nail polish on Mom's spanking-new coffee table. Mom let it go with the comment that now it was really ours. I suppose I didn't learn much about the people I no longer recognized. The memories were more like episodes from Father Knows Best.

The only things I'd ever heard Chuck say about our life then were pretty nostalgic, remembering the Fourth of July parades, his Little League games, our growing-up times in high school. I guess he had some bad feelings, but I didn't get to know him until he went away to college. On his very short visits home, we would talk all night in the kitchen about what college was like and the Viet Nam war. I looked up to him and felt important when he talked to me like an adult. I visited him many times after I left for college and on into our adult lives—when we introduced each other to Chinese food and many books about history and philosophy, not so much math as when we were children—though that would change when we reached our seventies sent cards to each other on "prime" birthdays. He loved history in high school but became an engineer. He had that kind of synthetic intelligence that programmers don't always have—the kind that can penetrate the humanities with a clarity and outspokenness that comes of working in a field that has right and wrong answers, and at the same time requires nuanced detail. He gave me advice. In high school "don't wear socks." Later on, "tell the truth."

His perceptions were accurate and surprising, but I didn't often didn't take his advice. I wore socks, I didn't mow my lawn, I didn't ask for alimony in my divorce, I quit my jobs one after the other. I married an antiwar ex-con, another engineer. But Chuck remained loyal.

I was sorry when we grew up and learned about ourselves and were blown away by the four winds of adult life, with less and less contact, seeing each other only on holidays, and even then not much. It would've helped me understand what was happening in the adult world which remained opaque to me for decades.

One day when I was in kindergarten, I was playing on the seesaw with an older girl—a first grader. She was taller than I was, had long black hair and the dark, shiny eyes to go with it. My own hair was short and fine and blond, and I admired her. Older. Better. I felt important when she agreed to play with me, and when she sat down on her side of the see-saw and sent me flying up into the air, I was free. She bent her knees then and pushed into the air, but I wasn't heavy enough to make it all the way to the ground. She thunked back down and just stepped off the seesaw altogether and went and sat on the swing, waiting for me to put myself back to together and join her.

"Why'd you do that?" I was still brushing off, and was stunned.

"You have a lot to learn," she said.

"What do you mean?"

"There's lots of things you don't know yet," she said low and grim. "Wait until you're as old as me. You'll see."

I couldn't imagine all the things that had happened to her, but she didn't mean reading and spelling, that was for sure.

"Tell me."

"No," she said—haughty now, unkind. She looked away up at the blue sky as if she could see things there. "You wouldn't understand anyway." And left me on the swing. We never played together again. I still admired her. Then I forgot about it.

So childhood took its slow, windy way up and out, while I watched and learned how to imagine and think contradictory thoughts and wonder and compare. My mother smiled and read poems to me to teach me what more she knew that I didn't. One of my favorites was by Ogden Nash — I still know it by heart:

> Behold the hippopotamus,
> How wond'rous strange he looks to us.
> But in my moments dark and grim
> I wonder how we look to him?
> Hold, hold oh, hippopotamus,
> We really look all right to us,
> As you, no doubt, delight the eye,
> Of other hippopotami.

My father went to work and then on the weekends took us in our small overalls to dig dandelions out of his perfect lawn while he supervised and mowed. My mother taught me how to have fun, and my father taught me that everything was hard, but had to be done anyway. You had to bring everything you had to the task, and do it perfectly, or the consequences could hold some disaster that remained unclear to me.

Yet he taught me to do my math homework with a pencil and not a pen.

"The younger generation uses pens and messes their papers all up. When you make a mistake, you can just erase it, so you can see how you got the answer. That's how we learn." he told me.

—

Reaching the Alzheimer's sign after that fifty-five-year round trip, I got off my bicycle and parked it. I missed that family life. It was what I was losing, not the memories, but the life I lived in them.

I went twice a day to the Alzheimer's unit, in midmorning and again around dinner time, and stayed an hour or an hour and a half. I had nothing to do but sit with Dad and watch what was going on in the ward. He didn't initiate conversations with me, but would usually respond if I asked him to identify an old classmate in his yearbook or count some coins.

But sometimes he would initiate. Once he said out of the blue, "I guess I lost this one." I told him we all lost this one, and he shrugged. There is a rare, clear memory of another time I arrived in the evening. We were in his room getting ready to brush teeth, when he caught my eye and hung his head.

"I was a bad dad," he said glancing up to see what I thought.

"You weren't that bad," I said and gave him a smile and a hug. "You always were too much of a perfectionist, but that has its good points." He didn't smile at that, and I knew that I had never forgiven myself for missing the grade by even one point.

He'd never said anything like that before in his life, so I was curious. They say that Alzheimer's does something to your forebrain that stops it from filtering out emotions. I wondered whether he had always had doubts about what kind of a father he was, or they only came out when his filters were down. Too bad: I would've liked to have had this conversation with him in my twenties.

Most of the time it was boring or irritating in the Alz unit. I found myself at war with the nurse Betta Norce who ran the Alzheimer's Unit. Everything about her rubbed me the wrong way; she even spelled her name incorrectly. She was not fond of me either. That was obvious in the way we smiled at each other.

Much of my time there was spent listening to what the literature called "word salad." When I don't know the person who's talking, the meaning escapes me, but I believe it's always in there. Because other times I can understand word salad, even with strangers.

I sat listening to a resident tell me a story. It gave me a break from focusing on Dad, and gave him a break from the effort of connecting. I relax. The only things anyone knew about her was that she lived with her son one state away. When he died, her daughter-in-law dropped her off here by herself. It's easy to listen without any hooks or snags, her full sentences empty and free.

"But anyway, I liked my dog. And this little dog was somebody else's dog. I don't know who it was and so I ... it wouldn't stay by me like other people's dogs. It would come over to my dog. And so I told that lady, I said, 'I can't do it because,' I said, 'somebody will hurt it.'

"And she said, 'Anybody hurts this dog they're gonna get their head knocked off.'

"And I said, 'My God, do you like that dog? I like that dog that much more.'

"She said, 'I like that dog that much more.'

"And anyway, I guess it was two weeks after that I saw her house and it was coming down like it was gonna be broken. But anyway, it came over to my door and I saw it."

I knew Dad well enough that I could guess pretty exactly what he was talking about. The dog lady's family probably knew the story she was trying to tell too. But I still understood what she was trying to say.

—

It's funny that the toll the Alzheimer's took was on the rest of us, not as much on Dad. He was taken care of and, except for occasional out-of-control rages, was happy—or at least during the time I spent with him he was.

Except once. When I complained about the medication they gave Dad that made him slump in his wheelchair with his head on his chest, they explained that he would get angry and they had to do something. The unit had too many demented patients who were easy to rile up. They were two to a room and there was not enough staff to address the problem in any other way.

But I hadn't seen him get angry. I asked the nurses if they would call me the next time they could not handle him. So the compassionate nurse called me one day and asked me to come. When I arrived, Dad was yelling at the top of his lungs for Mom. His anger had only ever before been visible in his face—it didn't come out of his mouth. But now, it was definitely SNAFU. He was wheelchair-bound, so not dangerous

"Let's go find Mom," I said and rolled him out of the unit, under the doubtful eyes of the nurses. We went as quickly as possible through the hallway to the closest door to the outside, Dad rubber-necking into every room we passed, and continuing to yell. I walked outside with him for too long, waiting for him to calm, finally giving up and taking him back, ashamed to allow the nurses to give him the offending medication. But that only happened to me once.

It wasn't my dad they were treating. It was some kind of monster who didn't know himself and had no control, couldn't even see that what he was doing was something he didn't want to do. Parts of his brain were not working.

The science says that Alzheimer's is not contagious, but the science is wrong. We all caught Alzheimer's, for Trudy and I raged and repressed. We both became forgetful and I know that some of my memories of that time are distorted—something that always amazes me, because the memories seem so clear and have been with me for such a very long time. Much later we were able to recover from our Alzheimer's—another slap in the face of science.

One day when the dog story was over, (she would start again and go on and on if I let her), I got up to try and make some friendly conversation with Nurse Norce.

Ruth the Witch was over in the TV area, and she had just accepted a paper cup of milk from one of the CNAs. Ruth looked down at her cup, then up at me, and aimed herself at me like a hornet, stretching out the hand holding the cup. Norce sprang into action, hurtling her girdle through the swinging gate on the side of the nurses' station.

"Watch out! Watch out! She's going to spill it on you!"

But my mother taught me long ago not to cry over spilt milk. Nurse Norce appeared to be upset about something other than a little stain on my clothes, and it's not that Ruth might trip and fall. I thought I knew what she was worried about.

And milk is not the only thing she was spilling. Ruth was also spilling glee from her eyes, her smile, her whole face. I side-stepped, took the cup from her hand, and sipped. "Deee-licious!" I grinned. "I needed that."

Ruth's lips stretched flat and pressed together below those bright blue eyes. She was all there in those eyes. And she was smug.

"She just wanted to give me some milk," I pointed out to Norce.

But she had already taken the cup away from me, and snapped at Ruth, "Now you can't have any more for yourself." Okay, so that's what Norce was worried about. She wanted to conserve milk. Ruth and I didn't care. We were friends, and friends share.

I glanced over at Dad now. How much of his aggression was prompted by Norce's need to control her patients? She didn't see him, just like she didn't see Ruth. Her medical education had bleached her clean of compassion, and the lawyers had dyed her with fear.

I'd broken my ankle once and knew how perceptions could distort. "Shall I cut up your meat for you, Sarah?" an acquaintance asked one day when we were out to lunch. She saw a cripple, not me. Really humiliating.

I'd seen Dad's irritation escalate into aggression so severe that it required sedation. Most sedatives have side effects that can severely affect the patient's health. My father's sleeping patterns were disrupted by doses of Ativan, which dislocated him in the daily schedule. When he was awake, he ate microwaved scrambled eggs, sometimes as much as three hours old. When he was knocked out during the day, he lay awake at night, requiring more sedation, because there were only two and occasionally one attendant on duty, and he was a "danger." Once, the sedation came as a relief to me, because he sat at the locked door to the unit banging on the bar that opened it to get out. There was a brightly lit EXIT sign above it, and I thought he was just trying to follow directions. But I suppose I will never know for sure.

—

I do have to admit that Dad was a danger to himself *and* others the time he pulled the fire alarm and the fire department responded. When I got there several nurses were guarding him, now sitting in his wheelchair by the alarm.

He just pointed at it, and I looked. It was one of those red ones with a handle that pulls down to set it off. The word *PULL* was embossed on the handle. "It says: PULL," I pointed out. "He was just following directions." And he wasn't really a *danger*, it just cost a lot of money to have the firemen come. And, instead of hiding it or removing PULL, they solved their problem by putting an iron cage over it that he could not open. This solved their problem, but he continued to be frustrated.

It seemed to me the nurses were doing useless things, like taking notes, logging meds taken and not taken, and also logging me: the trouble I caused when I visited. They did not log how happy Dad was to see me, or how calm he was when I was there—no "danger," and not demanding much of their attention either.

And did they notice how happy I was when I saw recognition in his eyes, when he wanted to hold my hand when I sat next to him at the supper table? Watching the animal movie with him in the darkened lounge reminded me of a time watching movies all night together. We were both sick, and neither of us could sleep, so we watched zombie movies and ate ice cream.

Eventually one of the nurses recognized that he was dehydrated. He was always asking for water when I visited, and I would go over to the nurses' station to ask for a cup. They gave me one of those little cups they put a patient's pills in—I'd say less than two or three ounces. I'd stand by the water fountain, and fill and refill the cup until he stopped taking it. One day, Nurse Norse told me not to fill it up more than once.

"But he's thirsty?" I tried to make it sound like a question, but there was no hiding my exasperation.

"He has to urinate too often when he drinks that much. It takes too long to transfer him to the toilet."

I got somebody or other in a position of authority to let me bring in a quart of water, which they kept in the refrigerator. They were supposed to give him at least a quart a day, but they didn't. It just sat in the fridge. And then he got urine infections.

It wasn't hard for me to tell when he had one, the way he grabbed his groin and made a face. Once, I asked them to give him some medication. But the response was, "How do you know he has an infection? We can't do that without a urine test."

"When can we get one?"

"We'll have to call the doctor."

"Okay, then. Please call me when you know."

On the bicycle trip home that day, the memories came easily and clearly, and in chronological order, beginning more than a year before, before we moved him, and before he was diagnosed with Alzheimer's.

—

Dad was at the largest hospital complex in the state, in the recovery room from back surgery. They gave him a dose of his usual medication for acid reflux in his IV drip. He turned out to be allergic to the medication given in a drip, and went nuts. They had to move him to the acute unit and tie him down as he yelled and thrashed, strapped down with a wide leather belt that look plenty used.

A few days later Dad settled down enough to go back to the regular ward for a few days, where a newbie nurse was sent to change his catheter. I was there and saw her bungle it, injuring him—he bore it without comment, looking up at me with wondering, teared-up eyes. I called another nurse who took over.

Later that same day, the business office called Mom down to sign papers permitting the procedure and absolving the hospital from any liability. The papers were time-stamped before the procedure was done. I couldn't resist having some fun with the financial officer. Acting puzzled, pointing out the inaccurate time, I told Mom to change it before she signed. Of course, she didn't—she was a well-trained nurse herself and followed hospital protocol. The officer looked askance at me—and at Mom, relieved.

Dad had thirty-six doctors in charge of his case in twenty-eight days. After the regular ward, he was moved to the surgeon's floor. Then he had a heart flutter and was moved to the cardiology. I spent whole days with Dad, as his watchdog.

One day, a nurse comes in with some medication to add to his IV drip.

"What's that?" I get up and block her way. I have never seen her before.

"It's his acid reflux medication."

"Is it the same medication he had during his back surgery?"

"I don't know—why?"

"He's allergic to it."

She gives me a bewildered look. "No, he's not."

"Yes, he is. He spent three days in the critical care unit tied to his bed when they gave it to him." I felt the explosion of his body against the wide, leather straps.

"He's been taking it for years."

"I know, but he takes pills. When they put it in his IV, he had a reaction,"

"It's not in his chart."

I take a step toward her. I am as big as she is. I feel dangerous. "Let me see his chart, I'll show you."

"You're not allowed to."

I hold still with some effort. I don't want to let her near Dad.

"Can you look at it?"

She just stands there.

"Call the doctor."

"I'm not going to do that, now get out of my way."

"Where is it?"

"Outside the door."

I decide to just stand there, and she leaves. When she comes back, the doctor is with her.

"What's the problem?" *He asks, pretty relaxed.*

"I want to see my father's chart."

He walks out the door and gets it for me himself. "May I see it?" *I say, holding out both hands. The thing is in a black notebook, fat enough to intimidate. Hundreds of pages. He hesitates, then moves next to me and shows me the first page.* "All allergies are flagged on the first page of the notebook on big red stickers. It's not here."

"Well, it should be! Who can we check with about this?" *He lets me take it from him then, and I flip through looking at the dates and finally find the page, show it to the doctor.*

Without any acknowledgment to me, the response is, "All right. Scratch that order." *He says that to the nurse. To me he says,* "Can he take it orally?"

"As far as I know."

The nurse nods her agreement, and as she follows the doctor down the hall, I hear her say, "It wasn't on the front page."

"I know," *says the doctor, uninterested.*

I don't know what kind of treatment they substituted, or maybe it was none, for within a few days or a week, he had surgery for stomach ulcers, and was moved to a different floor.

I ranted until the surgeons let me lie on a bed in the same room with a curtain drawn between us during the surgery, but I wasn't allowed to get off the bed or speak. Looking back, it's hard to believe that memory is accurate: Did they really let me do that? It calmed me down, though it didn't restore my faith in his medical treatment.

I wanted to get Dad out of there and into a more stable place. The next day I approached a different nurse and told her I wanted to talk with all the doctors who were treating Dad.

"You can't." I wasn't surprised

"Okay then, can I see his HMO doctor?"

"Normally, they don't come over to the hospital, but I guess you could ask."

I called. Dad's lady doctor was still on maternity leave, but another doctor came right over.

"What's up?" he said. I filled him in on Dad's hectic month, then asked whether he would be willing to call the other docs for a meeting all together.

"Why not? This is the first time I've ever been asked to talk to the doctors over there. I think it's a good idea. We've been trying to do it for ten years."

So the meeting was arranged, with much ado about how difficult it was to schedule six or seven doctors, some of them surgeons, at the same time. I imagined we'd meet in one of the hospital meeting rooms, with a wide, polished table and coffee tray. Instead, they found space in a broom closet. The closet was the size of a very tiny room. It was dim and smelled musty, overlaid with another aroma like metallic soap. It always surprised me how unclean are the places where we keep our cleaning paraphernalia. Here, in a hospital, the contrast with the halls and rooms outside the closet was stark. It was crowded, too, but at least had a blackboard and chalk.

"I've never been here before," the HMO doctor grinned as he joined me in the broom closet. The other doctors filed in behind him. After everyone was in place, I took up a piece of chalk and jumped right in. I'm sure they had all been forewarned about the troublemaker.

"Okay. We're here to make a plan. What's our objective with Dad?" I wrote the numerals from one to six on the blackboard, drew a line under

them and wrote GOAL at the bottom of the board, then looked at the cardiologist sitting next to Mom. He pretended for a moment that my look signified nothing. Then, slowly, he said, "Stabilize the arrhythmia." No question in that voice.

I wrote nothing. "Next?"

"Heal the ulcers and get him back on a regular diet."

"Nope. What do you say?" I looked at the back surgeon next to the ulcer surgeon.

"Get him into physical therapy for his back."

"Nope. Next?"

"Get him off the catheter."

"Nope."

And so on around the room. Nope. Nope. Nope. Even the doctor from the HMO office across the street was at a loss. They only offered the kind of just-in-time attention that auto manufacturers paid to their inventory.

At last, I got back to Mom, who wasn't expecting to answer—she wasn't a specialist after all. "Mom? What would you like us to do with Dad?"

She didn't have to think. "Bring 'm home!" she said. I wrote that at the bottom of the board.

The doctors quieted down and looked at each other. Then they began to talk among themselves about how each of their specialties could help Dad go home. Mom and I left while they were still going at it. And, although he had to go to a nursing home for a week or two, he returned home in December, almost two months after the surgery, and by January we were gone from the state.

That particular HMO came under attack a couple of years later, because they accidentally operated on the wrong patient, who died.

—

Those bicycle memories were painful to relive, so I was relieved to be home. The next day a nurse called to tell me that the doctor had finally ordered the test for the urine infection, and later that day reported that it was positive. "But the doctor doesn't want to give him too much medicine, because if they use it too much it would stop working."

Didn't they think he was going to die? I'm sure I did something tantrum-like at that point—yes, I think I called the social worker at home close to midnight and yelled. Whatever—whether I was right or they were, I didn't see many urine infections after that.

I continued to watched the endless loop of their parade. More than tired of thinking my own critical thoughts, I decided to go out one night and distract myself, get away from it for a while. There was a live, local talent show at the refurbished theatre downtown. Tonight, violins would play under the chins of gangle-elbowed or fatty-thighed youth. Here dinner theatre retirees would sing and young mothers of malnourished but Sunday-School-attending babes would tap-dance. It was easy to spot Ray, a.k.a. the Videoman, mid and center with his kempt blond hair and blue eyes, setting up his equipment. His father had just become my dad's roommate.

I sidled across the row and sat down next to where he stood fiddling with his tripod.

"Hey, Sis." Ray always beamed; he is beaming still. "I guess we're sort of related now that our dads are roommates."

"Hey, bro." As the evening wore on, I became more and more comfortable with Ray. At intermission, I said, "Let me ask you something, if it's not too bold." Ray kept working and smiling.

"Shoot, sis."

"You have brothers and sisters, right?"

"Yup."

"Do you get along? I mean, do you cooperate in your dad's care?"

Ray dropped his hands into his lap and turned on his stool to face me. "You know, that's a good question." There was a hitch in his underlying cheer. "We kinda haven't got along ever since my older brother became my older sister."

"Huh?"

"Yeah, in fact, he builds nursing homes. I mean she does. But my dad was so angry with him. They hadn't spoken for years. When it was time to choose a place, Mary wasn't there. I could understand it was confusing for Pop. Marvin had a family. He was fifty years old. Pop just didn't get it. And then everybody took sides. It wasn't pretty."

"But what about now? I mean, who makes the decisions about your dad?"

"Oh, my mother can still do that. In fact, a couple of us tried to get her to put him in a home a couple of times. But she wouldn't do it. Not 'til he fell and cracked his head on the lip of the shower stall. And now she feels so guilty, she doesn't want to go see him. Mom's relieved of a great burden. Dad was really mad at her when she left him there. But she's still competent. So we just try to help her any way we can." Ray swiveled his stool and bent back to his camera.

Ray's father, Dr. Jones, had practiced general medicine in the county for fifty years. He had delivered one of the CNAs on the unit, who took great satisfaction in returning his care.

One day, Dr. Jones stood humbly in front of the nurses' barrier. The feet on his smudgy glasses bit into the side of his nose. He repeatedly removed them, rubbed the sore spots, and tried to speak to the male nurse behind the barrier. He failed to come up with sensible language to make his request for the two little pads to put under the feet of his glasses.

The nurse, a compassionate man, looked up but did not see what was bothering Dr. Jones, and attempted to distract him.

"Hi, Dr. Jones," he started respectfully, "How are you tonight?"

The doctor nodded vaguely, pushed his glasses up on his forehead again.

The nurse changed tactics. "Tell me, do you have any children?" If they can still speak, patients can usually remember their children. And they don't remember if you've asked before. I liked this nurse a lot.

Dr. Jones looked up and pulled his glasses back into place in front of his suddenly focused eyes.

"Yes," he said

"How many?" asked Nurse Nice.

"Three," said the doctor, now really pleased to be engaged in a conversation.

"Nice size family. Any sons?"

Dr. Jones's face clouded over again as his shoulders dropped, and he quickly turned away. The nurse shrugged good naturedly and let his demented patient go, bowing his head again over the paperwork. How could he possibly know that a simple question would evoke pain and humiliation in his patient? He was not trained to treat pain and humiliation.

—

Still another day on the unit. 4-3-2-1*. Handle, hip, I'm in. Bud sits against the left wall, a big ol' smile opening his face. Not hollow, not vacant, but translucent, light-filled, water-eyes turn on me, as if the light going in is not registering but has just reversed its direction and is now coming back out of his eyes. I've looked into the same eyes in photos of Zen Buddhist monks and nuns. Bud is happy. Or maybe he is soma happy, and doesn't have to come back to reality to suffer the consequences. Medication here is until-death-do-you-part.

A tall man stands betwixt the nurses' station and the euphemistically so-called "living" room. He turns slightly to one side, then to the other. I recognize him. I met him just before the turn of the century, at the office where I worked for a short stint. The owner's husband was this man's son, and brought him along for the day. The tall man sat on a bench in the hallway, calmly watching with no comment.

Now he looks a little lost, not knowing which way to turn. Nurse Nice says from behind the counter, "Sarah, this is Paul Neder. He's your dad's new roommate." Looking for Dad out of the corner of my eye, I step forward and hold out a hand. "Hi, Paul. I'm Sarah. My father is your roommate."

Paul takes my hand in his and with an urgent pressure pulls me into the arc of his other arm. Then he lets go of my hand and traps me in both his arms. I can feel him shaking slightly and hear him draw quick, meager breaths. Now it dawns on me that the look in his eyes was not lostness, but terror. He leans on me. I hug him strongly back, trying to make myself bigger, and start to rock him side-to-side a little. I put my temple to his chin and coo, "It's all right. You belong with us. Your family will be back soon." But he still holds on to me like a capsized sailboat, still adrift, unable to believe he is near any solid ground.

The instant he touches me, some kind of thunderless lightning galvanized the air around us. I'm certain I didn't see this, because I know my back was to the counter, but I know Nurse Nice leaped over it. Two aides rush down the hall toward us. They are all yelling. Paul grabs me more ferociously. I keep rocking. But they rip his arms away from me and up into the air, like he is an outlaw: *Reach for the sky!*—then pin them to his sides. I am a little surprised they don't have handcuffs. Nurse Nice cranks his neck far enough to make contact with me at the edge of his eye and jerks his head toward the exit door. "Go. Get over there." I do as I am told.

I was out of it, back near the door I had come in. No one wanted to make room for me. The aides were trained to have lawyer's eyes in their heads, to see injury where there was only a daughter trying to comfort a father. Paul became dangerous in their eyes, but not in my arms.

—

Months later, after Paul was dead, I sat with Paul's son, Tom, in the living room of our rental house. It was a ratty living room, with multicolored brown shag carpeting and furniture that was cheap and worn out for the most part, although we set our teacups on a lovely oak coffee table with turned legs and glass inserts on the top surface shaped like tulips.

I had invited Tom to come and talk about his experiences there. I had known him as my insurance agent for a few years. We now sat trying to be informal, with the balls of our feet on the coffee table, looking other places than at each other.

Tom was embarrassed when he asked me not to repeat what he told me. He set his teacup on the coffee table and leaned back in the high-backed chair. He took his feet off the coffee table and set his tea cup down, leaning forward again and putting his elbows on his knees to steady himself. He looked down between his shoes, as if looking at a tiny play there on the floor.

After a too-shallow breath he spoke. "He was in the unit less than a day. What really made me mad was that they didn't really know what to do at the Alzheimer's unit. They said he attacked another family member, and that's why they had to kick him out."

Now I leaned forward too. "Was that the only reason?" I whispered.

He did not raise his eyes. "Yes. 'Danger to himself or others.' You know, they have to prove that before they can evict them." Tom trembled a little and turned his head swiftly away and down.

"But they never said anything to me about it." I tried to get his attention back. "It's not true. And they didn't tell you who the 'family member' was? It was me. I'm certain of it. Let me tell you what happened: It was more like being at the scene of an arrest than in a hospital. It was traumatic for both of us." As I finished the story, some tension went out of my body, but some stubbornly remained. "What happened to him? I didn't see him again."

He sighed. "You'd get different stories about that from me and my brother. He was the one who went to visit every day. He was the one who got all weird so none of us could talk to him anymore."

I chewed on the thought that I had become that weird in the eyes of Trudy and Chuck. "Would you mind if I call him?"

"Of course not."

There was a silence while we both sat.

"I don't know," said Tom and stopped. He continued after an uncoordinated pause, in a clipped voice. "My brother is the one to talk to," he repeated. "He was the one who pushed, who took care of him. I didn't agree with him. He would leave work when the nursing home called. He did too much."

My stomach turned. Was I doing too much? My mind spun like a pinwheel throwing off sparks. What's too much? Why did Tom think his brother did too much? What would he think if I told him how I felt, that I couldn't live with myself very long after Dad died if I had any doubts about the way I behaved toward him. Did I love well enough? Was I loved enough?

But Tom was more interested in telling his tale than in judging me. "The day after they put him in the Alzheimer's unit, they took him out of it and put him in the mental unit. It was pretty far to go, and I went down with my mother, but they wouldn't let us in. He had to be isolated for a week or two. He was locked in a padded room. They took everything away from him—even his belt and shoes. There were these big men working on the unit. They gave him a lot of drugs, and after a while he came back to the nursing home.

"He couldn't get out of bed, so they didn't have to lock him up again. My brother tried to get him off the drugs. We all thought they were too strong, but Steve was the one who complained. Dad lasted about a month, then just stopped eating. He made it past Christmas, but he wasn't really conscious."

Tom stopped and looked up finally. He had been staring at the floor all the time he spoke, observing these past events and describing them to me as they happened beneath him, Lilliputian on the floor.

"But it was me! He didn't attack me—he was just scared!" I was self-righteous.

"They didn't put a name on the report. I don't want to know," said Tom. I thought he might cry. "Call my brother and ask him what he thought."

It was clearly the end of the story for Tom. He got up. "I'm glad I got to tell it," he said, thanked me, and let himself out. I never called his brother. I felt awkward, what would I say? "Did you love your father too much?"

—

It was five o'clock in the afternoon, and I had stopped by to say hello to my father in the Alzheimer's Unit of a local (if not "hometown") nursing facility (if not "home"). The word "facility" means competence and ease. I put calling a nursing home a "facility" in the same category as Orwell's Ministries of Peace or Truth. It's more like a "hearsing" home.

I usually didn't visit at this time of day; it was too hectic just before supper, and there were too many other visitors. They all distracted each other's parents, wives, husbands, children, senior companions, nurses, CNAs, and themselves. I thought about how hungry and how tired I was—how much I was looking forward to being home and cooking some dinner for myself, then going to bed with a good book.

The residents were sundowning. Correction: we were all sundowning—that is, we were all at the end of a busy day—alzies, staff, families. And we were all tired and hungry, although to varying degrees.

Sundowning is a technical medical term. As the sun goes down demented patients get crazier. When I first heard it, it sounded to me a pleasant sort of thing. Sundowning, I thought, must mean something like finishing up, relaxing, getting a little sleepy and slow. But it means exactly the opposite; more like suddenly finding yourself surfing the wild, wind-whipped waves of your own anger and neediness. Like the childhood rage that often came over me, just at bedtime and after a day too full for me to take it in all the way, a day I had enjoyed so much I didn't want it to end, and so felt let down that it was ending. Partly, I was too tired, I couldn't do whatever I was doing anymore, like playing ping pong or tag. I kept thinking I could do it, but my arms and legs didn't go, although I could see clearly that they *could*, they *ought*. It was both too much and not enough.

I could be set on my ear by the smallest request, or even remark. For instance, my mother might gently coo, "You're getting tired, aren't you honey?" Well, NO, Mom—not in the sense that I want to STOP what I'm doing and rest! Or, it might be seeing succotash on my dinner plate, or even just a stray bit of hair that insisted on creeping into the corner of my mouth as I chewed. I could usually just grump it out, unless someone spoke to me. Then the wave crashed forward carrying all of me with it and turning me over and over. At the same time something heady was unleashed that roared out of my mouth at everyone and everything within the range of my child's hand, eye, or needy soul. It was the feeling of being violated by everything, even myself, but mostly by the very fact that other people existed in my space. Even when they weren't doing or saying anything, they couldn't help me get what I wanted, and they were in my way. In point of fact, they were to blame.

So I knew sundowning when I saw it that day with the Alzhammered. The aides and nurses were rolling most of the twenty of them toward the narrow opening to the dining "area." Dining area. Who wants to dine in an "area," or sit in an "area," or do anything in an "area"? Areas, like zones, have boundaries around them which you aren't supposed to cross. Restricted Area. But room—give me room, lots of room, and a starry sky, anytime, over an area. A room is an appropriate but not limited place. Its where you ARE supposed to do something: live, sleep, eat—no, dine.

Some or all of the aides, like me, were thinking about their own dinner, which would follow the residents' meal. Some residents were still being hurried on the toilet. "Susie, what are you waiting for? Finish up and come to dinner," I could hear Leslie say to ninety-nine-year-old Susie down the south hall, first door to the right.

Harold chuckled at my elbow. "Bet she really doesn't want to know what Susie's waiting for."

"Bunny!" Warned red-haired Donna over in the TV "area." Bunny, who was recovering from a broken hip, was doing her best to stand up and walk to dinner. "Bunny, sit back down in your wheelchair and wait 'til I can get over there."

I looked around for Dad. As usual, he was one of the first ones there, and he came, quietly eager. It was his favorite time again, time to eat. I decided to help. I went halfway down the linoleumed hall to Dr. Fred's room. He sort of knew who I was, and if he forgot, he would remember as soon as I began to sing the fight song from the college we had both attended, albeit thirty years apart. Though he often looked like he was seeing only the inside surface of his unwashed glasses lenses, his blue, twinkled eyes focused a little more when we sang our song together. Fred knew all the familiar old words and even though they were nonsensical, they were somehow comforting.

I didn't sing it now, as I aimed Dr. Fred's wheelchair at the dining clog. It was already too noisy. We all jostled, the wheelchair-bound more so than the walking. For the nth time I wondered why they had enclosed the area with a half wall, so that only one or two could pass through the opening. Most of the tables were inaccessible just when they were most wanted.

Just at the nub of the knot, Patty came a-shuffling up. She was a Philly broad. You could see the brassy hair of fifty years ago beneath the gray waves stuck in her skullcap hairdo. You could hear lots of small children tangling around her ankles when she spoke in sharp authoritative tones. So we were all three from the urban coast bawd and brawl—Patty, Dr. Fred, and me. Patty wanted to talk to me. She pushed her way past a couple of aides and around the side of the seven-foot-tall, rolling, stainless-steel dinner cart.

The "cart" felt more like an armored car. Imagine if you were served food off of those things in a restaurant or in your home. How would it make you feel? Like "dining"? Metallic. Clattery. The shelves are too close together; you can't see the way the food is presented. It is too obviously mass produced—not intended to be enjoyed—merely eaten and checked off the list of your "intake" for the day. Then the cart is easily cleaned. You are in jail. You are in the intake area of the jail.

Anyhow, Patty wedged her way past the rolling fortress and made straight for me, yelling something that was unquestionably important, ignoring Dr. Fred, not just pulling my attention away from him, but ripping it off him, leaving his skin raw and his hands angrily startled, like those of a little boy when somebody bigger and stronger succeeds in wrenching a small toy out of his clenched fists.

Dr. Fred sat there with his mouth open, his fishy eyes staring through two smeary lenses. And in that instant, as I turned toward

Patty, he summed up sundowning for us all in one exasperated, hurtling exclamation.

"Will you PLEASE," he shot at Patty, "keep your mind to yourself!"

Chapter Three

THE BIG TROUBLE

There's nothing left for me
Of days that used to be
They're just a memory
Among my souvenirs
Edgar Leslie

Mom lived across the street from Dad's Alzheimer's unit in an assisted living facility which was part of the nursing home campus. People could live in the assisted living until they were too far gone, and then be moved across the driveway to the Alzheimer's unit to be pushed the rest of the way, gone for good.

Mom was not interested in visiting Dad. After a few weeks of sleeping all day and all night, she finally let me persuade her to go. Dad was glad to see Mom and recognized her, no problem. But when it was time to leave, he lost it and started to yell at her not to go. Mom beat a retreat, and I stayed a moment until Dad forgot about it. When I got out, and the locked door finally closed behind us, Mom looked battered. "I don't think I'll do that again," she said and started to cry. When we got back to her room, she took off her engagement ring and put it in my palm and folding my fingers over it. "You're taking care of him now," she said, and breathed a big sigh. "Thank you." I took the ring, and put it away for someone in a younger generation to wear without the blight of memory clinging to it.

I tried again to get them together, rolling Dad in his wheelchair over to Mom's apartment building, taking him up the elevator and to her door.

I pushed him in and settled him in the living area, a place homier than Dad's situation: carpeted, with her own furniture and doll collection in it, and with people to talk to who didn't have Alzheimer's.

"The museum," Dad said, after looking around briefly.

I glanced at Mom.

"He always hated the old furniture, even the ones his own grandfather made. I had to fight to get him to let me keep grandma's drop-front desk and the corner cupboard," she said pointing to the open desk where she had been answering some letters.

I nodded, remembering how difficult it was when we were children to get him to take us to museums—and only on vacations, never, ever when we were at home. He didn't have any use for them. History was bunk to him. A Henry Ford kind of engineer: progress, speed, forget about where it comes from, just get where you are going.

Trudy wasn't around for this conversation, and usually never when I was, if she could help it. She was off, handling the money and legal papers, as she had been since their arrival. I was in charge of Dad's care, and we didn't talk at all, except when it was absolutely necessary, and even then, not often face-to-face. When Chuck and Trudy decided to create a living trust, Trudy left the papers in the back of my car (so she wouldn't have to see me, or so I surmised). When she did see me, it was usually painful. I was hurt that I hadn't been part of the decision. Reading my diaries now, (really, they are just scribbled notebooks, not unlike what exists in my memory), I see there was no way I could know whether Trudy could help herself or not. Just as she didn't really know what I was doing, thinking, or feeling.

Once the assisted-living director called me to ask whether I knew that a batch of photographs had been put in the dumpster. "I pulled them out for you—shall I put them back in your mom's room?"

The next time I went to visit, I saw a larger pile than I expected. One in particular I was grateful had been saved. It was a photo of a family picnic on my father's side. There were a couple dozen relatives, and I had referred to it often when making the family tree. But it made me angry that Trudy had forgotten how much I was interested in family history.

When I asked Trudy about it later, she just said, "I was cleaning with Mom and she didn't know who they were. I didn't either, so we threw them away." Reasonable, I guess, but I still took it as a slap in the face.

When I didn't see Trudy, I can't say that I wasn't happy, because when she criticized my thoughts or actions, it seemed like she wanted to kill me. Guy and I had bought property almost twenty miles out of town, and had started building. We had borrowed some money from Mom to buy a tractor, which angered both my siblings. We hadn't yet settled that controversy, but that was easy to resolve. She and Chuck just took equal amounts and we were even, but she was still icy cold.

Well, I had no part in the decisions about money after that and it felt like she was stealing something from me, not money but something more important. Maybe that's what she was feeling too. I felt somewhat guilty for feeling that way privately. We moved forward, updating each other and our brother without the discussion I longed to have with them. Just the facts, ma'am, though we were careful to get each other's agreement over any big decisions.

And she stayed cold, all the time, or at least all the times I saw her. We bumped into each other once in Mom's apartment, and somehow or other the topic of Dad's guns came up. I thought she had taken all of them with her to her house out-of-town. She said I still had them, or a couple of them. Neither of us backed down until Mom got up and walked over to point at the two hand-guns on her table in the living room behind a bowl of fruit. Did we keep glaring at each other? I don't recall.

"Don't you think it odd that neither one of us saw something right there in front of us? That we didn't think of asking Mom until we were already far into an argument?" I didn't want to sound so defensive. I didn't want to hurt her. Did she think I did? I wanted the arguing to stop, even if it meant we never saw each other again.

Trudy made a face that made me realize that much of my confusion came from assuming that she loved me. I shivered. Did she think I didn't love her?

I started to keep a real journal, though it came in fragments, sometimes as much as a vignette, but never a sustained story. There wasn't a coherent plot or integrated characters. I wrote and wrote, and it all fell to pieces like broken china. *The story isn't over yet,* I thought. *Maybe I won't be able to write the whole story until they are both dead.* Much later, after they both had died, Trudy would tell me that when she walked into Mom's room she felt like she was walking into a brick wall, seeing the three of us together again like we were when she was growing up. After she said it, I felt that memory too, in some dim way. It was her memory, but I started having it, overlaying it on the ones I had of our happy family. Still, it remained opaque, I couldn't hear what it was trying to say.

Another time I left Mom at the door of her apartment in the assisted living and went down the turning stairs and pushed out the door of the building, leaning hard against the oversized, metal handle that ran the width of the door. I ran into Trudy under the portico, coming at me like an SUV gone loose, with her brown hair disgruntled and her eyes aflash. She had a newspaper in her hand and began waving it in my face.

"What's this? What's this?" There was a big black permanent marker circle around the kudo I had sent into the local paper. It read, "Thank you from our family to the staff at WholeCare for your great care of Dad." I had signed it from the whole family.

"Who gave you the right to speak for me?"

I cringed. The absolute line drawn through the sand. I couldn't deny it, couldn't absorb it, couldn't stand it. I took a step to push by her, and then pushed past my anger instead. Taking a deep breath and from somewhere deep I managed, "I'm sorry," in a shaky voice, but without looking at her. "I called them when I realized what I had done and asked them to change the signature to just mine. I knew you wouldn't like it, but it was too late."

"Oh. Okay then." She shouldered by me and pulled the door open to disappear up the stairs.

Later, too much later, Trudy explained to me that Dad had taught us to be angry when we were crossed, and she thought he had been raised the same way. It seemed like an inhuman thing, not something someone would have been born with. Not something you'd figure out for yourself either, because it didn't work that well. Obviously, it was too hard to resist for both of us.

I was back behind the wheel of the hatchback and strapped in before I could relax the crouching shoulders, breathless belly and tensed legs that made we want to leave my body. I took my journal and kept writing. It was funny. I didn't get angry at the nursing home in the way I did at Trudy (well, twice I did). The anger at the institution was resistible somehow. I could work to change Dad's treatment and ignore the pawns who were only doing their jobs. I was at a loss to change Trudy. Why? I had less traction with her, my own sister. Now I think she may have thought the same about me.

—

The nursing home invited the families of people in that unit to start a support group in the building. We met in a conference room in the nursing home with antiseptic air closed in by windowless walls. While we waited for everyone to get settled, a man about my age who slumped back and down in his plastic chair was describing a new concept for the care of the Alzhammered. I sat up straight in mine and listened while he described the concept: a small, ten-bedroom house with a kitchen in the middle where people work who were not medically trained so much as trained to accompany people when they were on their last journey. When doctors and nurses came for necessary visits, they are required to knock on the door and be let in, rather than just appear and start poking.

"That's very nice, Randall," our facilitator interrupted. "Not what we do here," she added, not looking up from her notes, "But I will tell the administration to take a look." I caught Randall's eye and made a writing motion with my right index finger in the palm of my left hand. He nodded and pulled a piece of paper out of his notebook, scribbled something quickly, and passed it to me. "Dr. Thomas Greenhouse project. There's a book in the library—*Eden Alternative*."

The facilitator took the time to give us a dirty look. I felt like we were passing forbidden notes in sixth grade.

I nodded and sat back in my chair. It was time to go around the table and introduce ourselves.

The first to go was the facilitator. "WholeCare has decided to hold meetings of family members every week so that you can share your joys and frustrations. All of you have parents or other loved ones here with us. We will give you this room for an hour each week, and we'd like to know how we can make your loved one's experience better. "Let's introduce ourselves, shall we?" she said without looking up from a paper in her lap. Was she reading from a script?

There were mostly women around the table, women about my age and of varying shapes and sizes, hairdos or none to speak of, dressed for work or play. Most of them were sad and a little scared about the large number of deaths lurching about the room, and how much scarier our own parent's death was than anyone else's. But we had something in common, so it was easy to talk. We were the ones who came often enough that we had started nodding to each other in the hallways. No one talked about themselves, or how they were feeling. It was odd. They clearly were not happy about their parents living in this cleaner-than-clean place on a regimen that prescribed eating, bathing, sleeping, and medicating each at the same time every day. Even when we could visit. That's what I thought, at any rate.

"I'm worried about my mother," I said. The facilitator frowned. "She's not visiting my father and I..." Several people nodded and murmured around the table. One said, "Mine too."

"She has not been to see him for a few weeks, most of which she has spent sleeping in her new bed. He's been asking for her every time I've been in to see him but is easily distracted from that thought. The other day she gave me her wedding ring and said, 'You're the one taking care of him now.'" I got a little choked up as I finished.

"That's horrible!" The facilitator butted in. "That's sick!" Everyone else fell silent. The facilitator frowned at me. "We're here to talk about your father and WholeCare."

"I thought you said we could feel free to talk about anything we want?"

"Well, yes, if it has to do with what's going on here. If you want to talk about your mother, you can meet among yourselves."

"Okay, then. Uh, let's see. The nurse on the Alzheimer's unit doesn't want me to take my dad out to lunch. He needs to get out of here once in a while! And they won't give him physical therapy because he's not *improving*. What's that about? Can't he have physical therapy so as to just hold his own? He needs to walk. He'll lose control of his bladder if he doesn't move."

"That's standard policy," she replied. "The insurance companies won't pay for physical therapy unless the patient is showing improvement. The therapist is required to keep notes." She was still looking in her lap.

I didn't feel surprised so much as hopeless. "But he has money to pay for his own therapy?" I attempted.

"We can't do that. Not all the patients have enough money for that. It wouldn't be fair to them."

"What?" I lost any cool I had ever had for this woman and this place. "I thought we lived in a capitalist country? Where people who have more money can do what they want with it?"

She just ignored me, and I gave up. "Let's go back a step, and try this again," she continued. "This is a support group, not a place to question WholeCare policy. You are all here to help each other through this trying experience." She was right. She wasn't here to argue with somebody who had no standing. It felt to me much like dinner time when we were children: go to your room if you can't behave.

By that point I couldn't figure out what we were supposed to be talking about, so I made a funny face and excused myself from the meeting, Randall following suit along and one other woman. We met briefly in the hallway outside, where Randall gave us more information about Dr. Thomas and the Greenhouse Project. "We should try and get WholeCare to look at his program," he said. "It addresses some of the things you were talking about in there. That's what I want to talk about."

"I don't think there's much chance this place will look at it," said the woman. What did you say the title of that book was?" So we took down each other's phone numbers, but no one ever called me.

I read the book, and later went on a weekend retreat with Dr. Bill

Thomas, a physician who invented the concepts of "Greenhouse" and the "Eden Alternative" for end-or-life care. He and his wife, a nurse, introduced dogs and plants and birds and revolutionary training for CNAs which gave them more power to make decisions and encouraged them to treat Alzheimer's patients with respect. I told him about my problems with the medical professionals: I thought he would understand, himself having fought the medical profession on the very issues I complained about.

After listening at length all he said was, "Well, *you* were there." I thought he didn't believe me.

Flying home, I was struck by the ambiguity of his response: I was a witness, he couldn't gainsay my experience. But my very presence at the scene changed the nurses' reactions, made them defensive. Well, tough shit. They weren't interested in helping Dad and they weren't interested in helping me either. And they should have been. So I kept resisting and fighting.

Later in the year, I was able to persuade WholeCare to let me bring in a physical therapist, as long as the therapy took place in Dad's room when his roommate wasn't there and the door was closed. This worked. After the therapist left, I would walk with him up and down the halls so that he did not entirely lose the strength in his legs. He needed a modicum, so that he could get in and out of the Jeep when we went out to lunch.

—

While the Alzheimer's unit pretended to keep order and make sense of the strangers in their midst, things went no better for me outside the nursing home. Trudy and I had pretty much fallen back into a pattern that worked for me as I imagined it worked for Trudy. We both visited Mom, but not at the same time. We both emailed Chuck separately from our separate computers.

We were in a lawyer's office, asking questions about wills and POAs and trusts. The lawyer sat behind a desk, and I sat on the left, facing him but halfway turned toward Trudy, who sat on the right, her chair facing the front of the desk, intent on the man who was speaking.

"Wait," Trudy said, "I want to write this down." I started to tear a sheet from a yellow legal pad in my lap. Trudy was rummaging in the front pocket of her overalls, one of those pockets just big enough to get one finger into that is the signature of that brand of clothing. I started to pass the sheet of paper to her. She looked right at it, but not at me, then pulled out a gum wrapper. "This'll do," she said.

It was so odd that the counselor looked at me and raised his brow. I wrote in my journal "She hadn't just ignored the paper, she hadn't even *seen* it. I shivered." Now, of course I don't remember it quite like that. Of course, her comment makes no sense unless she *did* see it.

So Trudy took care of money. I took care of Dad. Somehow those two projects logjammed.

—

Another day my sister and I stood outside the one-and-a-half story frame house in town, where I had moved in with Guy and his three boys. The spring sun was coughing out some sunlight and the trees were tatting lace with it, letting it fall on the mud and not-yet-growing grass of the front lawn. Trudy looked me levelly in the eye.

"Do you have to visit him *every* day?" she said, as frozen as ice.

"Why not? I have the time. I'm only working half time now. And it's all right with Guy. We can afford it. He supports it." I thought, also coldly, *What do you care when I visit? You don't visit him at all.* I did not ask myself why I cared so much about what she *didn't* do.

"And what happens when you move out of town? Then you won't be able to do it anymore. He'll be worse off than if you'd never visited."

"Why do you think I won't come in after we move?" She just stood there. "When I lived out at the lake, I came to town all the time. I don't mind it. Besides, he has Alzheimer's, what makes you think he'll remember?"

Trudy stood gaping at me, then snapped her mouth shut, turned, and marched away. I looked after her, and then I understood. Maybe she wasn't willing to drive all the way into town from her new boyfriend's place. More likely she just didn't want to visit at all, but I got to do what I wanted too. So, what's the problem here? We were both wrong in some way that I would not fathom for another decade, another dysfunctional family, and another way to breathe freely again.

—

One Sunday, when Dad and I were at a sandwich shop, sitting at a table by the window, Trudy and the boyfriend came in and took a booth on the inside wall, right across from our table. She didn't make eye contact. Dad looked at Trudy for a few seconds, looked back at me, and shrugged. She turned her back and pretended not to notice her father and sister were there. I finally got up and went over, fomenting a confrontation I could have avoided. Why did I push her like that, I ask myself now.

"Won't you come and sit with Dad? He doesn't understand why you are ignoring him."

"I thought we agreed you were going to take him to the pie place."

"They aren't open on Sundays."

"So?"

"So, I brought him here. He likes to watch the trains, anyway."

"But that's not what we agreed."

"Things change." I wished that they hadn't, but I wasn't about to tell her that.

"Well, I came here to have lunch with George. Not to see Dad, or you. You don't have a right to be here, so leave." My heart snapped shut.

I went back to my own table. I ate, but not much, and remained silent as if anything I said could be held against me. I needed to get out of there as soon as I could.

Trudy finished her lunch and stood up. She came over and said hello to Dad, who invited her to sit down. Her boyfriend did not join in. She left. Dad looked at me, and shrugged as if he didn't understand why she did that. Or, maybe he didn't even recognize her. I stopped eating and fell into a reverie.

—

Decades before, sometime in our thirties, we'd had the usual discussions about how our parents had failed us, but I was speechless to discover that not only did she not love Dad, she seemed to hate him, pretty much. But why? He was handsome, funny, and generous. He supported the family and took us on summer vacations. He taught us to count, to add and subtract by using the Church's collection every Sunday to pit us against each other in a competition to see who was fastest and most accurate.

Trudy was youngest, so I tried on the idea that she had just been too young to keep up with her older sister and brother. She'd also been pigeon-toed and had to wear braces. Neither Chuck nor I had those handicaps, but we both wore glasses while Trudy didn't need them, and I spent much more time and received much more pain at the dentist than she did. (Just now in the hundred and twentieth edit of my memoir I at last notice that this last sentence is wildly mean and untrue.) Why wasn't she just indifferent towards the man? I couldn't see that she might feel imperfect in a family whose standard was unforgiving. It never occurred to me until it did, that we all weren't perfect.

Or was it animosity towards me? That made some sense. Times I had forgotten came to me, how I teased her mercilessly when we lay awake at night, the times we argued, times I left her behind to be with my friends, the time I sprayed perfume in her mouth, but it still didn't feel like that explained her fury at me now. Later, I would revise that judgment, and try to forgive myself for making it.

More recently she had stopped by the house in town. She came into the living room, and Guy and a close friend of his were there as I came down the stairs. Just as if they had rehearsed a dance, they formed themselves into a barrier around Trudy, and I stood there awkwardly talking to her over their heads. And when she held out a bag of bagels as a gift, Guy took it from her and handed it to me, unsmiling. They reacted to her as if she was dangerous, a threat to me somehow. That was over-the-top, even for me.

—

"I'm done, "said Dad, after a few minutes, calling my attention back to the lunch table.

I looked down at my uneaten BLT. "Let's go then," I said—and getting up, went to the other side of the table to take my post behind the wheelchair.

Later the same week Trudy and I agreed to meet down by the creek, behind the main street of town, for lunch. We sat down, unwrapped sandwiches, and I asked her what was up.

"You disregarded everything I told you."

"I thought he'd like to see the train."

"But I told you not to over-stimulate him," she said. True, she was a therapist and knew much about the psychology of people with disabilities, such as what could trigger them.

"But he enjoyed it. No?" I defended myself. "The only problem was you. You apparently didn't want to sit with us."

"It was my lunch. He has enough. I wanted to have lunch with George."

Well, I thought with a rush of anger. *We are alive, after all. Adjust! It's not about you.* But I didn't say it.

I got up and turned away. There wasn't much point in this disagreeing about who had acted more stupidly. Trudy got up too and surprised me by suggesting a walk. And I accepted, hoping as I always did, that something would come of further talk. I wasn't sure what. We didn't even agree on the simplest of perceptions, much less on what we ought to do. Part of me was curious to understand Trudy's feel for what was happening. Part of me was afraid that it would only lead to a barrage of unmanageable, snap accusations.

We walked slowly along the edge of the lake and fooled around with nebulous topics. Several times we went back and forth on the semicircular sidewalk dividing the beach from the parking lot. It wasn't a hostile conversation, but we didn't get anywhere.

The third time we gained the end of the sidewalk, I turned to face her. "But I need your help with this! I can't do it all by myself."

Trudy grimaced swiftly, gave a gentle roll of the eyes and a just perceptible inclination of her head toward one shoulder, a stretching and thinning of the lips into a straight line, then a squint. The skin around her eyes sagged at the outside corners. It was the first time I noticed she was starting to wrinkle, even though she was already almost fifty years old.

We started back along the way we had come, staring straight ahead at the lake. "You don't listen to me when I do tell you," she said. I looked at my sister's closed face, her wavy brown hair moving in a gentle puff of air. If I had heard her say that to someone else, I would not have recognized her.

"What do you want? I don't know what you want."

She stopped and turned toward me. "I don't want to know anything about him. If I want to know something, I'll call you. Don't call me."

Fine with me, I thought. As I watched her walk away, I thought I was losing her forever. But who was it I was losing? Despite all the singing I had done with Mom, the sky had fallen after all.

Chapter Four

REMEMBERING

In Alzheimer's disease, the amygdala is generally affected later than the hippocampus. So a person with Alzheimer's will often recall emotional aspects of something even if they don't recall the factual content. They may therefore respond more according to how they feel about a place or person than in a more logical way.
Alzheimer's Society

Memory is deceptive because it is colored by today's events
Albert Einstein

When Dad first got here, he still knew who everybody was (or we didn't notice if he didn't), along with lots of other people: his nuclear relatives, the people in his college yearbook, the teacher he loved in first grade. But other things weren't right with his memory. At home, he had collected twenty-five little plastic boxes of dental floss, for example, and even more larger boxes of Dr. Scholl's foot powder, which we found on his side of the bathroom cupboards, stacked up where they belonged. He was clearly off, but was that dementia? Guy and I started to do this even before we were on Medicare. I buy salt. Then he buys salt. Then I can't remember if I bought salt, so I buy more. This looks like the start of dementia, but it doesn't have to turn into that. There are lots of weeds in my garden that mimic the plants I want to grow, but they don't end up to be what I planted.

I never know what I'm going to remember. Oh, my memory's okay and everything, I just don't know when it will strike—or if, when I call it, it will come (just like my dog). Sometimes I'll go five minutes and sometimes several hours or a day, and suddenly it's there, clear and bright as over-bleached blonde hair, and I can say just what it is. When Mom started to forget something, she'd say, "Just wait a minute—my memory is like that trolley rack at the dry cleaner's where they hang up the cleaned clothes. If you wait long enough it'll come around." And she made a circle around her head with her index finger, like the motion for being crazy, but above her head pointing down, instead of at the side—at right angles to crazy.

I started to read Freud and got curious about connections in the thoughts of Alzies. If you only knew them well enough to know who they were, what they had experienced, what they meant, then maybe what they did and did not say and do would made some kind of sense. Maybe the regular people, the ones that aren't Alzhammered, can't tell what our mothers and fathers forget and what they remember? Why not try to figure it out?

So I decided to do an experiment and spend a couple of hours a day in the Alzheimer unit with my father—and with my mother in her apartment and out and about with me in town. Dad's nurses called this "denial," but I knew what I was doing. I started to keep a notebook of what I saw and heard.

When we moved Dad out here, we brought with us a couple of his old radios. When one of them didn't function, I took it to him in the nursing home. He was in the dining place when I set it on the table in front of him, plugged it in and turned the knob to on. Only, it didn't come on. He immediately turned the radio around, took the backing off, and pulled out a tube, one of the ones that didn't light up. Then he got up from his chair, walked about twenty feet straight back from his chair to the hallway, turned right and went into the first room on the right, which was somebody else's room. I followed, and marked his confusion.

Immediately a CNA was taking his arm and leading him back to the table, chastising him for going into another patient's room. He went with her quietly looking back over his shoulder and let himself be seated in front of the radio again.

Standing there watching all this, I could see him at home sitting at his desk in the den. If he got up and walked away from his desk and through the living room to the front hall, then turned right, he would be at the door to the basement stairs. And at the bottom of those stairs was his workshop, the place he kept his collection of old, working radio tubes.

The next day, I brought him the box of old tubes we had also brought along, and he fixed it.

—

I started to formulate a theory about Alzhammered memory. Forgetting is like rinsing off in the shower: the ordinary activities of daily living and the impermanence of human experience wash off and down the drain. We forget the small stuff. Not remembering is different—more like not *seeing* the grime that's still there—like the flashbacks that my neighbor Larry has because he has PTSD. The fear doesn't disappear, it's always still there, but he doesn't talk about it. Alzheimer's is partly not being able to say what you mean. Remembering can be in your body; in a way, the experience remembers you. Alzheimer's is more a silence than a blank slate.

Much of the behavior of the other inmates still didn't make sense to me, but when I thought about Dad this way, I could usually suss out what he was up to. He wasn't a danger, well, maybe to himself, but at least not to others.

One day my mother called me from the assisted living across the parking lot from the nursing home where my dad was a kept man in a backward sort of way. He wasn't the one who was prostituting himself for money—the nursing home was. My mother often called me, just to talk, though I knew it was really because she wanted to hear a voice she recognized. She knew who she was when she was talking to me. And I knew who I was too.

She was laughing. "You should see the little boys running around having so much fun!" I pictured one of Mom's windows on the second-floor of the assisted living, overlooking the parking lot beside the Alzhammered Unit.

At first, I panicked. "Little boys?" I said. "How little? Are their mothers with them?"

"No, not them," she said. "The ones with FOUR legs."

"Oh, dogs! You mean dogs?"

"Yes, dogs," she hummed it. "They're having so much fun." Her pretty smile lit up the phone line all the way to my kitchen.

I quickly got used to her new language. It was playing, like the way we had done crosswords together, only more fun because it was my mother sending me clues from farther and farther out, and when I got the answer, it was more rewarding than any puzzle I'd ever done before.

I parked next to a red pickup in a downpour one afternoon, and she looked up into the bed of the truck which held an over-sized, drenched, black dog and laughed. "Look at that RED CHICKEN!" she said, turning to see whether I laughed with her. I understood exactly what she meant. On our way to church on time, I looked in the rearview mirror and said, "I need to comb my hair."

She replied, "Let's go. You look like us."

She'd look up out of the front windshield and, seeing a bird swoop by, saying, "There goes a song!" Or when I came to pick her up for her haircut: "Let's go fix my beauty." And because she was happy and go-lucky too, these kinds of mistakes were not failings for either of us. They added something to our times together. I could guess the trains of thought even when there were four or five cars missing between the engine and caboose. Every time, I could put the pieces of my mother back together again into a whole person. So they were happy times. Things went well when I was with the Alzhammered, but there were other things that were going wrong.

—

One time I overheard the CNAs talking about Dad liking his bath so much, and I thought, hoping it might be true, *maybe they'll give him more than one a week....* "He's so hard to handle," one of them said. It was true: he was a large man—six feet, two inches tall in his prime—and bound to a wheelchair. He could help a little when he wanted to stand, but even two people would have a hard time keeping him from hitting the floor if he didn't. I heard myself judge those CNAs. "Just do your job. You have no right to complain." Of course, I only said that to myself. They simply agreed that they wished they didn't have to give him a bath so often.

I heard Dad once starting to talk about "Bikini." The CNAs got all fluttery, waving their hands close to their shoulders and running away from him, like they were afraid of him, then it dawned on me. He wasn't talking about bathing suits. He was talking about Bikini Island where the first atom bomb tests were carried out after World War II. My father was there on a US Navy ship, one of the first Americans to personally witness an A-bomb explosion. He was there as an official government witness along with other men from the Army Corp of Engineers. He was the most interesting thing that had ever happened to him in his life.

That's what I mean. He forgot he had the Dr. Scholls, but he remembered the A-bomb. The social worker at the first nursing home he was in didn't know to ask about Bikini when she filled out the form with me about Dad's personal history, and I didn't think to tell her, so the CNAs didn't know any better.

Dad didn't talk much about the A-bomb when I was growing up. Just once or twice, and then all he said was that it wasn't such a big deal as they made it out to be—that he had eaten a can of baked beans that was left on deck, and he hadn't died of radiation poisoning or anything. He thought it was more dangerous climbing up and down the rigging to get on and off the ship! He made fun of the people who wanted to apologize to Japan, and he made fun of the people who thought there were long-term health consequences of the radiation. Nevertheless, Bikini was a big enough thing that it stayed in his memory, and he talked about it more and more as the dementia took hold, up until just before he died. Sometimes it seemed like the only thing he could remember. When the first nursing home kicked him out for being "a danger to himself or others," a nurse came to interview him for a new place. He tried to tell her about it, but she just looked puzzled.

And he got what he wanted out of the A-bomb. When the orders came through for him to go to the test, he said he wouldn't go unless they promoted him to lieutenant. He got his way, and I do believe the promotion was proof to him that he was good, and that was more important to him than being present at one of THE major events of the twentieth century. Perhaps that's because he didn't see the A-bomb as being such a bad thing. Certainly, my mother didn't. She always said if it wasn't for the A-bomb my father would have had to invade Japan and maybe die, and maybe she would've had to die too, and where would I be?

The copy of Dad's promotion letter made it through many cullings to end up in the top of my barn in 2000, with all of his report cards and Sunday School attendance certificates, and all of the checks he had written since he opened his first bank account at age thirteen. His life was well documented. Nothing was missing. If it wasn't in those documents, or in the thousands of slides and tape recordings he had made of his family and friends and vacations, it didn't happen. If it wasn't in the files, it wasn't true. There wasn't much about their private lives that made it through. Love letters, their happy times and good times before we were born, didn't play much of a part in my picture of who they were. Even my mother's sixty plus years of Daily Aid diaries, which she kept every year staring about the time she married, contained what was happening, but rarely revealed how she felt about any of it. They were less like memories and more like, well, documentation. Just the facts, ma'am, facts that gave me little sense of the reality they measured.

As it turned out, my life was there, too, in those files I had not known about, much less remembered, until I was in my fifties. There were checks for house payments, food, clothing, cars, furniture, and the anonymous cash. I don't remember exactly when we started paying for things with credit cards. But I do remember once when I was very little watching Dad pay for something I wanted very much. It was a balsa wood airplane that came in pieces that you had to assemble yourself. But you didn't need batteries, it would fly when you held it by the belly and sent it gliding off. The only problem was, I was too little to put it together. We took it out of the box, and before I could even touch it, Dad picked up the pieces and did it for me. He let me have a turn flying it, but that wasn't same thing for me, and it ended up on a shelf above the desk in his home office. No one would know from the documents that he bought it for himself and not his children.

I looked back at the check register. One check was made out to the hospital where I was born, a day or two after Mom brought me home. I cost $30. My brother cost $32—*circumcision, perhaps?* I thought. Understanding that my dad had paid for me to be born was something I had never considered. The people in the place and time I was born into paid for their babies. Did they look at us differently because we cost them differently?

—

There can be other reasons why people don't say things besides forgetting or not remembering them. Already at sixteen or seventeen I couldn't face any situation which called for a lie. I was out pranking with a group of friends on Halloween (soap and toilet paper kind of thing), when we were rounded up by the local police. I didn't know either of the officers, and I don't think any of my friends did either, but who knows? They lined us up, which was a pretty long line, maybe ten or eleven of us, and I was at one end of a line of teenagers in cutoffs with straw hats on, the minimal Halloween costume required of those of us who were "cool." I am amazed when I remember it was on a Tuesday night. Beyond that, all I remember is that it was dark, dry and warm, and that we were standing in a macadam street in the middle of town. There were flashlights.

I didn't know what to expect, but as it happened the officer started the questioning at the other end of the line. The first suspect, or victim, simply denied any guilt. As the officer questioned us each in order and in turn, and as each one denied our guilt, I became more and more afraid that when he came to me, I would not be able to lie. My mouth got dry. I couldn't swallow. After several long minutes, he arrived at me with a unanimous testimony that we were innocent.

"What is your name?" the officer asked. When I told them I was my father's daughter, that's all he wanted to know. We were scot-free. I still couldn't swallow and left my friends hooting in the darkness behind me.

—

The most important person not to lie to was my mother. Lying to her was even more difficult for me than lying to the police. I never could do it, and only rarely even consider it—she knew me well enough that she knew when not to ask questions.

Woodstock, that was one time. July 1969. My friend Jill was on her way to pick me up at 6 a.m. in the morning, and my mom got up to make me breakfast. Jill had told her mother that we had a place to stay, but we didn't, we were just going to go and see what happened. She told me to tell my mom the same, and I had. But when Jill appeared at the door, smiling and eager to get going, Mom gave me a hug, and I got scared.

"I'm not going," I said, and Jill said, "Why?" I shrugged, and she shrugged and turned around and left.

"Why aren't you going?" asked Mom, putting her arm around me patiently.

"Because," I lied, "We don't have a place to stay."

Mom shrugged too. And after a moment of thought she said, "We all have to learn how to lie."

But I wasn't disappointed. I knew the chances that going without a plan might end up not being that much fun. I watched on TV instead, and tried to find Jill in the crowds. I had a good seat for the show and was glad to be home and warm and well-fed, and not wet and cold and hungry without a place to pee in. And I was glad I hadn't lied. I had never lied to Mom nor she to me, and I couldn't bear the thought of that happening.

—

Can you lie even when you are telling the truth? ("I love you," says Dad.

Does he? Is he lying?) Remembering. Forgetting. This is life as I knew it, in 2000 AD.

Then one day it hit me. This story was not just about Dad and Mom, Trudy and Chuck. It was the nursing home, the doctors, the professionals who didn't recognize Alzheimer's in people other than their patients. And if that was true, it must be about me too. Now reality had made its chaotic appearance, and I wanted it to go back to the old, comfortable order I'd been used to for fifty years. Looking back on it now, it makes sense to me, but at the time it ate me up until I was nothing but a crumb. My mother had it worse, even though both parents didn't remember me at times. My father was angrier, but he always remembered some of the important parts and even knew who I was just days before he died. Mom lost everything, though she didn't know she did.

I didn't believe that Trudy was lying and neither was I. We had Alzheimer's: couldn't say what we meant, what we remembered. Trudy and I would be cured, but only after seven or eight more years of silence.

Chapter Five — SIGN HERE, PLEASE

You promised that you'd forget me not,
But you forgot to remember.
Irving Berlin

After I allowed myself to admit that Trudy didn't care about Dad, things got easier. I carried on, sometimes burdened, sometimes lighter-hearted, but always glad to know the code that opened the door to the Alzheimer's Unit and escape the reality hail outside. Often, I wondered, *who was the crazy one?* Dad didn't even know who I was anymore.

1-2-3-4, hip to the metal bar, I'm in. It is eerily quiet in the brightly lit ward. No one is moving. In a way it is devoid of life in here, I think. Only when the activities director's around is there any speaking with the inmates, or singing, or everyone sitting quietly while she reads a newspaper from a town that most of them did not ever live in before and the rest have no memory of. If it wasn't so well lit, it would be dark in there. From another angle, there are long stretches where the patients are not doing anything except what is right in front of them. If there is nothing upsetting right in front of their faces, they're fine.

Shortly after Dad arrived at the nursing home, we needed to move the automatic pension and Social Security payments from the bank in his hometown to the one in ours. Who knew that the powers of attorney held by both my mother and brother were no good with the federal government? I didn't understand this, despite my doctorate, but queerly, I found I could accept that the government had no faith in our legal system. In order for Mom to move the Social Security payment from the old bank account to the new, she was told to appear in person at the so-called "local" Social Security office forty miles away, which was "manned" by an answering machine. We left several messages asking for a call back. Without Trudy or me there to help, though, she couldn't explain her question well enough to the clerks mainlining the databases at the other end of the phone. And, naturally, the offices would not make an appointment at a certain time to call you back. Of course, they claimed they would do that—or rather, the national hotline said that the local office would do it. In fact, it didn't happen.

As for Dad's pension, the blue chip company sent a simple form for him to fill out and sign. No, Mom or Chuck couldn't sign for him. Hmm. Neither government nor the private sector would honor a duly executed legal document. This boded ill for what promised to be a legally and financially complicated future. The feeling of insecurity was excruciating. Mom looked at me with pleading eyes; I was used to them by now. But what had I gotten myself into? Was Dad really crazy? Or was I the crazy one?

Some would have simply forged a signature, but I was my father's daughter, I came from a family that told the truth. He would have wanted me to be honest about this and not sign his name for him.

That wasn't always true of me. I had a few affairs with married men and lied about it—even to Mom, who knew anyway. When I brought the man and his wife and kids home with me once, she was welcoming and we all had a good time. And the next day Mom told me the story of a man in the small town they had retired to who lived with two women. "He loved them both, and neither of them seemed to mind, so everybody just let it be." I was dumb-struck, not that she knew, but that she was giving me her blessing—or at least an idea of a way through.

But no! I didn't lie. No one really asked me about it. They didn't want to know the answer. They didn't want me to *say* the answer out loud, where they would have to accept it or not. They preferred to ignore it. Of course, the three of us minded the situation we were in a lot, so it fell apart.

Even authorities, when they know what you're doing, let you go if it's too much trouble to hold you to account. Once I went off to hitchhike with a boy. On our way home, we were picked up by the police. When they called Dad he said only, "You should always have your driver's license with you." Turned out that's all the police wanted proof of who I was, not whether or not I had broken the law. It was good advice: when people know who you are, or think they do, you can get away with things. The authorities not only let me go but drove me at speeds exceeding the legal limit to the next bus station while we rode silently in the back seat. I said nothing, and we hitchhiked home.

So now I helped Mom fill out the form, and took it to my father in the Alzheimer's unit. I placed the form gingerly in front of Dad and said, "Dad, we're moving your pension deposit to the bank out here, and they need you to sign this paper."

He balked, his forehead wrinkling both horizontally and vertically at once, a facial expression that covered confusion, even fear, on top of disapproval. "No," he said, bristling. He pushed the paper away.

I tried again, and again he pushed it away. I slumped back in the plastic chair and looked out the window. Through the yard and over the eight-foot-high solid wood fence, I could see only the gray, featureless sky. Gradually, I stopped seeing even that and saw instead myself talking to Dad at a time two years before, during the spring after Dad had gone into the hospital for his back operation.

—

That afternoon, I sat in his den, staring out into another gray sky. Mom hadn't said a thing, just looked at me with her clear child's eyes. She did not want to make medical decisions for Dad, though she clearly understood that someone had to. She had been confused and tongue-tied during the weeks after his operation, repeatedly thanking me for staying with her. Time after time, I had witnessed her deferring to the doctors without asking a single question. Because she was smart, I knew she must be scared. So I had asked Dad to sign a medical power of attorney for one of his children. It felt awkward; he had always made not only his own decisions but also the decisions for the entire family. But it also felt like the right thing to do. Though I appeared to him to be an alien, I hoped I could convince him that I was an alien with a good heart.

He was irate. Sweat burst from his skin like rain from a thundercloud. Even though he was sitting in his desk chair with his back to me, I seemed to be looking up at all of his six feet, two inches—into his angry—face from my former five-year-old height. I steeled myself for a battle I knew I had to win. But the steel I was able to muster wasn't enough.

Turning toward me, he mumbled something about "trusting your mother," which trailed off into a shamed look that pleaded with me to go away and be quiet.

I didn't know what to do next. He didn't want to admit that he didn't trust us, and his fear continued to rain down on me and soak me coldly to my own bones. Finally, I said, "Well, think about it," and turned to go.

"I don't need to think about it," he snapped pretty nastily, but I knew he had no choice.

I waited five days before bringing up the subject again. I reminded him that my sister was expert at dealing with the health care system, which she had done professionally for most of her life. I told him I was going to sign one for myself, if she would agree to take on my health care too. He wouldn't budge. I felt the issue was so important, I finally exploded.

"You're not this stupid!" I yelled at him. "I'm ashamed of you for putting Mom in that position. It isn't fair. If you can't sign it over to one of your own children, then pick somebody else you do trust. I'm sure one of your old friends around here would do it."

He ducked around to face his desk and said nothing. Why didn't he trust his own daughter?

A few days later he had three copies of medical powers of attorney, *one with each child's name on it. He called me into the den and gave me mine. There was no more discussion. I had won. He felt beaten, diminished, lost—now that he had to depend on someone else.*

—

Looking at the empty sky as I sat next to my father in the dining room of the Alzheimer's unit, I remembered how much he'd feared signing those medical powers of attorney. I guessed that the fear must be that much worse now, when he couldn't even understand what the paper meant. It struck me for the first time that he may not have understood exactly what the medical powers of attorney had meant either. I felt ashamed for having bullied him into signing them. Nothing seemed to feel right anymore.

I put my hand on his and slowly repeated the daily litany. Did he understand any of it? Perhaps the sound of my voice, calm and reasonable, would make him feel more at home. "We think you had a stroke. Trudy and I came back and brought you and Mom out to live near us. Mom lives across the street, I live ten blocks away, and Trudy is right outside town. We are moving your bank account out here so Mom can get at the money. Now, won't you sign it for me?"

At this last question, Dad peeked up sideways at me and took the pen. "Okay," he said, unexpectedly relaxed, his old handsome self.

"Right here on this line," I said, hopefully fixing my finger just above the spot.

And he signed. He signed my name, Sarah Measwell. "There you go," he said proudly and set down the pen.

When I laughed, he looked pleased. He was also pleased, I might add, to have won this one.

As for myself, he knew who I was again for a moment! Wasn't so bad, in fact, I felt grateful that I could take care of my dad at the end of his life the way he had taken care of me at the beginning of mine.

Chapter Six

LOSING CHUCK

How come you do me like you do do do?
How come you do me like you do?
Austin and Bergere

My brother came to visit. He brought his son Frank with him. Frank wanted to go skiing. I wanted Frank to visit Dad. Chuck said he didn't want Frank to remember Dad that way.

"But," I remonstrated, "I saw Grandma that way, and I still remember her the way she was before."

"You were older."

Frank went skiing.

Dad had been expecting his son all week. Most days when I said to him, "Guess who's coming?" He would answer, "Chuck" with a grin. If he didn't know I'd tell him, then he'd say, "Oh yeah, you told me that." I was surprised and pleased that Dad remembered him so well. I didn't know how many years it had been since they had seen each other. The next morning, I preceded my brother by about twenty minutes to the Special Care Unit (so-called and false).

When I got there, Dad was gleaming: shaved, combed and rarin' to roll. Jessica, the activities director, was relieved to see me. "Thank God you're here," she grabbed me by the hands. "He's been a handful, and they didn't know when to expect you."

Dad is fit to be tied, literally, as far as the staff was concerned. He squirms in his wheelchair and goes from one door to another asking,

"Which way will he come in?" He won't leave his post to go get his jacket, hat, and gloves, so I go and get them. Finally, Chuck arrives. Dad is so happy, he cries. I don't claim that it is an easy moment for Chuck; most members of our family, and not just the males, are not given to crying in public. I have never seen my brother cry, and my father only once (when his mother died) and my mother twice (when she fell on her face and broke a front tooth, and when someone cut down and made off with the full-grown blue spruce in our front yard right before Christmas). The tears appeal to me now, because I see Dad recognize someone he loves, look forward to an outing, and feel himself honored and respected, even if he does forget them in the next moment. Someday the scientist will prove what I can see in front of me, that it helps Alzies to have these experiences. They'll find it releases endorphins or something.

While Chuck speaks with him, Nurse Norce motions me to a table about twenty feet away. "Did someone call you about the bruises?" The CNAs had recently discovered some bruising on Dad's lower back.

"Yes, I spoke to one of the nurses about it. I think he used the door jamb on the Jeep to slide out of the seat one day when we went out to lunch."

Norce tells me with a smile that it might be better if Dad didn't go out so much. I am polite, even sweet. Inside my head a voice is yelling so loud that I can't hear myself talk, What's wrong with her? Can't she see how much Dad enjoys these outings? My God, he's beaming! He hasn't had a urine infection for three months! He's happy! He actually looked forward to seeing his son all morning!

Outside, my voice is saying, with a calm edge to it, and with so little breath I'm surprised she can hear me at all, "He hasn't had much Ativan recently, and if you look at the chart, you'll see that when he does need Ativan, it's not correlated with going out."

"Well, he gets tired, you know, and they have to think about everything that happens during the day that drains his energy. And what if he broke his leg?"

Inside: Of course he gets tired, they all get tired, don't you get tired?

What do you think naps are for? And as for broken legs—well, he's fallen a half dozen times here and never when he's been out with me. At least I don't leave him alone wearing socks on a linoleum floor. My legs are weakening. AAUGH.

Outside: "I understand that you have to think about my father's safety. I appreciate your very professional handling of him and the extra effort you go to point out perspectives that I may not see. From your position, it's a great worry about broken legs. From the family's point of view, we have to balance the risks with his quality of life. Right now, I think it's still safe to say that he's doing very well by riding around in the Jeep with me. But I certainly appreciate your bringing this up."

As I speak, I notice Jessica out of the corner of my eye. I feel her eyes focus tightly on the magazine she is reading to Patty. But her ears don't tighten, they seem to expand, to take in everything we say. Her body says, "I have an opinion about this, but I'm not going to say anything, I'm not going to say anything, I'm not going to say anything." She's having a hard time keeping her mouth straight.

Once more I feel like a prisoner trying to escape, caught in a moving spotlight, afraid to be shot. I fear the day when the nursing home authorities will formally diagnose me with being in denial and try to keep me from seeing Dad altogether. I hope this will not happen before he dies. So far there has not yet been an Alzheimer's family member gone postal. It will happen when one of us becomes demented and a frontal lobe stops functioning. Then, nursing-home staff beware. A danger to myself and others.

As we left I am able to breathe again and try to concentrate on keeping Dad talking about his memories with Chuck. We had a wonderful lunch. Chuck finally caught on, asking Dad about people and places in his home town that Dad could remember and converse about. Dad took part and even initiated some things. I am grateful that my brother has seen him like this, seen the smiles and the head shakings, heard the laughs and the characteristic way Dad phrased his sentences. Chuck could see why I was doing what I am doing. I try telling that to myself.

As we got into the Jeep, Dad said, "Let him drive." I handed the keys to Chuck who mumbled through his mustache, "It doesn't matter who drives."

"No. He wants to sit next to you. He wants to talk to you."

"Okay," Chuck, still mumbling, caught the keys I dropped into his hand, and climbed into the driver's seat. He didn't talk to Dad, who is nevertheless content to sit by the side of his only son. I count the lunch a success from Dad's point of view. That's all that matters anyway, right?

—

On the morning before he left, I took the brother into the neighborhood across the street from where Mom and Dad lived, to show him a small residential assisted living place run by local people. Ten private rooms with living and dining spaces, it looked normal from the outside, just another house on the block. The train ran behind it, so I thought Dad would be happier there.

Chuck wasn't interested. He hardly greeted the director and had no questions.

"Would you like to see the larger room? It will probably become vacant fairly soon," she asked him at the end of the tour.

"No. That's all right. I think I get the idea," he mumbled, not meeting her eyes or mine.

On the walk back to Mom's, he gave me some advice. "You should concentrate on your own new family, now. You want to go back to the way we were in the fifties. You can't do it."

"I don't want to go back to the way we were in the fifties. What makes you think that?" I groped for a context that would make some sense of what he said, to correct some misperception he had of me. It was true that I had brought every last thing I could possibly load into the moving truck of their belongings, but that was only because it made me feel good to remember them when they were in their prime and I was young. But I said, "I just want to take care of Mom and Dad. It's like I can pay them back for everything they did for me. It feels good. If Trudy thinks I'm taking better care of them—"

He didn't let me finish the thought. "NOT BETTER," he hissed, reddening. "Different!"

"It's Trudy's word. Not mine." I defended myself. But was it? No value judgments allowed here, though they called like sirens to us all. Although I had been surprised by their seeming indifference to Dad, I got the message that they were not going to play their cards the same way I played mine. It reminded me of a roommate I'd once had. We both loved to play hearts. But she had added a twist to the game. Without telling anyone, she set her goal to come in second. This was in fact a more difficult thing to do than simply to win. Her strategy was to promote the leading hand rather than her own, and try to thwart the third in line—just the opposite of the normal strategy. It made the game much more complex and interesting—if you knew what she was doing. For those who didn't know, the way she played her hand made no sense and invariably frustrated their own strategy. They couldn't count on her. That reminded me of a much criticized mayor of Chicago in the late sixties. "At least you could count on what he would do."

"It doesn't matter whose word it is," Chuck retorted. "Look. You want to go back to how we were in the 1950s. Get over it! Families are like those pod plants in *The Body Snatchers* that mature and then explode, sending their seeds far away from the plant to grow new families. The new plants don't have anything to do with the parent plant. Their time is over. Mom and Dad are a dyad spinning through space together. They have each other. You need to connect with your new family and take care of Guy, not Dad."

So what's wrong with the 1950s? At least for us, we didn't have to work, everything was paid for and all we had to do was bring home high grades and do anything we wanted to. Right now, I wanted to thank him for his advice and at the same time reject it, but I couldn't think of a way of wording that without sounding sarcastic. And I was horrified. Pod people? What had happened to the brother who'd watched *It's a Wonderful*

Life with me Christmas after Christmas at home with Mom and Dad? Maybe the body-snatchers *had* landed on his house. I had a pang at the thought that Chuck was describing his own marriage. Then I remembered that they visited his wife's family frequently and were close to her sisters and brothers and their children. I had another pang. This time for myself. I'd failed many times to manage a connection with any man that was not fraught with argument and recrimination. I'd failed to have children. I was envious.

"That's not my experience," I said, using a phrase my yoga teacher had used when she disagreed with me and didn't want an argument. I tried to not to think about it. He just didn't love Dad anymore, that's all. It was time for him to go catch his plane.

I felt like a puppet or a billiard ball. No matter what Trudy said, it felt like an attack. Whatever I said to her, she took it as an attack and that made me think I meant it as one. I had seen in email that interpreting anything to mean its exact opposite was child's play. With nothing in common, there was no way of communicating with each other. I wrote long essays explaining how I felt and why I acted the way I did. Trudy did not respond to these at all. Chuck wrote me a letter once. Why did I throw it out? I didn't want to remember it.

—

The next day, the three of us scheduled a meeting in the bare conference room across the hall from Mom's apartment. We sat around an eight-foot-long table, finished to a high gloss and without a scratch on it. Windows ran the length of one wall, but they could not be opened.

I chose a seat along one long side and my brother sat opposite me. Trudy pulled out the chair along the short side and, edging it around to Chuck's side of the table, sat down.

The details of what we said are hazy, but the general thrust was money. And then there was that moment when Chuck left his chair and stamped along his side of the table, leaning forward, head and elbows bent, fists tight. "You think you're a saint," he said, red-faced, more from embarrassment at being angry than the anger itself. "You want us to think so too."

A saint. I thought it was harder to become a saint than that. Trudy *would* have been a saint if she had done what I had done under her circumstances. My circumstances were just as different from hers as bubble gum from broccoli. Not that I like either better than the other. I chew on both. I had wanted Trudy to be a team with me in Dad's care. When she rejected the care, she had rejected me with it. Why? I was happy to take care of him—I wanted to. No sacrifice there, I didn't feel I deserved to be beatified and Trudy didn't either. Chuck was the one who thought I was a saint. Why? And Wow!

We were in there for hours, with the windows shut tight, our eyes moving sideways and down, never looking into a face. Mom opened the door once and, blown back by the fire inside the room, said only, "Come see me when you are done," and backing out the room, she shut the door quietly with both hands on the doorknob, pulling it after her.

Finally, I made my plea. "We've talked all this time about the money," I said. "How does all this make you feel?" I might as well have been bouncing a basketball off a brick wall.

—

That night I had everyone over to dinner in our stuffy dining room. We managed to surf through the food okay but came to verbal fisticuffs over coffee and dessert.

"Just leave him alone," said Trudy. "Why do you have to go visiting *every day?*" I realized this wasn't easy for any of us. It was dangerous. Mom checked in and out, falling asleep at the table, then seeming to wake up, but still dreamy.

"I want to. Why not?"

Chuck said, "This is what Dad wanted. He bought insurance to cover nursing home care."

"So what? He didn't think he'd be there for years getting drugged. What do you want if you get Alzheimer's and have to be locked up in a place like that?"

Chuck hesitated.

Trudy was ruthless. "Just give me drugs and leave me alone. I don't want to be here," was her only comment, and I wanted to believe her. Trudy had always been a straight arrow about how she felt, and, I also realized, I had not. But I still did not accept her words, believing instead that she didn't know how she would react.

"What about you, Chuck? Wouldn't you want your daughter to visit you?" His jaw dropped a little and he looked at me dumbly for an instant, then said, "We shouldn't be doing this in front of Mom." I looked over at her, but she was just sipping her coffee brightly with nothing to say, apparently trusting in the Lord.

I let it go and hurried them off. After they left, I had a few beers in a too-many hurry, and a spat with Guy before bed.

****

Chuck was set to fly out on a Sunday. We arranged to meet for breakfast at a local café at 9:30. That morning Trudy called at 7:30.

"Can we make it a little earlier?"

"Sure. What time?"

"I can be there by nine."

"See you then."

I arrived at 9:00 and ordered coffee. At 9:45 they arrived and sat down. No apology. No acknowledgment that they were unapologetically late. I felt like Charlie Brown just after Lucy has pulled the football away *again*.

We ordered and after the food was set down, Chuck looked down in his lap. With clenched teeth and tears in his voice he said, "I was so mad at Dad. I went home in June. It was Mom's seventy-fifth birthday. He asked her where she wanted to go to eat dinner. She said the old hotel. But then he said, no, he didn't want to go there."

This was the Dad I remembered. One time a guest of mine who had never been in our neck of woods was visiting and asked to eat some local ethnic food. While they went to MacDonald's, I stayed home and nursed my cut-off nose.

Chuck went on, "Then I realized that he was demented, so I let it go."

There was an uncomfortable silence, until I broke it. "You need some therapy. Of course, this was always Dad's way. Not his dementia." I had let it go as Dad's dynamic twenty years before. Dad's and *my* dynamic.

And then, my brother and sister talked to each other for a half an hour. About how awful Dad had been as a father. At first, I tried to comment, but they didn't want me to be part of the conversation. Finally, I told them in exasperation that I had thought the same of Dad twenty years ago and had gotten some professional help. I thought they should seriously consider some counseling. I knew as soon as I said it that it wouldn't take but went on, hoping they might remember my words that might have some effect later. And it turned out, Trudy was in counseling around the same time that we met that morning, but I wouldn't know that until more than ten years later.

About three years later, I realized that they were trying to talk about emotions, as I had requested in our meeting. But it wasn't about me, so I didn't see it at all, much less as an improvement.

—

At home again with the bottle until I was drunk but calmer, I sat with Guy on the sofa by a dying fire. A fire's a peculiar presence, a protection and a danger. Warms us most all our days and nights, providing light as well as heat, and life as well as protection. Yet we never speak of it—in silence Guy dressed for outside and took the old pink, paint-chipped wheelbarrow to the woodshed to fill it with split wood. In silence, I stood by the door to let him in and shut it again against the cold. In silence, he handed me the cedar log by log, and I stacked it into the rick. We both tended the fire, we were both aware of it certainly, and in summer when there is relief from the business of the fire, I notice its cold absence when I walk by the stove. I remember what it was to live in those other places with their furnaces fed by dead gas, their filthy oil contained in basements where we couldn't see what was keeping us warm. Every time you turn a furnace on it is a jolt, not just to the ears, but to the body, and they require only once-a-year tending that you could uneasily forget, the cold heat provoking no conscious twinge of thought. Their fires were hidden fires. We used our TV as a cold fire, too, woosh, it turns on like a gas log with the same steady drone of produced and directed sound.

"I can't feel at home without a real fire," I said and turned to brush my teeth before bed.

Someone once told me that when you floss your teeth, what really happens is that you break up colonies of bacteria that combine somehow with odd particles to cause your teeth to decay. It doesn't really matter that you get the food debris out as much as that you break up the colonies every day or so, to keep them from organizing for tooth-war. Then I remembered another thing—that people take aspirin for headache but more times than not it's dehydration that brings on the headache, and the water relieves it, not the pill. What if everything people do is like that? You think you're doing one thing and it turns out you're doing something else. It was obviously time for me to go to sleep.

I crawled in next to Guy, who had beaten me to bed, but his feet were still ice-cold. I laid my head on his shoulder and sighed.

"What's up?" he asked pulling in his chin and trying to move his cheeks out of the way so he could see the top of my head.

"I don't know. I just don't understand what Trudy and Chuck are thinking."

"Don't worry about it. You don't need to know what they're thinking."

"Maybe. I found some emails from Trudy and Chuck today." I had had great difficulty reading them. My eyes kept glancing off the page. They were too painful. After reading them, I was wrung out. "They just don't want to take care of him."

"Yes, and they felt guilty about it. They let the guilt out on you."

"I know," I said. I had never thought of that before, and didn't believe it.

I lay back flat, staring at the ceiling and tried to work with the conflict.

So what? So what? So what? So, I guess, when I insisted on giving Dad better than "adequate" care, I was constantly pricking them, poking them, a source of infection. How else could it have been done? I couldn't convince my sister and brother that his care was inadequate, though they left me alone to take care of Dad as I pleased. And Chuck even supported me in one plan-of-care meeting we had had when he was visiting. Everyone was telling me I was wrong—not just them.

—

I flashed on a day the staff had cornered me in Dad's room, three or four of them at once, to talk to me. One of them was a nurse who had illegally given his daughter marijuana for her pain, been tried, and found guilty. I liked him. Surely, he understood why I was trying to take care of my dad, as he had bucked the system taking care of his daughter.

The staff—there were four of them—stood in a semi-circle facing me, blocking the door. The double room was not large, perhaps only fifteen feet wide and a little more than twenty feet long with large windows facing, but not opening on, the walled yard outside the unit. There were two beds, two night stands, and two dressing tables in it. As I turned to straighten up, they crowded my personal space, and the hair rose on my arms and neck.

The spokesperson (the nurse I liked) started to speak in his gentle voice, the one he used with my father, about how I was not helping my dad, how I was obstructing their care, how I ought not to come as often. My stomach hollowed out and fell away. While my conscious brain told me that they were wrong and that I wouldn't stop, a wave of what I can only describe as love for all of them came over me. It was a warm feeling in my heart causing my brain to freeze up. But my body, unfrozen, crashed through their living wall, and left.

Patty Hearst, the rich girl who had been kidnapped by a revolutionary band in the 1960s, had something like that happen to her. I'd just had a brief brush with Stockholm Syndrome. For me, the threat had been real, though not as lasting as Hearst's was. What lasted was the idea that

I had to change what Americans think Alzheimer's is, and what medical providers think is "adequate" care. A daunting project, given how these medical providers perceived me. I had requested a copy of Dad's nursing notes a while before. When they handed them over ten days later, I wrote in my diary that night:

> This day I sat in the library parking lot and read nursing notes. I was astounded at what the nurses had written! That I said Dad had struck me in the face! That Trudy had tried to get a signature from Dad duplicitously! That the ambush of the administrators in Dad's room had been a plan-of-care meeting!

This begged the question whether the nursing staff also had Alzheimers?

I knew there were other family members, even at WholeCare, who were as critical of their Alzheimer care as I was. It convinced me that I wasn't the only one who had a painful conflict with my family over love and not just money.

—

"But it can't be like this for everyone." I sat up in bed and turned to pout at Guy. "There must be some way to have a connection with each other. Even if there's no love lost."

"Why don't you email Brad?" Guy offered, pulling me down and snuggling down against my shoulder, protecting me with an arm slung across my waist.

Brad was an old friend of his—a wily, twinkly old sailor, artist, and backgammon player. His mother had recently died in a nursing home. His story of crawling into her bed to hold her while she fell asleep had enabled me to offer the same comfort to Dad, despite the whispering nurses' assistants. I found, in fact, that I enjoyed the nurturing on my own account, probably as much as Dad did.

So now I emailed. Flinging my story and feelings out to zigzag around the dark skies above the nation, and who knew? Perhaps around the world, I concluded, "How did you and your brother get along while your mom was dying?"

Back through the void zagged a succinct reply, "We held separate memorials. Love, Brad."

The many books about Alzheimer's that I read at the time contained not a word that the illness would infect our entire family. Many of the memoirs were dedicated to siblings who had helped and supported, appreciated and cheered on a daughter caring for an Alzhammered parent. Not mine. We would argue over money and over Dad's care, but that was only a cover for the deeper rift between us.

We forgot who we were and that we were special and lucky and not subject to the forces that bound the rest of the human race. Still, we dealt with it the way we dealt with everything the family faced. We didn't speak unless we had to, and never about the things that were riveting me.

I was fifty-one years old when the Big Trouble started. Half a century had gone without my learning a single thing that would help me to live through it, much less understand it.

Chapter Seven   PSYCHOTHERAPY

*Look at the world through the eyes of others,
and seek to understand experiences that are not our own.*
Azar Nafisi

*We have learned from the study of dreams and pathological
states that even what for a long time was believed forgotten
may suddenly return to consciousness.*
Sigmund Freud

I knocked on Tilda's door and remained standing, even though there were chairs pushed against the hallway's smokey green wall. They were hooked together by their bottom rungs like pop-it-beads, and whenever I sat in one, they all rocked unevenly, heightening my sense that *something is not right*. A white-noise machine lay on the floor at my feet just outside the closed door. Tilda was with someone else, and I would have to wait until that person exited through a different door. As if I cared about other people's problems.

    I had scheduled the appointment months before, because so many women I knew recommended her. In the meantime, I had tried to find another therapist. I felt so anxious, I didn't think I could wait. But the waits were long at most places, and during the one appointment I managed to get, the psychologist grew more and more anxious as I told her all about my dysfunctional family and the dysfunctional family at WholeCare.

"I just don't think I can help you," she said, ushering me out of the consulting room at the local hospital. "You just have too much to deal with."

Amazed by her, what, honesty? It wasn't youth or inexperience that was at work. I felt abandoned. "Do you know anyone else who would see me?" I asked hopefully.

"No, I'm afraid not."

So I waited until Tilda had an opening in her schedule and started seeing her regularly. She gave me a battery of psychological tests on a weekly basis, some of which measured my levels of depression and anxiety. They didn't mean much to me, as they didn't apply specifically to what I was going through at the time.

But I was patient.

The first time I saw Tilda, I told her I had come to resolve an issue with my sister and brother. I no longer recognized the people I loved, but I loved them and clung to them, determined to understand their motivations and my own, which I felt were pushing buttons I couldn't see.

I sketched the situation with Mom and Dad, and quickly moved on to the main thing that was bothering me: the meeting where they only wanted to talk about money. I pour out all the worrisome things I had learned about Trudy. By the time I was done, I had almost convinced myself that this was just one more challenge I could face.

"Trudy says she wants no responsibility."

"So, take her at her word?" Tilda smiled.

"But she wants to manage the money, that's a *bit* of responsibility, isn't it?"

Tilda let that rest.

"What was it like for you as children?" she wanted to know.

"It was pretty normal."

She arched an eyebrow. "Tell me about it."

I had been worrying over the old memories until I had nearly worn them out, so it wasn't hard to tell her about that. In fact, it was fun—playing games with Dad, singing and joking with Mom, the good times we had, the education, support and encouragement.

"How did you three get along?"

"I thought we at least trusted each other, but we fought like normal kids, I guess. I'd always had a vague sense that Trudy and I weren't sisters like other sisters were: We didn't share clothes or perfume or makeup. We only talked to each other on the phone irregularly as I remember it. Who knows how she remembers it? We didn't discuss boyfriends or husbands as much as I would've liked, though she married twice and divorced twice. Just the facts: I'm getting married, she's divorcing, but not much about who we were marrying and divorcing. When she told me she was divorcing, I cried, and she made a funny face. We weren't intimate. But we did have the same childhood, so *some* of our memories must be the same."

Tilda made a funny face.

"We did like each other, so when I was forty-one, she invited me to come and live with her and her husband here. I was losing my computer software company, and she was there for me. I lived in a cabin on her property that we built together under her husband's supervision, and we shared food and bathrooms in the big house, went out together to eat and to movies—until I moved out after a year to live with Guy. So she was always there for me when I needed help."

Tilda nodded while she took some notes and I went on.

"We had our fights and competition like any siblings do, I guess. And we helped each other and had fun. While we were in college together we didn't have much contact, except riding home for breaks. She hung out with different people and took different courses. I was interested in humanities. She studied science— stuff like that."

Tilda listened patiently as I went on, asking for clarification intermittently.

Near the end of the hour, I returned myself to the present when I saw that she was *politely* listening but fiddling with some papers in her lap.

"I'd like you to take these and fill them out for me." She explained the assignment briefly. "It's a trauma map."

"A what?" I had never heard of such a thing.

"A family tree where you note the traumas in different people's lives." Tilda smiled.

There was a list of examples, things like abuse, addiction, divorce, injuries—things my family hadn't experienced. Well, there had been injuries—but just the usual broken bones.

"We didn't have any traumas in our family. We were just ordinary."

"If you didn't, that would be pretty special," she grinned and nodded at the list. Also interspersed on the list were things I didn't think of as traumatic: untimely relocations, embarrassment at school, punishments.

"Anything, you know, like deaths, accidents, divorce—stuff like that. Even weddings and births, happy times, can be traumatic. See what you can remember." I had never realized that these things that happened to everyone were traumatic, but I would go ahead and do what she asked.

"Same time next week?"

—

So the next week I was sitting down on the client's chair, pulling out the forms, which had run over onto two pages. I had the marriages and other good things, and the deaths and other common things all marked by each person. I skipped over them and moved on to the ones that seemed like real traumas to me, and described them out loud to Tilda:

"My father's cousin Sam had been divorced after her husband had had an affair with a woman who lived with them while was studying nursing with Sam. I remembered my mother's response: 'Your grandmother always liked Sam's husband. She was the only one in the family who liked him.'

"My great-aunt Rhea on my mother's side was a lesbian. She lived with another woman in a house they built in the next town over from where I grew up. When my father was transferred to the area, they helped us settle in a smaller town nearby, and Mom took us to visit them weekly or more when I was little. When I was researching the family tree in Aunt Rhea's attic, I had found some notebooks with dirty jokes in them and decided they were lovers. They shared a bedroom with two single beds in it. Rhea had never married, but her friend had married a guy named Joe, and the marriage was almost immediately annulled. Rhea confided in me that the sex was what scared her friend. Ever after that, Rhea was not interested in men. In any event, certainly, the family never breathed a word about this possibility, which seemed obvious to me." Another story, I told myself. True or not true, it made sense of my great-aunt's life for me.

"My mother's mother died of a stroke when she was only fifty-six. My mother's father died of a stroke. That was traumatic for us! My mother went to take care of him in the hospital, and Dad had to cook and get us all off to school in the mornings. He sent my brother to school once in his jacket with no shirt and wearing a pair of pajama pants. When we went to pick her up after Grandpa died, we had a car accident. I was about five.

"In high school one morning I saw a garbage truck turn too fast and flatten the convertible that had swerved in front of it. The car belonged to the brother of a girl on the bus, but he was unhurt. She was hysterical and when the police arrived, they took her home.

"A boy whom I babysat when I was thirteen or fourteen drowned at a picnic when he was two or three years old."

There were traumas crawling all over me!

Tilda studied the forms in her lap. "Most families have traumas like these that are part of everybody's life," she said, not looking up. The interesting thing is most people also deny that they've had them, until they stop and think about it. So, sorry, you're not special after all!" she grinned. Then, studying the map more closely she asked, "What's this about your father's father?"

"He was shot in the back while working on the railroad the same year my father was born."

Tilda looked up and waited for me to continue.

Shifting in my chair, I added, "He had a gun in his holster, but the holster strap was not snapped. When the train stopped suddenly, the gun fell out, hit the floor, and went off. Killed him instantly."

Now Tilda sat back on her sofa and narrowed her eyes. "Do you believe that story?" She looked me straight in the eye, not blinking.

I felt my face tighten around my silence.

"Sounds pretty unbelievable."

"Huh. I never thought about it. I guess so." Then I remembered something else.

—

My dad's mother already had Alzheimer's by the time I began to ask her about that side of the family, but she wasn't in an institution yet. I had gotten to her in time. I had found old family photos—lots of them, in her old, roll-top desk that eventually wound up in our living room. Grandma and I had undertaken a project of labelling them. One day, as we finished up, she became agitated. (It's odd to see your grandmother so agitated!) She asked me if I had found a letter. When I said "no," she asked me if I had looked in the secret drawer. She told me not to tell anybody else and just bring the letter to her. I didn't know there was a secret drawer, so I rushed home.

I couldn't find the secret drawer, until my mother came home. When I asked, she said, "Oh, we found a letter in that drawer."

"Where is it?"

"I threw it out."

"Did you read it?"

"M-m-m-m."

"What did it say?"

It was from my grandfather's partner on the mail car where he worked for the railroad. Dated not long after the fatal gunshot, he had asked her to marry him. Why did Mom throw it out? She thought it would upset Dad.

—

Tilda just looked at me without saying anything, so I moved on, reporting the continuing difficulties of my situation with the sibs. As we wound down, I told her about my experiment with left-handed journaling, a technique a friend of mine had recommended. I stood to leave, still talking while straightening my jacket.

"You ask yourself a question, then start writing with your left hand as fast as possible. It looks like scribble, so then you go back and write above each squiggle a word it resembles. So I came up with this: 'Kill the family's continuing monopoly.' I don't know what to make of it." I handed her the scrap of paper from my jacket pocket.

"And what does monopoly mean to your family?" she asked, hand on the doorknob, just as the last word came out of my mouth.

I took a sudden deep breath. DUH, but I didn't answer. As I turned to go, she said, "Think about it," and I left.

Monopoly. The shoe, the ship, the iron, the dog. My father was the "champeen" and had handed us down a vintage set with real wooden houses and hotels, not the hollow plastic ones. He had taught all of us how to play. Mom had rarely taken part. No, never. She never played a game of Monopoly with us. After a while, Dad had stopped playing, but we continued, especially in the summertime, when our lives still had the extra hours and hours required to finish a game. To this day I can rattle off all the rental prices from Mediterranean to Boardwalk.

So what? I thought as I left Tilda's office. But everything came home to roost in that imperative from my leaky unconscious. I had the reputation of being the unchallenged winner of Monopoly among the siblings. I had taken Dad's place as the *champeen*. I had bullied my way to the title by mocking and deriding my sister and brother when they would not agree to my offers of Illinois for Pacific Avenue. I even cheated, stealing money from the bank—something I did not admit to Tilda.

Had I now taken Dad's place as the champeen, or even head of the family? Was I still bullying my sister and brother to get my own way? There was no question in my mind that they thought so. Did I think so too?

But we each took what was important to us. I didn't care what Trudy did with the money. I wanted her to take care of it. But she didn't want me to take care of Dad. She wanted to put herself as far away as possible and forget about him and our past. Because I was trying to be the *champeen*?

—

"Look at this," I said, handing Tilda a letter from Chuck before I sat down. She took it from me and read it silently, not looking up until she was finished. I had just opened it on the way over to the appointment, and was confused and shamed. I only remember one line from it: "Who made you sheriff of Dad?"

Tilda took some time to read it before she looked up. "This is the meanest letter I've ever read," she said softly with wonder in her voice, and watched me. That relieved some of the pain I had carried with the letter to my appointment. Psychologists usually do not deliver such value judgements about anybody, at least in my meager experience. It was normal to feel so hurt after a letter like that. I wasn't as crazy as I sometimes thought.

And she delivered another blow. "He doesn't care," she said simply, and illuminated a dark corner of me which now could see that I had resisted thinking just that. How could Chuck not care about Dad?

Now that I thought it under new light, the letter made sense to me. It was mean, but at least I could see what was happening. I could deal with it. And I didn't believe that Chuck was mean. I could figure this out.

"They don't care about Dad," I said.

"Why do you think they don't?" Tilda leaned forward and picked up her pen.

"All I can think of is that Dad used to make fun of Trudy's physical differences: pigeon-toes or "fat ear lobes." And she couldn't keep up with us in math, we were so much older. They sent her to school when she wasn't yet five. I don't remember that he was very critical of me in so many words, though he was pretty judgmental. He teased us if our grades weren't perfect; he compared us with each other, even giving us bigger allowances for better grades. And then there was the time Chuck had an accident with the car and wanted me to tell Dad about it, because Chuck thought Dad wouldn't get mad at me. He was right. And when I banged the car up once, Dad never asked me about it, just had it fixed.

I sighed. "They are leaving me alone pretty much, so what am I upset about?"

Tilda was still watching me. She said, "They don't care about you."

—

"Hi Tilda. There's some good news to report this week. Dad knows who I am again! He also knows who Trudy is. Yesterday he said to me 'You and your sister are far apart.' How does he know that, Tilda? Does he know she is not visiting him? He never says anything. But he has been reading my mind off and on too."

"How so?"

"When I told him Mom had trouble depositing his retirement check in the bank, he started to explain to me how easy it was to deposit a check. She went to the dentist, and on the same day he asked about her teeth. I hadn't mentioned what she was doing at all! The most surprising thing—I had been out to see a friend of mine who had broken his water energy system by blowing off the four nozzles on his water wheel with too much water pressure. When I got to the unit to visit with Dad, he asked me about the broken shower. I started to ask a passing CNA if one of the showers was broken on the unit, but he interrupted me, 'No, the four showers,' he said."

I paused, cocking my head. Dad wasn't the only one who could read my mind. I'd been at an Alzheimer's meeting with local panel of experts taking questions about Alzheimer's. I don't remember the question I asked, but in her response a counselor had named many of my family members by their first names: not just Mom and Dad, but my extended family. Although I was acquainted with the counselor, I was certain that I had never mentioned them by name to her. And if I had mentioned them in passing, would she have remembered them? And if she did, how would she know how they had reacted to the family Alzheimer's? I gulped and she looked surprised: "Oh, did I name your family members?" From the look on her face, I could tell she recognized the ESP too.

This was too much to tell Tilda. She'd think I was crazy and I didn't need that, so I didn't tell her about it. Funny how crazy it seemed at the time it happened, there among all those sane people. When it happened with Dad in the unit, it had seemed natural, even likely.

Tilda was asking me something else: "... hard to tell if he doesn't remember your mother. She hasn't been in to see him for how long?"

I just nodded and moved on to describe some recent dreams.

"Trudy is standing windblown on a dirty ocean beach in a wedding dress, waiting for Dad near the surf. I am on the other side of the spit of land from them, in a changing room. There is sand in my bathing suit, so I take it off and go into the water. It's warm and I feel relaxed and free."

"What do you think that means?"

"Trudy is trying to take care of Dad by following the rules laid out by WholeCare, and it's not working out."

"What do you think your bathing suit means?"

I had to think about that for a minute. "I'm bucking the rules. I take it off and take care of Dad the way I like. That makes me happy."

"Do you think it makes Trudy happy to control the money the way she likes?"

I hadn't thought of that. Money had been a bone of contention in the family, but I needed more time to think about that. As I walked home, another memory struck.

—

I was old enough to get my first full-time job and young enough not to have much choice about what it would be. Dad helped me find a job as a solderer at a local company that made fire alarms, and then we opened my first bank account. Depositing all my paychecks in the account, I spent the summer dreaming about buying a stereo system like the ones my friends had. When the summer was over, I went to Dad to get his help in choosing one, but he told me that the money I earned was to go toward my tuition.

I don't know why, but this time I took issue, finally convincing him that I would keep the money left over from the stereo for school. He helped me pick out one of the least expensive units available, which cost about half the money I had earned.

He must have treated both of my siblings the same way. Chuck had wanted to go to Europe one summer when he was in college, and Dad said he had to get a job. I don't think he went that summer, but he did go on his own at some point. Then he laid down the same conditions for me when I wanted to go. I got a job in Amsterdam that summer, but I quit it near the end of the summer and traveled. He was a little easier on Trudy when she held out to get him to pay for that trip "because he loved her." I guess he didn't treat us as equally as I had imagined.

Chapter Eight FUNCTIONAL

Ring around the Rosie
A pocket full of posies
Ashes, ashes
We all fall down.
Traditional

I was just beginning to understand Dad's Alzheimer's. When I visited the Special Unit (sounds like a military op) I felt like the nurses and I were also crazy. They saw things one way and I saw them another. I saw people who were confused and wanted some personal connection, who often didn't know where they were and wanted to feel safe. The nurses wanted to do their jobs and help sick people—and to keep control. I wanted to make Dad feel safe and to reconnect with him. What I did caused chaos. They got in my way, and I got in theirs. It was hard to tell where the Alzheimer's ended and our own craziness began.

Things were easier for me when I visited with Mom and the other residents of the assisted living who were not diagnosed with Alzheimer's. I knew Mom had it, but at least she was not a danger to herself or others. I could see a lighter side to the disease. When I got out of jail and into a world where people functioned not that much worse than Dad, I found myself with people who were just forgetful and could still be happy and free.

For once, I wasn't on a schedule. I had gone to yoga that morning at the assisted living, where my mother and Guy's mother Gurlie both lived. It was "chair" yoga: no mats, no blocks, no straps, not even any tights or sweat pants. What made it yoga, I guess, was that it was slow and everyone held still for long periods of time. Also, there was namaste at the end. Most of the ladies (all residents except me and Mark, the husband of a resident, and not demented) followed the simple instructions most of the time: "Stand up, point your toe. That's right, now point the other toe."

"What?" said my mother looking down at her feet while she wrinkled her forehead.

The instructor Abby was an experienced woman, full of enthusiasm. "This one," she said touching the left big toe and lifting Mom's heel with the other hand.

"I know," said Mom irritably.

Abby could also charm the boredom off Mark, who seemed to enjoy being in the class even though he argued with Abby about how worthwhile it was. He clucked every time she gave an instruction, no matter how slight the movement. "C'mon Mark," she would smile. Bathing in the light of her eyes, Mark complied.

Usually, the time dragged on and on for me as I did my duty toward the elderly. Twenty minutes of yoga would seem even longer than my forty-five-minute sessions with Abby in the real world. Today, without any plans for the entire afternoon, I concentrated on pointing one toe and then the other—slowing myself to the pace of the other women—paid attention to the breaths I took when instructed to, and was surprised at how good I felt at the end.

Afterwards, Mom and I usually lunched together with Guy's mother Gurlie and today we had invited Mark and his demented wife along. Then Sylvia, another resident, decided to come along, and then Fran, an appendage of Sylvia's, of the same short height and bird-like build, differing from Sylvia only by the shade of her darker gray hair. Fran did not say much, but watched carefully when other people spoke.

So seven of us traipsed out, Fran locking an elbow into one of Sylvia's and matching her toddle for toddle. "Seven at one blow," I thought, remembering the little tailor. Only two of us knew what we were doing, or thought we did: Mark and me. We had a quick huddle before the others caught up with us. He would drive himself and his wife, and I would take the other four women.

Phase one of the outing began: loading everyone into the car and conveying them to the restaurant. We started off well. Mom and the other three women jumped into the back of Gurlie's Buick. My mother-in-law took her time getting into the front. She was a large woman, as tall as my husband, and was made even larger by her oversized purse, in which she kept only her regular-size wallet and a pen. I could never get her to carry kleenex, despite the drop of mucous continuously suspended from the end of her hawk-beak nose. She put the purse down on the front seat and stared at it. Nope. That wouldn't work. She passed the purse to the ladies in the back seat. Then she tried to get into the car while holding her cane.

Gurlie was never without it, an aluminum affair which was adjustable, though Gurlie would never allow me to change its length. It had four feet with rubber covers on their ends, which stuck out like the legs on a cartoon caterpillar, bent at 90 degrees. It didn't fit in the front seat. Finally, she passed the cane as well into the back, where they wrestled it to the floor.

Gurlie couldn't hear well in the noisier spots in town. The Thai restaurant had quiet booths, but when we met at their door, the sign said CLOSED. We were only a block away from the health food store, which had a lunch counter in one corner. I considered how much time it would take to load them back in the cars, how much risk of falling, hitting heads, sitting on purses, versus the adventure of the slushy sidewalk. Usually, they were too slow to walk a block and still leave enough time to eat, but today I had no need to hurry.

So we gamboled down the avenue and around the corner, arm-in-arm-in-arm, as wide as the sidewalk. Gurlie had brought along her cane, but, as usual, it never touched the ground. Nevertheless, it seemed to do something for her balance, like a tightrope-walker's pole.

When we reached the restaurant, we pushed together three small tables, assembled one-too-many chairs and settled down. Phase One: accomplished. It seemed like an hour since we started out. I sat down to gather myself for Phase Two: ordering, and looked up at the menu posted on the wall.

"What would you like, Mom? Gurlie?" I asked as I slid into one of those old-fashioned, chrome and cracked-vinyl-covered kitchen chairs around the tables at Brown's health food store and lunch counter. I was beginning to enjoy taking care of my mother. I had decided to quit my job to take care of my parents and Guy's mother, who also lived in town. Gurlie wasn't demented or didn't appear to be to me, just cozily confused. Sometimes Guy reacted as though he thought she was, and it was a relief to him that I was doing it.

Everyone had not quite settled down. they were still fussing, smoothing their skirts, futilely pushing their purses into the legs of the chairs. It always surprises me how lively the demented can be: I had lost ten pounds these past months trekking around and around the heathered-green halls of the assisted living after my mother, passing the same paintings of mirror-eyed children, the same empty meeting rooms decorated with dried-flower arrangements in which no one ever met around the unscratched tables, the same closed and numbered doors. I had little idea who lived behind them.

Everyone, at last was still and understood that it was time to eat lunch, and I was certainly ready. I asked again, "So Gurlie, what are you hungry for?"

"What?" said Mom, leaning in my direction.

"Gurlie? Why, that's *my* name!" said Mark's wife tiny Gurl, giggling. With her short, dark cap of hair clapped tightly to her skull and small, not-quite-beady eyes, she reminded me of a junco. Twitching her head, she scooted her chair closer to Mark, and leaned forward, her elbows on the table, ready to chat. "My mother was Danish you know, and she named her daughters after princesses. But they always called me Gurl. That's short for Gurlie, you know."

"Yes, Gurl," drawled Mark, a tall drink of water. "You've told us that before." He shook his hanging white-haired skull, at the same time shrugging an over-sized pair of tired, khaki-clad shoulders. Gurl gave a large, uncomprehending smile to the table before her eyes focused back on Mark.

"Well, I know I've told YOU," Gurl rebuked Mark with her finger as well as her tongue. "But THEY haven't heard it before." She was wrong but wasn't lying. She had Alzheimer's. At least her stories were interesting, though: a Bulgarian father who fled the Czar's conscription; an upper-crust mother who was a socialist. I didn't mind listening. Mark ignored her and stood to remove his jacket to the back of his chair.

"So, what are you hungry for, Gurlie?" I asked again, addressing my mother-in-law.

"Who's Gurlie?" said Gurl. After a pause, Gurlie lowered her head, waving her hand just above it.

"Well, me too! Isn't that funny," Gurl finished.

"You've told us that before," grumbled Gurlie, not one for tact when truth was hanging in the balance.

"What?" said Mom, leaning forward and cupping her ear.

"Have I?" said Gurl, and fluttered a little. "I don't recall."

"There's soup..." I ventured, this time not naming any names.

"What kind?" said Gurlie. I fought off an impulse to give her only one choice. Make it easy on myself. But there was no need. And I always felt so patronizing when I limited their choices, as if I were out with a bunch of kindergarteners.

"Cream of potato and minestrone."

"Minestrone," said Gurl. "My mother made the best minestrone. She was a vegetarian, but she didn't make my father eat it. He was a Bulgarian. Or us, either."

"It's a good thing she didn't," I deadpanned, as I had done with her times beyond counting.

"Why?" she wanted to know.

"Because then your father would've been a vegetarian Bulgarian," I laughed out loud, and Gurl howled ferociously as she rocked back in her chair.

"I never thought of it that way."

"What?" said Mom.

I mentally checked off the greatest benefit of Alzheimer's. I could tell the same jokes over and over and still get a laugh like it was the first time.

"What's minestrone?" Gurlie broke in.

"Vegetable soup."

"Or what?"

"Cream of potato."

"Well, I don't know," Gurlie puzzled up her face. "They both sound like vegetables to me." Gurlie was from Nebraska where the land is flat, the sunshine is clear and words are unambiguous.

"One has cream," I tried to distinguish them somehow in her mind. Maybe I should have said, "One's white."

"Oh, cream. Well, let's see, what was the other one?"

"The other what?" put in the other Gurl.

"Ooh, uh, well, I can't remember what we were saying."

"Where are we?" asked Gurl.

"Right here!" grumped Sylvia. Everyone else, except Mark, nodded at the satisfactory nature of her answer.

I jumped at the opening and turned to my mother. "Mom, want a—"

"Yes." Mom was a little deaf, but she cut me off before I repeated the question. She always agreed to a spoken question addressed to her if you looked her in the eye. She was fundamentally optimistic and always seemed to know a question when she didn't hear it.

"How about a black-bean burger?"

"Okay!" she laughed. "That sounds good."

"I'll have that too," said Gurlie, relieved.

"Okay," I said. "Me too. Now we're getting somewhere."

"Where?" asked Gurl.

"We're ordering lunch," put in Mark. "What do you want?"

"Oh, I don't know. I'm not really hungry," Gurl yawned, which made me want to yawn too. I stifled it, refusing to look at the clock.

"You've got to eat something,"

"What are you having? I'll just have some of that."

"No, you won't," said Mark flatly. "That's MY lunch." His mouth pursed itself with resentment.

Gurlie and Sylvia had been paying close attention. Suddenly Gurlie said, "I want soup and a sandwich, but that sounds like too much."

"You can have a cup of soup and a half-sandwich," I informed the table. "It's a special."

"Can you get a *bowl* of soup and a half-sandwich?" Gurlie wanted to know. I considered ordering a bowl of soup and a whole sandwich and splitting the sandwich with her, then realized that this was way too complicated an arrangement to explain in what remained of the afternoon.

"I'll ask," I said instead. I went to the high counter in the back of the room. The woman who was taking orders smiled at me and leaned over the counter just as I took a breath to speak.

"No problem," she whispered behind her hand. "We'll give them whatever they want."

Another satisfaction I derived from Alzheimer's. People liked to help us. They liked me for taking all these dotty ladies out for lunch. I liked myself for doing it too. Strangers wanted to take part, so that they could have fun and like themselves. So they helped whenever they could.

Forward I plunged into the valley of indecision. It wasn't so much that they had trouble *making* a decision as that they couldn't remember two things at the same time. Mom had solved the problem by agreeing to whatever was being offered in the instant. She just agreed to everything. Then, if she didn't like it when it arrived, she rejected it. What luxury! I wished I could make all my decisions like that. I mean, see the options in the flesh and then accept or reject them, not beleaguered by racing thoughts about wasting time, wasting money, how much fat, salt, and gluten.

By the time I returned to the table, Gurlie had discovered that she could see the menu posted on the wall if she twisted around in her chair. This meant that we had to start all over again. For the next half hour I explained the options of salad and half a sandwich, soup and salad ("How big a salad?" they wanted to know), seven different kinds of sandwiches, and four different dressings for the salad, on the salad or on the side. Mark sat mute at the far end of the table, leaning his leaden head on his right fist, arm bent at the elbow. He looked like he might drop it any second.

With some consternation, Gurlie ordered a whole sandwich and a whole salad. I went to the refrigerated drinks section and took out seven SOBE pink lemonades. I couldn't face explaining the options: there were myriad.

"Look!" I said enthusiastically, before anyone had a chance to ask questions. "Pink lemonade!" They all smiled up at me, except Mark. I glared at him and he accepted the lemonade.

Phase three consisted of actually eating. But it wasn't as easy as you might think. My bowl of soup arrived.

"What's that?" asked Gurlie.

"Soup." I said, thinking that I'd give her as little information as possible in answer to her question, that way avoiding more questions.

"What kind?" Foiled again.

"Cream of potato."

"You didn't tell me about THAT."

I took a deep breath to answer, then paused to gather myself. "Would you like some?"

"Naw." She looked disappointed.

"You can have whatever you want."

"Naw. It's all right."

The woman brought Gurlie's salad.

"What's that?"

"That's your salad. See, it's got dressing on the side."

"What kind of dressing?"

"Blue cheese."

"Well, that's okay, I guess. I like that. But it's too big. I can't eat all that AND a sandwich."

"Just eat what you want. You can take the rest home in a doggie bag."

By this time Mom had drunk both her lemonade and mine. She looked like a chipmunk with her cheeks packed with black bean burger. She was happy.

Gurlie wasn't.

"I thought *I* ordered a black bean burger."

"Do you want mine? I don't mind. I'll trade you."

"Naw. I guess not."

Mom was a fast eater and quickly finished everything in front of her—which meant both her lunch and mine. I was hungry—it was past two o'clock—but I didn't think I could explain that to the ladies at the table. Besides, they might all think they had to order again. Gurlie had just completed putting the salad dressing on her salad and was about to take her first bite.

It went on that way, while I carefully kept my eyes off the clock. I just sat smelling the grilled cheese sandwiches and minestrone, the blue cheese and raspberry vinaigrette dressings, the SOBE pink lemonade. I moved into it. Everyone seemed happy.

After a while Mark said, "I've got to go. My meeting's in five minutes."

"I'll take Gurl home," I offered. "I don't mind. It'll be fun. If you think she'll be all right with all these strangers."

"Oh, I guess it'll be all right." He grinned a handsome, resigned smile.

The counterwoman came and laid each check gently at each elbow. There was a chorus of: "I didn't have that." "This is mine." "What did I have?" "I only have a twenty." Fran quietly put in only two dollars for her five-dollar lunch, looking slyly sideways at me as she slid the bills under the pile. In the end, I made four dollars.

I began packing the extras in doggie bags. When I got to Gurlie, she had finished half her salad. I put the grilled cheese, untouched, and the rest of the salad in a bag. "I want the chips, too," she insisted. I threw the four chips in on top.

I was first out the door into the fresh air, but stood waiting to help the ladies down the block to the car. Mark was at my heels, shrugging on his jacket.

"I don't know how you can stand it," he paused, looking down at me.

"Well, I've served on lots of committees! No, seriously, I just think of it as if it were a fragrance. All you can do is move into it and breathe. It can be kind of relaxing if you let go."

He smiled as he turned toward his car. "I'll try to remember that," he said and escaped for one of the two hours a week he was without Gurl. He could step outside the fragrance for a while.

Slowly the women made their way back to where the car was parked and began a discussion about where they were going to sit.

"Why don't you get in the front, Gurlie?" I threw out a decision, hoping someone would grab it, and I could reel her in.

"Gurlie?" said Gurl. "Why, my name is Gurlie!"

"What?" said Mom.

And away we went.

Chapter Nine   LOSING DAD

Of course, the rest of the time I was in a world that smelled very, very bad to me, so much so it was hard to take a very deep breath. My power was about to be tested again. The second summer Dad was in the nursing home something was very wrong. In my daily visits to the unit, I had irritated Nurse Norse. It started one morning when the psychiatrist was sitting in the nurses' station and wanted to try a Parkinson's drug on Dad. When I told him the drug had already been tried at the nursing home before we moved him here, he denied it, saying, "The nurse says they didn't."

"Give me his chart." I put my hand out on the high counter of the nurses' station. The top of the shrink's head was an inch above the top of the counter. He reached up and handed over the heavy notebook, keeping his head down and continuing to work as if he'd dealt with family members like me before, and knew I would fail to find anything, that my memory was making it all up.

While I paged through, I remembered back to the hospital over a year and a half earlier, physically blocking a nurse who was on her way to adding Zantac to Dad's IV drip and arguing my way past a doctor.

If the doctors and the nurses didn't read the charts, who did? Evidently, professionals who could only read stickers. I found the page that listed the Parkinson's drug and showed it to the shrink, adding unnecessarily but irresistibly, "Betta, wrong again." At least he acknowledged my find and did not order that drug again. He ordered Risperdal instead, and ordered me not to visit Dad for two weeks.

Risperdal is a drug made out of rat poison. It's side effects include: drowsiness, dizziness, lightheadedness, drooling, nausea, weight-gain, tiredness. "If any of these effects persist or worsen, tell your doctor or pharmacist promptly. Dizziness and lightheadedness can increase the risk of falling." When they gave it to Dad, he sat with his chin on his chest, drooling, unable to raise his eyelids. Why would you give someone a drug like that? To treat Parkinson's?

"If I don't visit, will you hold off on the Risperdal?"

"No."

"But we have to do the experiment. If you do both at the same time, and Dad's behavior improves, you won't know which one was effective."

The doc nodded. "You're right." But he ordered the Risperdal anyway and gave the order not to allow my visits.

I reiterated, "I'll not visit then, for two weeks, but when I come back, I will not be convinced by any result. You won't have any grounds to keep me out."

I realized later that my absence probably affected more people's behavior than just Dad's, and I'm not talking about the other patients. Perhaps that was the psychiatrist's goal; just to defuse the situation. But it turned out that the Risperdal only infuriated me more.

—

One day, I found Dad sitting in his wheelchair, unresponsive and barely breathing. I tried to rouse him, but no luck. I turned to the nursing station to call for help, and Betta, not looking up from the chart she was studying, dismissed me, "He's all right."

I went back to Dad and gently pushed an eyelid open. The eye was rolled back in his head. I yelled and Betta came over, bending to take his pulse. A look of alarm spread quickly over her face, and pressing her lips tightly together she ordered a nearby CNA, "Let's get him into his room." Once there, the blood pressure cuff didn't find much pressure. And they did something, I can't remember exactly what, and a little later he was awake and asking for a banana. Still, Betta didn't write up the incident. I gave up and started to count pennies with Dad, one of his favorite pastimes.

We were at a stand-off. I remembered Brad saying he used to hold his mother while she fell asleep. This sounded like a comforting thing to do, so I tried it.

The notes that the nursing staff kept about Dad started to include descriptions of my behavior. That I caused his episodes of anxiety and dangerous behavior. Once I took him into an empty TV room to watch a show about animals. I turned off the lights; that way his attention did not wander from the TV screen, and anyway, Dad and I had spent many hours when I was growing up watching TV movies together. It was calming for me as well as for him. I was surprised to find in the nurses' notes about that night that what I had done was not normal, and they worried that I was harming him somehow. They diagnosed me as being in denial.

—

At the beginning of August, Mom called one morning. She was incoherent and had not a trace of a smile in her voice. "I got a call from them. Oh, Sare, what will we do?"

"What's wrong, Mom? What call? Who called you?"

"No, no, not a letter. I don't know who."

"Not a letter?"

"I just had to call you."

"Okay, Mom, I'll come over right now. Okay?"

"They do! Oh, please hurry, it's today!"

My leap over and down our front steps flushed out a black cat from the bushes at the same moment that a car took our corner too quickly. The cat was dead in a matter of seconds. I was grateful that the driver stopped and said he would take care of it. I felt bad and wondered if this was a piece of bad luck only for the kitty.

When Mom opened the door she said right away, "They want him out!"

"Who?"

"Dad."

"No, I mean who wants him out?"

She was holding a letter in her hand, and I snatched it away. She was right, WholeCare was evicting Dad. He had to be out by the next day.

What the fuck were they thinking? I had the POA for Dad's healthcare, Trudy did for the finances. They never sent letters to Mom. They never even called her. They would know this was the kind of thing you wouldn't do to a spouse suffering the first signs of her own dementia. Wouldn't they? I called, but the only thing they would tell me was that he was a "danger to himself or others" and had to leave.

"What kind of danger?" I asked, trying to let go of the clutch of anger in my chest and thighs.

"He took a swing at one of CNA's the night he arrived."

"That was a year and a half ago! The man's in a wheelchair! Didn't the CNA step back? He can hardly move since you've started giving him Risperdal."

"He's uncooperative in the bath."

"Surely that's not dangerous! He can't stand up for heaven's sake." It didn't occur to me that there were things he could do in the bath that were uncooperative and might be dangerous. He never threatened me that way. But then again, I never gave him a bath.

I didn't have anywhere to turn, so I took a breath and called Trudy. She surprised me by arranging for a lawyer to get an order to keep him there until we found another place. The search was slow and awful. Trudy and Mom and I visited other facilities, some as far from us as three hours. I didn't want him that far away, and neither did Mom, whether or not she visited him. One mental hospital that was hours away had the Alzheimer's patients on a ward with violent Huntingdon's patients who were imprisoned in wheelchairs that had a kind of cage on top. That's where Trudy wanted to send him.

Finally, we found a place an hour and a half away which had built small houses like Dr. Thomas's greenhouses, with only ten residents apiece. The Alzheimer's house was peaceful. The other residents had moved there from regular assisted living houses for the not-yet demented that were laid out in the same configuration, with the same paint colors and same pictures on the walls. People who could no longer care for themselves were moved here, without disruption. The entrance for workers and families was tucked into the end of a short hallway, without any signs indicating that it was an exit. The fire alarms were tucked away where only the staff could find them. People slipped in and out without attracting the residents' attention and went straight to their family members' rooms without having to pass a nursing station or engage with the CNAs. There was a walled garden off the dining area, and a small, dark room with a fish tank. Residents were fed on their own schedules, and Dad wouldn't have to eat spaghetti every other day, or rewarmed scrambled eggs.

I felt lucky, but Trudy stubbornly clung to the hospital at a greater distance. I thought, she just wants to be rid of him and will not visit him. She hasn't visited him when he's been in town, why would she start now? But it was the power thing. I was trying to make the decision for all of us. That's what I told myself, and then I had to decide which was more important? Could I give in and let my sister make the decision? Nope, I knew I couldn't leave Dad alone that far away in a place worse than where he was—and Mom unable to see him.

So, we decided to let our brother have a vote, but it was clear that we couldn't do this all by ourselves. We hired a mediator.

—

"I know the mediator you are going to see," Tilda said. "Do you remember the personality test I gave you?"

"No. Which one was that?"

"The Myers-Briggs Type Indicator. It measures your personality on four dimensions. You are an ENFP: extraverted, intuitive, feeling, perceiving. From what you've told me about Trudy, she is opposite to you on all counts: introverted, sensing, thinking, and judging. You will have a hard time agreeing, especially in a case like this one.

"Your mediator understands these types. Tell her what they are, and then ask her to intervene when you start to react with your feelings when Trudy is in her thinking mode, or when you are looking at things from your perceptive stance, and she is judging."

Well, that worked, sort of. Once, when it got hot, the mediator paused the meeting and said she had to make a quick phone call, and asked us to wait out in the hall. Back in her office she got the brother on the phone. But, in the end, the brother would not vote (also characteristic of what I guessed was his type) and Trudy and I held our respective grounds. That left Mom.

I didn't want to call her in. She would be forced to choose between her daughters, or so I would perceive it. But there was no other option as long as neither of us would give in. So Mom chose. And she decided with me for the place closer by. Trudy and I had traveled down our parallel roads, and it was hard to say whose road was worse. I wished I could have softened that blow, but then I'm a feeler, not a thinker. Perhaps Trudy did not feel the blow I thought she would. Or perhaps she was feeling a different blow.

The nursing home never recognized the trouble that they had caused our family; the reason they gave on the legal papers for the ejection was that he was "a danger to himself or others." Maybe so. Still, I didn't see why moving him so far away would solve our problems or his. But it would soon be over for Dad, and hopefully Mom's situation would not cause the same kind of dysfunction. And we had no choice.

—

The Alzheimer House sent a nurse to come and interview Dad and give him a physical. She was a lively, red-headed Irishwoman in her forties. Dad, who was his charming self, told her about Bikini, and I made sure she understood what he was talking about. It did not take long to get the approval and schedule the move. After we got him all moved in, she told me that the reason WholeCare was in such a big hurry to get rid of him had nothing to do with me. She had discovered a decubitus ulcer on his rear end in the physical examination.

"Technically, I was not allowed to accept him as a resident. These kinds of things are manageable, but they almost always get worse. A nursing home can lose its license if one is discovered. They were afraid of that."

"So why did you take him?"

"I liked him. And you... and I thought the family would all be better off if we took him. We'll get him a kind of mattress that should help."

"Why did the place accept him though, couldn't they lose their license?"

She looked intent for a short moment, then made up her mind. "I didn't report it."

So, I thought, she risked her job and probably *her* license to help us out. Or she understood that we all had Alzheimer's and this was the best treatment for all of us.

—

Dad taught us how to play monopoly, and when he wasn't top dog anymore, I had to step in. That caused us much danger to ourselves and others. Trudy and I had both tried and run headlong at each other for a little over a year.

I keep an occasional diary, but since I do not keep much of it *in* a diary, I often find sticky notes, bookmarks, (or even gum wrappers) with my scribblings on them. One from that pivotal year with my sister surfaces while I am writing this twenty years later. In it I advised myself,

> Playing with red trucks; in the mud while the grown-ups are watching for danger. I can have fun and build something and not worry, or when I am not worrying, I can build things.
>
> Dad said, "never hurry, never worry." The rejuvenation comes from becoming young again, where young equals

not knowing what to expect—it can be fun not to know, to make room for filling up again.

Pour out all the old worrisome things I have learned. Turn over all the rocks, all the runes, all the tunes, the tunas. Delight in living the challenge. Trudy says she wants no responsibility. So—take her at her word.

What is it that I do that blocks communication and gives others power over me? Stop smiling.

And I signed it, so I would know it was me who wrote it. Later, I would understand it was not about my power at all. It wasn't me who was under attack.

—

I fought hard to have Dad's doctor prevent the nurses from sedating Dad for the trip to the new house and to let me drive him rather than send him in an ambulance. Mom went with me.

When we arrived at the new place, CNAs came out to help transfer Dad to his wheelchair and roll him into his private room. All the rooms were private here; it cuts down on the agitation that happens when Alzies don't recognize the person in the next bed. Dad was asleep, and the transfer was difficult. When we finally got him to his room, he still was unresponsive.

"Better take him to the hospital," ruled the nurse who had brought him here. "I think he's faking, but we have to be sure."

The new place packed us some sandwiches for dinner, even giving us a choice. Of course, we chose BLTs, and while they hustled to make them, we wheeled Dad out to a van, and he was lifted into the back with Mom, while I rode shotgun. The official vehicle was required by the lawyers and insurance companies governing all our moves. It was late by then, and rainy, and Mom and I were tired, but we pulled up our shoulders and carried on.

Dad was all grins and looking out the windows into the rain-blurred street lights and the soaking dark night. Mom looked uncomfortably dutiful and did not respond to the puzzles I presented her with.

We arrived at a small Catholic hospital after about twenty minutes. It was packed! The woman behind the plexiglass was worn. It was late, and she looked past retirement age. We sat down to fill in yet another version of Dad's medical history that would be added to the unread files. The hospital did not even have enough room for all the people in the waiting room, much less the extra burden of paper.

Someone moved to give Mom a seat at the end of a row of plastic, connected chairs, where there was room for Dad's wheelchair. There was nothing to do, and Mom and I had run out of things to say at the end of a day that had started too many hours before. But Dad looked eagerly around at the other people and the room—curious and very happy to be out with us. I entertained myself reading the placards on the wall with names of people who had given money; others were posters with health tips warning about the prevalence of diabetes, heart disease, and child abuse—the signs and what to do about those conditions. I was sad to think that child abuse must be almost as prevalent as diabetes and heart disease to win a place on these waiting room walls. There were things more dysfunctional than WholeCare or our family.

They took us all into a dim examination room, not a small private one but a large room with sheets dividing it into spaces you couldn't see into, though everyone could hear everything going on in other spaces. There was nothing wrong with Dad. The doctor smiled, did all the tests, and we relaxed. He turned toward Dad. "Are you enjoying yourself?" And Dad nodded. Chuck called while we were there, and Dad had the extra bonus of speaking with him. By the time we arrived back at the Alzheimer's house, Dad was ready to sleep, and Mom and I made our way to a bed-and-breakfast to spend the night. I slept. He was safe in a place that recognized him and Mom and me.

It was far enough away that Mom and I went only once a week, and as far as I know, Trudy did not visit him at all. Mom developed migraine headaches and was treated for them.

After a few of our weekly trips, we were sitting at lunch with him one day. There was his tray with the gray food on it and a baby bib tied around his neck. My father was no longer there; he did not stop to use a fork or spoon, eating with his hands. Both of them. With stuff like applesauce as part of the meal, he was really messy and, of course, did not even notice the napkin. Mom and I sat by and watched for a minute, and once I tried to wipe his face. He just swatted my hand away. Was Trudy there? I think so sometimes.

I was glum, but Mom was angry. "He's an animal," she said with hiss. This was so unlike her that I immediately stood up and told her it was time to leave. She was glad to do it, and Dad didn't notice at all.

The doctor was willing to stop some of Dad's meds. I thought that it would be a good thing to let him go rather than struggle to keep him alive, but the doctor said there was no guarantee he would die. "He might just have a stroke." That would be harder for everyone to handle, so we continued the medications.

A month or two after he arrived in the Alzheimer's house, he was moved into a nursing home not far away.

—

Guy and I were in the middle stages of building our house in the woods on top of a mountain. What with the other stresses in our lives, this stress would break me periodically. One day, I packed my bags and headed up to the building site to tell him I was leaving him. I arrived and parked in front of the barn, taking a moment to be sure I wanted a divorce, when my cell rang.

Dad was dying. Time to come.

I left with only a word to Guy that I didn't know how long I would be away. I was prescient in packing that bag and did not have to drive home first before heading out for Dad.

The nursing home let me stay in an empty room on the same floor as

Dad. He was no longer able to do anything but lie there on a bed pushed into the corner of a large and empty room with no one else around. When I tiptoed in, he surprised me by asking with closed eyes, "Who's there?"

When I answered, "Sarah Smile," he did.

"That's my daughter," he said as he opened his eyes. But before I could answer he closed them. "Sarah Smile," he said, contented. I knew then that even though he was dying, everything was going to be all right.

They moved him into another room where I slept on a mat. Trudy took a second shift the next night, and Chuck flew in to take a third. I returned the fourth night. Once, when I left to get a meal, I heard him call out "Sarah..." in a tone that signaled to me danger and held a pleading direction for me to come. I rushed back to find him still unconscious. I still hear that last, unconscious call.

About one o'clock in the morning I awoke to a nurse leaning over me. "Your father has gone," he said. "Would you like a few moments alone with him?"

I nodded.

I sat on the floor and looked at the body. It was unnerving; when I looked almost away from it, so that it took up only a corner of my eye, it seemed to breathe. When I looked straight at it, it was still, but wasn't it about to take a breath? And sure enough, when I looked away it did.

I went out to ask the nurse to call the brain bank, where we had donated his brain. I waited with him until the orderlies arrived and zipped him up in a shiny black bag with a toothy zipper. I must have said goodbye, before I left.

We arranged for his body to be cremated. The undertaker asked at one point whether there was anything we would like to put into the box with him to be burned. I give him a photo of me, Dad, and Mom playing with me in a creek when I was just barely walking, not mentioning the request to my siblings. Glad I brought everything with me. I still feel guilty that Trudy and Chuck were not in the photo. But then again, Trudy wasn't interested in the family photos, so I felt justified.

—

When Dad died, all his possibility stopped. He was over and turned to stone just as he was, without any joy and without repentance. Silent now forever, he was he who he was for each of us. My image of him with Alzheimer's began to fade, and even twenty years later I still see him from the perspective I had of him when I was a child.

But the trouble he caused us continued on the trip back to bury him. Trudy decided she and Mom would travel separately from me. We all stayed in different motels. Mom traveled home with me. Oddly, I had developed a bad case of tinnitus, and I couldn't open my jaw very far the whole time I was there. Couldn't hear, could barely eat or talk.

We never did talk about how we felt about Dad, but I found out a little from the short speech Chuck gave at his funeral. He admired him for what he did at work: build missiles and protected us from the Russians. I talked about the tile I had had made for his gravestone, with images of the things that had been important to him painted on it: a TV set, an iron, a CB radio, a car, an airmail stamp. Around the edge it said, "Here lies the body of Dorothy's Ron. He liked to turn things off and on." Trudy said nothing.

Arriving home numb and exhausted, my attention began to be turned to the unfinished kitchen in the new house. It was completely bare, no cooking possible until the new custom cabinets were installed. Day after day, I painted the shelves and the inside of the cabinets and drawers—without any music, any radio, even anyone to talk to. But I had plenty to think about while I worked. I gnawed on the bones of my sister. Who was she? What had I done to alienate her? I was by turns angry, sorry, sorry for myself, proud of what I had done, confused. One moment I promised myself never to speak to her again unless she apologized. The next, I considered apologizing myself, but I didn't know what for. All I had done for the last two years turned over and over in my head—what my siblings and I had done, said, thought, over and over and under and around with no resolution coming through. The only relief I had were thoughts of my step-granddaughter.

The telephone rang. It was our carpenter. "I have a bone to pick with you," he started. "Just got to get this off my chest."

"Shoot," I said. I put down my paintbrush. Was I going to lose him now, too?

"Well, there's three things. First, when I agreed that you could buy the materials for this project, I lost some of my profit. I get a contractor's discount at the lumber yard, but I don't pass it on to you."

"But we paid you higher than you asked for your hourly rate." I paused. "Do you want to renegotiate?"

"Right." He thought about what I'd said.

"I did agree to it, I just wanted you to know."

"The second thing is that you were supposed to pay for that order from the plumbing contractor. You paid it two weeks late! He was mad and called me. Bad for my reputation."

My turn to think. "Okay," I said. "You are right. My fault and I'm sorry. Is there anything I can do to make it up to you? Give him a call myself and apologize?"

"No, that's all right. I just wanted you to know. Thanks for the apology. And last, you hired young Pete away from me. He's my guy, and he wasn't available to finish up the Rachlin job."

"I'm drawing a blank there. Must've been Guy who did that. I'll have him give you a call."

"Thanks," said my friend the carpenter with relief in his voice. "See you Thursday."

The line went dead, and I just stood for a moment looking at the phone in my hand. Huh. I think I just had an adult conversation. The call confirmed my feeling that there was nothing wrong with me.

Whatever is wrong must be with Trudy then. I can't do anything about it now. It's too late. She's gone. I'm probably the only person in the world who can't say anything to her without breaking the boundaries between us. She needs to take control, stop playing Monopoly with me. She might come back to me, or she might not.

The obsessive thoughts I'd been having for almost two years stopped in that moment and did not return. Just like that, I was cured. Dad was gone. Chuck was at his distance, a little farther than I liked, and keeping it. There was no worst anymore. I could ignore all of it and focus on Mom and my other family.

Chapter Ten   MERCY

Looking back now, it's hard to believe that Trudy and I didn't speak again for practically nine years after Dad died (no—more like seven—I'm confused). Oh, sure, we visited Mom and were polite when we ran into each other, but we tried to avoid those accidental meetings. I broke my ankle during those days, and she brought Mom up to visit me but only stood back and took no part. Once she asked me to bring Mom to a performance of her band. And once on my birthday, she met me at Mom's with a small present—a blue ceramic jar with daisies on it to add to my box collection. Looking back now, I can't say that I made as much effort as that. She occasionally disagreed with me; when she didn't, I unfairly thought they were times when she wanted to do things my way anyway.

One day, at the end of a church service, the minister pointed out that there were slips of paper in the pews. She asked us to write down a person's name we would like her to pray for. Just the name, don't sign it. Don't put any reason either. I surprised myself by writing down Trudy's name, even feeling a little silly. But it made me feel so good—why would that be? I don't believe in traditional prayer. I think now it was because I didn't have to make any judgements about her, just ask someone else to pray for her, that's all. I could do that. This small gesture freed me to think about her again and miss her now and then despite our distances from each other. I would have liked to share more of our time with Mom with her too.

I visited Mom as often as I had Dad. There were still books to keep. Mom continued to have lunch out with me, shop, do all the things we had loved to do together (sing!), but she deteriorated quickly after Dad died. I don't know how often Trudy visited her, but any visiting by her was a whole lot more than Dad got. Trudy saw her only when I wasn't at the assisted living place and avoided me everywhere else in town.

On a trip home from an outing, I was trying to distract Mom with old family stories.

"Hey, Mom," I turned my head from the road and grinned. "Remember the time when you and Dad came to my wedding when Guy and I got married? Dad locked himself out of the car while it was running," I laughed and glanced over at her.

She looked a little puzzled, so I searched for something that had happened longer in the past. "Tell me about when you and Dad got married."

"He was so handsome," she smiled wistfully, looking straight out the windshield. But that was all I got of that story she had told me enthusiastically dozens of times before. And then, after a moment, "I don't know about that guy," she said, dropping her head slightly to look at her hands. "He doesn't come around anymore."

I hesitated for a moment, the words, "He died, Mom" on my lips, when I caught myself in time, and instead changed the subject, saying the first thing that came into my head. "What was your mother's first name?"

"Mary," she remembered, relaxing back into the seat and raising her chin, "Mary Harriet."

When we arrived at her apartment, I hurried into the rooms ahead of her, snatching the photographs of Dad we had carefully put on the kitchen counter, the coffee table, her dresser, even in the bathroom, thinking they would bring her happiness. Bummer. I would never speak to her about him again.

Instead of going home to a book as I usually did, I went home to TV, where Guy was watching the World Series. I threw myself down next to him, just as a public service announcement came on:

Older Woman: "What did you say your name is?"

Fifty-Something Woman, who is holding back tears: "Rosita Maria Sanchez."

Older Woman: "What a beautiful name! And who are you?"

Fifty-Something Woman: "I'm your daughter."

I asked Guy to mute the sound for a moment.

"You know, when Dad didn't recognize me," I mused. "It didn't seem to upset him. In fact, he looked pleased that I was his daughter and didn't understand how he came to be so lucky. It made me cry. It's not the fear that I might get Alzheimer's—yeah, it could be, partly, I guess. But having Alzheimer's didn't seem to bother him, most of the time. It was other things. But when he didn't recognize me, I felt like we were both gone."

When Mom opened the door to me the next morning, her face was scrunched up and she didn't breathe right. She was in pain. "I can't," she said. She turned and fled into the bathroom, leaving the door open, and I followed. The bathroom was spacious and squeaky clean. She sat on the toilet grimacing. But nothing came out. When I helped her wipe I could feel the hard start of a BM pushing like a steel rod out of her anus. It was as big as a quarter and not budging.

"Okay, Mom, you are constipated. I'm going down to talk to the nurse. Do you want to come with me?"

She shook her head with a resigned "no" and, face hanging, went to lie on her bed, curled up on her side with her eyes closed.

The nurse was sanguine. "I'll give her some Metamucil."

"When did she last have a BM?"

"I don't know."

"But I thought you logged that?"

"Well, yes, but not every day. Don't worry, she'll be fine."

"She needs water."

"She'll get it with the Metamucil."

"Don't give her Metamucil!" Now I was angry, fuming at this stupid woman who reeked at that moment of all the rottenness of Western medicine.

I left and went back to Mom's apartment. I got her to drink a glass of water, and then asked if she'd like to take a warm bath. "C'mon, we'll go to Candy's," I said, not wanting the hassle of asking the nurse to bathe her downstairs in the one bathtub available for the dozens of residents.

"Okay," she agreed, "Let's go."

The bath seemed to give her some pain relief, and she didn't want to get out, but I needed to get her back and leave her so I could cook dinner for my family. After I dropped her off, I pulled over and called the doctor. Of course, it was a Friday night. Of course, it was after five o'clock. I sat and cried while I waited for the callback. It came after about a half-hour. When I explained the situation, the doctor told me to bring her into the office on Tuesday. Tuesday! I was in remonstration mode now. She's in pain. What don't you understand about pain? I imagined him shutting down on the other end of the line, wanting to get back to his own family and stuck on the line with a hysterical daughter. I agreed to bring her in and hung up. Then I called my nurse practitioner.

"Bring her in," she said. "We can dig her out." That's what happened. The nurse practitioner unlocked the empty office door, and her assistant, a midwife, "dug her out," while I stood by holding Mom's cold hand and watching her scream.

The nurse practitioner asked me about how I was doing with Dad's death. I started to cry.

"He had a good—and long—life," she pointed out, snapping me out of myself for a moment.

When it was over, Mom breathed normally, and smiled an exhausted and pain-free smile.

"I can't thank you enough," I told my two friends, and I thought they looked as beautiful as the freshest roses, standing there washing off excrement.

The next week, the doctor advised that Mom be operated on for colon cancer. He referred us to a kind specialist who looked at me with compassion. "Why?" he said. "She's demented. The surgery will weaken her and probably not extend her life. We should let it go. Okay with you all?"

"Yes," I said, relieved and speaking for us all.

We went on enjoying each other for some time. Mom was getting farther out. One day we had planned to go shopping, but when I got her room, I found a note: "Sarah—we are going down fast. I have 6 to 12 and probably more like 10 to 12. I'll be back as fast as I can! Love—Mom" The handwriting, spelling, and punctuation were as perfect as always. Did I know what she meant? Could've.

But we couldn't go on forever—just until Mom was found wandering barefoot outside the assisted living on a busy street. She forgot Dad, then she forgot where she was. At least Trudy, though scarce, was cooperating in Mom's care, and we set about again looking for another place for her. I was relieved that Trudy understood without any discussion that we were not going to put her back into the same Alzhammered Unit that Dad had been kicked out of. But it was the same story, the other places that would take her were too far away for us to visit the many times a week we both wanted to. We stalled for time now, while we kept looking.

Tricks worked for a while: a black mat to put inside the front door to her apartment so she wouldn't go out. An Alzheimer's catalog I ordered it from said that some people perceive this as a hole. But she soon enough discovered she could step on it, and it was time to try something else. Trudy and I bought a door alarm and arranged for an alarm to go off on the CNAs' belts when Mom opened the door. In a short time, all these strategies failed.

The head of the assisted living worked with us. She couldn't lock Mom's door (fire regulations for assisted livings), so we hired some women we knew to stay with her 24-7. When she went out the door, they'd follow and keep her safe and inside the building. Mom didn't seem to mind, except for one woman she didn't like who had to walk twenty feet behind her so she wouldn't notice. She was safe and wasn't agitated. Because it had circular hallways, Mom would walk for hours.

Of course, it was expensive to pay these monitors, but Mom had the money to do it, and it gave some extra cash to friends of ours. It also took lots of monitoring on Trudy's part, but neither she nor Chuck complained about money now.

Then, one morning she appeared very early at the director's office on the floor below her apartment, hair combed and completely dressed from the waist up, but wearing nothing more. Did her mirror show her only the top half? I wondered.

"She's a danger to herself," the director said. "There's nothing more we can do. It's time to move her into a place that can be locked. It's a legal thing." Along with the director, I was relieved it had happened so early in the morning. I was glad that she was so unaware of herself that she would not have to suffer the humiliation and embarrassment of what she had forgotten, or didn't even see.

We pleaded for one more week and crossed our fingers. Together we attended a seminar at the hospital that included a panel of local experts. One was the new head nurse of the Alzheimer's unit where Dad had lived. I hoped she would be better than Betta. She told the story of a woman who came to visit her mother every day. The mother no longer recognized her daughter, who would stand in front of her and cry.

"Why don't you go home?" the nurse told the daughter. "You're upsetting her. How do you think it makes your mother feel to see a beautiful stranger stand in front of her and cry?"

How would it make you feel to stand there yourself, I wanted to cry right now, right in front of everybody. How can you feel so much compassion for the mother and so little for the daughter? What kind of a person are you, anyhow? It isn't just about whether or not you are inconvenienced by this tragedy. It's not just about whether your patient is agitated or not, not about how difficult your job is. It's not okay just to medicate everyone in your care, or send them all away. How can a daughter trust the care of her mother to you if she herself can't trust you to recognize the most basic human suffering? She's lost her mother—for god's sake—who is standing right in front of her. Have mercy.

I'd given myself a headache by then. But help was on the way in the form of a young couple who started a new kind of house for Alzheimer care. Knowing who the new head nurse was at WholeCare, was a double reason not to put Mom there.

One day Trudy called with the news that a young couple was building a small assisted living with only ten single rooms in it. We got in touch with Jeremy and Dianne and arranged to see the place soon after. My first reaction to the building was to the décor: the same heathered colors and reproductions of bucolic paintings as everywhere else. But it was easy to let go of that reaction, because in a single room Mom could be herself, with her own furniture and dolls and no stranger sleeping in the next bed. She had a full-sized closet. Jeremy even asked what she liked to eat and whether she had any books and magazines he could fill the living room shelves with. The house was built around an open kitchen area that had a long counter dividing the living room and the cooking space. It was tantamount to one of Dr. Thomas's green houses.

"This way, the residents can help make dinner, or talk to the cooks," Jeremy explained. He was eager to get started and agreed to move Mom into the first room that was available (even before the finishing touches were complete).

A hardwood dining-room table was set off to one side, big enough for ten, where Jeremy served us tea and cookies. Two large doors opened out onto a patio and a yard with a six-foot high chain-link fence. Tall windows looked out on the yard from the table where Mom would eat her meals. Jeremy would hire more CNAs than WholeCare to work with only ten people and cook. He and Dianne lived next door to the building. There was an RN on call 24-7.

We moved Mom on a Monday. We had arranged to take her out to lunch while the moving company came and cleared out all her stuff from the assisted living and took it across town to The Nest. I stayed the afternoon, just to be there with her, but she didn't seem to be disoriented or even know that she had moved.

The next day I was there, working away on one of my indexing projects, when the voice of one of the residents came pushing through the door, "Why you're so blind you can't see—"

"I can't see?" boomed back Jeremy, in a tickled tone of pure cheer. More often than not, Jeremy spent his time with the residents rather than in his office.

"Yeah, you're so blind, you can't see—" Irma returned, with a lilting tease.

"You want a kiss, Irma? You want me to give you a kiss? Give me a kiss, now, and then we'll go to the toilet."

"Nah, I don't want no kiss." Her voice was warm with the attention and good humor pouring over her.

"There, let's go, now," said Jeremy, and the other voices took over, finally fading into the settled murmur of the air conditioning. A phone rang. Again. Again and again. But the caregivers were all busy kissing and toileting. The phone would have to wait for more important things to get done first. (What a concept!) I packed up and gave Mom a kiss too. She was with a new family here, and there didn't seem to be any dysfunction. And I was part of it! That night I turned off my phone before I got into bed, and for the first time in more than four years, I slept soundly.

And I continued to sleep soundly.

—

On Thursday morning, Jeremy called. "We haven't tried giving her a bath," he said. "But she needs one."

"Do you want me to come over?"

"Maybe it would be good if you were there."

When I arrived, one of the CNA's was struggling to get Mom into the shower. I decided to try to get her into the tub myself and sent the CNA out of the bathroom, closing the door behind her. But even with more privacy, Mom resisted. I undressed and got into the tub, and started to run some warmish water. By hopping in and out a number of times, I finally was able to coax her out of her clothes, into the tub, and onto the built-in seat, although she would not take off her underpants. Just as I had accomplished this, there was a knock on the door.

"It's me, Dianne," Jeremy's wife said through the closed door. "How's it going?"

"C'mon in," I said, "We're taking a bath."

Dianne opened the door, took a look, stepped in, turned around, and shut the door. When she turned back, she started to unbutton her blouse. To my astonishment, she stripped off all her clothes and joined us in the tub. I could not stop from bursting into tears.

"What? You don't have to do that," I said.

"I want her to trust me," Dianne said simply.

Mom trusted her immediately and forever after that day. So did I. I worried some that Dianne or The Nest could get into some sticky thickets if that story got out, so I didn't tell many people. But it was just the kind of thing I wanted for my mother, who had so often bathed me.

—

From Mom's room I could hear Jeremy in the living room.

"Hey Louise, you gotta go to the bathroom?"

"Well, I..."

"Well, doing some walking then?"

No response.

"Let's do some laps around."

Lousie doesn't say anything.

"Yup, yup, round and around, that's where we want you to go."

"UP... UP... one-two-three, there you go. There. You're standing. Now sit. You okay now? Just get in your chair, then you don't have to walk around. I don't know. Can you follow me?"

The staff also came to care about Mom, about *her*, who she really was.

Jeremy had hired me by that time to train the CNAs and cooks in Greenhouse principles, the most important of which was: Keep it resident-centered. There was a diagram with the Alzhammered resident in the center, and concentric rings going outward from there: first CNAs, then Jeremy and Dianne, then cleaners, then food suppliers, etc. The idea was that the closer you were to the center, the more your judgment takes precedent in what happens.

At one point, Mom was wandering around each night, poking her nose into everyone else's rooms. The CNAs asked me what I thought they could do to get her in bed. I didn't have an answer, but when I told Trudy, she said, "I'm not surprised. Mom was a nurse. She was just making the rounds to make sure everyone was all right. It was her job."

The next time I visited The Nest, the CNAs rushed up to me, grinning. "She went to bed last night—no problem," they beamed. "After we got everyone else into bed, we all went in the pantry and turned off the lights. She went right into her room and got in bed." Brilliant.

In another case there wasn't a good solution. Mom liked to crawl in bed with another patient, and since there were only single beds in the rooms, the CNAs were afraid one of them would fall out. They asked me to come one time when the two of them were in bed and see if I could persuade her into her own room. As I approached the bed, I heard Mom call her friend by my father's name. The woman was tall and skinny, like Dad had been when he was young, and slightly taciturn, also like my father. I was not surprised that it made Mom happy to be there again. I suggested that we buy a double bed for them, but the other family wouldn't go along. We left the CNAs to struggle as they could, and eventually they got her into a habit that masked the problem.

—

I took the tablecloths out of the plastic tub and shook them out, one by one. Trudy and I were hosting Thanksgiving dinner at Mom's new place. There were Grandma's linens with the family initial embroidered at the corners. There were some gorgeous tea-dyed, hem-stitched pieces—enough for a sitting of twelve. My favorite set was embroidered with multicolored Chinese pagodas. And they were all in perfect condition, appearing unused, except for Grandma's, which I remember she used for our Thanksgiving and Christmas meals at her house. All the others were in the same shape when Mom gave them to me as they were forty and fifty years before. I recognized myself: always saving things to be used later, at the right time, when it was an event that was so important that the good things would be appropriate. And nothing was ever good enough for Mom, or maybe she just used one set and saved the rest for a later that never came. Mom preserved everything to pass on to another life that might be more important than ours—a perfect one, not one that was just good enough.

—

Mom was happily undrugged for the five years before she died. That July arrived in a hot spell that usually waited until August to stifle us. The woods were still, except in the middle of the night when the chain saws were allowed to feed. Even the trees didn't move a needle, trying to breathe without overheating. When it was time for Mom to die, Trudy and I moved mattresses onto the second-floor balcony outside the office and brought sheets and pillows. We didn't need the sheets. Our brother came from far away and stayed elsewhere except when it was his turn to sleep in Mom's room on a mattress. Those nights, the two sisters took the balcony roost.

Mom lay in her room in a hospital bed, head raised, arms holding the blankets down close on either side of her body. Trudy sat at the head of the bed, holding a stick in her mouth, with a tip of dayglo pink sponge rubber. From time-to-time she withdrew it and dipped it into a paper cup of water.

I had never seen Mom like this before, unable to move, unable to help herself even to a sip of water. Her eyes moved widely in her head as she watched Trudy get up to refill the cup. Her eyes were full and opaque, my mother who loved me and who was dying.

I sang her the song she used to sing to sing me to sleep:

> Baby's boat's a silver moon
> Sailing in the sky

> Sailing o'er the blue lagoon
> As the clouds go by.
>
> Baby's fishing for a dream,
> Fishing near and far,
> For her line a pale moonbeam
> For her bait a star.
>
> Sail, Baby, sail
> Out across the sea.
> Only don't forget to sail
> Back again to me.

Trudy surprised me by singing it with me.

Sharing the balcony on those hot nights, unable to sleep, we talked, lying on our backs looking up. There was a hiatus in the silence between us we were so hungry to talk. We lay there both looking at the sky. I glanced over once and she was relaxed, her face calm in the moonlight.

I told her that Mom was better than a good enough mother to me. She taught me not to sit on public toilet seats without first balancing strips of toilet paper on the edges for protection. When the sex talk came, and even though it was clear that she didn't think sex before marriage would make me happy, she gently told me that it was all right if you loved someone and they loved you. After I had become sexually active, a local doctor told her I was on birth control pills. She told me he shouldn't have done that—my medical information belonged only to me—and then only asked one question: whether I wanted to talk about anything. I didn't. And when I tried to sneak out to go to Woodstock she said, "Growing up is sometimes learning how to lie." I pictured her in my mind as she stood at the door with me and looked her wistful way into her past and my future. I couldn't see what she saw, but in that rare moment she opened a little to me, nonetheless.

Trudy interrupted my thoughts. "It's pretty depressing when you see human beings just going on and on doing the same things over and over every generation."

I told her I had been at a potluck last night and there was an eighteen-year-old there who was pregnant. Her mother said she had had two miscarriages and an ectopic pregnancy before this one. She had been living with the father, who was married to someone else. Her mom tried to tell her, but she was determined to have his baby. Sounded like she thought he would get a divorce and marry her. Right after she got pregnant, she went away on a trip, and he took up with her best friend and kicked her out.

"Pretty common," responded my Buddhist sister. "But who knows? Maybe the baby will help her get an education. The Buddhists are constantly telling stories on this topic. There's one about a young man who lost his leg. Then the emperor comes to the village to conscript all the young men for war, and he doesn't have to go. You don't know what's going to happen."

"Like your friend Rodney."

She looked at me, blank.

"Did you know, Rodney got out of the draft to Vietnam because of that eye injury he got at your birthday party in high school?"

She laughed. "No, I didn't know that."

"Yeah. And my granddaughter is such a blessing to me! But she ruined two lives getting here. Or, well, maybe she'll end up saving Amos. Who knows? But it's so hard on Guy."

—

The next morning, we both stuck around by Mom's bed and took up the conversation. Trudy told me that she was glad for our earlier conflict, not getting along or—the words won't come to me—what was the word she used anyway? It was more like war. There was a hiatus in the war between us, as if because Mom couldn't hear what we were saying.

"But it forced me to look at my childhood," she said. "I didn't want to be there. The only way to get out was to make a different choice."

"I wanted to help you," I said. "Then I realized that I was the only person in the world who couldn't help you."

She started to raise an eyebrow but caught it. "I wanted to run away from it and I couldn't. I had never dealt with it before. I walked into a room once and Mom was there, and you and Dad were there. I had a physical sensation. It was awful. It was like being pulled back in at the same time I was hit by a wall. I had to force myself to stay. When I finally got to the point when I could just have the sensation and experience it, I realized it was the same as when I was a kid. It was me who put up the wall. I thought Dad loved you more than me and that you loved him more than I did. Well, that was probably true! Only it was me who decided..." She didn't finish the sentence, couldn't say, *not to love him.* "I made that decision."

I tried to remember if I had decided to love him, but there was nothing I could replay that sounded like that tune. A thought went by as on a tickertape: *...So I was the one in control, not him, not you...*

I said, "So that must have felt good, huh, to realize that it wasn't something that was forced on you with a judgment attached?" I was thinking that she must have felt that she wasn't good enough. Or as good as me. I remembered Chuck calling me a saint and how much it hurt me.

I thought she grasped my intended meaning when she said, "Yeah."

She went on, "It happened when I saw him and he didn't have any power anymore. I had never seen him like that before."

So it was possible to make a decision that wasn't his, I thought. I told her a little about my counseling about Mom and Dad in my early thirties. "I always thought that you and Chuck moved so far away because you didn't want to deal with it."

She dropped her head once. In agreement? Or shame.

Mom breathed and listened but showed nary a sign. Trudy left to go to her office and bring back medicines and lunch.

—

The Nest's nurse Laurie stopped by just after she left. She was surprised at the order for Fentanyl, a narcotic for pain, but bowed to the denser experience of the hospice nurse. None of us really knew what Mom wanted, less what she *would* want, or *would have wanted.* (Where are we, here?) At more moments than not, a shiver murmurs *this is about me and Trudy and Chuck, Laurie and Jeremy, and our letting go of her. Not her surrender, but ours.* Because there is no line anymore between allowing her to make her own decision and allowing ourselves to make ours. This is more like a Zen diagram.

We all made the decision to put on the Fentanyl patch, with Laurie thinking it would make Mom groggy. I was not convinced that she was groggy. She would open her eyes when moved or when someone would stick a swab in her mouth. When her eyes were open, she looked at you, and they were not empty. Disappointingly, they didn't carry any message, not even a signature. Just, *I am who I am, whoever that is*—God or Popeye. So making her groggy—is that allowing her to decide, or is it pushing her on? We can relieve pain; does that also mean we can relieve her of life?

"Sometimes," the hospice nurse said, "Relieving the pain—it allows them to relax enough to let go. They are tensing so much to protect themselves from the pain, they are holding onto their body." Is that like me all the time? Trying to remember everything? Remembering too much? Hanging on to my pain?

Or they get groggy enough that *we* can let go, I thought. No need to look into those Buddha eyes, full of nothing. I could stay here where she is so present and I with her, so that I can empty my eyes long enough to fall asleep. But I made my decision to go home and try to sleep where she is not present, except insofar as she has given her lungs and heart to me.

—

The hospice nurse asked, "Is she swallowing?" I started to answer, then shut my mouth and threw my look over to Trudy, who took over, telling her that Mom now responded with a suck-swallow-breathe reflex when we touched the moisture swab to the top of her mouth.

"Anything else I can do?" Jeremy asked me over and over again. But no, they were doing everything, even to staff bringing gifts, like an aroma-producing night-light. Life going on in the same space as death. Not like WholeCare, where the director forbade anyone from entering the room of a dying patient. She didn't want to "scare" the other patients. She wouldn't let anyone talk about it and did her best to quickly move dying people to the hospital, so no one would see. You think that didn't scare everybody?

One day Ruth, another resident who had also been a nurse, approached me. "Can I go in?"

"Of course, I'll get you a chair."

She sat with Mom for a half hour, then rose, picked up the waste basket, left the room and emptied it, then returned and put it back in its place. Trudy thanked her.

As she reached the door of the room, she turned. "Thank you," she said simply.

Chuck arrived and took his turn sleeping in Mom's room, and Trudy and I headed for our hot balcony. When we were settled, she rolled over on her mattress to face me, her head held up by her arm bent at the elbow over her pillow. "Once at WholeCare, Dad told me he loved me. It made me really mad. So, you had to be demented to say that to me?"

I had a hard time believing that was true. "You mean when you were a little girl? What about when you were an adult?"

"No, never."

I cast around for something to say. "I guess he started saying that to me when I was in my forties. It was awkward for him, he really had to force himself. But he did. Mostly on the telephone." I probably haven't said it to you either, I thought.

She went on. "It's sad really. For him, I mean."

I changed the subject.

—

The next evening all three of us were in Mom's room after dinner.

"How did it go with feeding Lily tonight?" I asked Trudy. Lily was another resident at The Nest. We sometimes gave her some attention when her son Ed wasn't around.

"Okay, I guess. At first, she didn't say anything, and once she said no. But slowly she let me get more aggressive with the spoon. I guess it's easier for me to feed her than to feed Mom." The left side of Mom's mouth shirred as one corner pulled back into her cheek.

"Did Lily just start to go downhill recently? She didn't seem very communicative."

"Yeah. Ed said she hasn't said anything to him for a while. But then he told me, one night after she was in bed he asked his mom, 'Are you peaceful?' and she sat right up and said clearly, 'Yes.' And then he asked her something like 'Do you have any regrets?' And she said just as definitively, 'No.' What a wonderful thing for Ed."

We both were silent for a little bit, before Trudy asked, "Did you ever ask Mom if she had any regrets? I didn't."

"No, but I doubt it. I don't think she every regretted anything in her whole life. Once Dad told me that he was a bad father, though." This last caught Trudy off-guard for a second; then her forehead wrinkled horizontally in a way that reminded me of Dad's when he decided to disbelieve a certain CBS news anchor. "Of course, he was demented already," I added. Trudy's face smoothed over, and she nodded knowingly, her mouth pressed firmly in a line, so I went on. "I said, 'No, you were good enough. You weren't perfect, but that doesn't mean you were bad.'" When I tell Trudy things like this, I see a look pass across her face as if, for an instant, she wants to argue the point. Maybe he was a bad father to her. She doesn't say anything. I haven't the faintest what it must have been like for her. I wish I could wipe it away, bewitch her with a twitch of my nose.

I got up and went outside to walk around a bit to ponder how she must feel. At home, I had asked Guy about having no father and how he felt about it.

"No one would listen to how I felt. When they used to say, 'You shouldn't feel that way,' it was better than saying, 'You don't feel that way.' At least they acknowledged that you had the feelings." I thought, not very much better.

When I came back, Trudy looked up from her perch by Mom's hospital bed. Mom was sleeping, or not conscious, anyway.

I wanted to talk more but not so intensely when Trudy said, "I was just thinking about Grandma.... I didn't like her."

"You mean when you were little?"

"Yeah, I hated to go stay with her. Remember how we each went to stay with her by ourselves? I hated it."

I was taken aback, then surprised by the memories of Grandma that returned to me.

—

I hadn't felt any great warmth for Grandma, except when she dried me off from a bath in the bathroom with black-and-white checkered pressboard wall tile; a tiny 8 x 10 window opening into the alley above the tub; a sink standing on chrome legs thin as a storks', and an oval cardboard box of lily-of-the-valley body powder sitting on the back of the toilet. Once she puffed me with it and I loved it. But she did it only once, and I never asked her to do it again. It was hers, and impolite to ask for more. She'd give me what she wanted to give me and that was enough for her.

She worked hard keeping house, cooking, and baking—knitting, tatting, and keeping track of a distant, younger generation on the afternoon soap, The Edge of Night. She sat in a blue-Naugahyde, overstuffed rocker. Her sister, Aunt Katie, had a yellow one. Aunt Katie's had a matching footstool, but Grandma's didn't have that.

Next to her rocker was a guppie tank sitting on an antimacassar sitting on a magazine table that had a tilted pocket that held the TV Guide. The table and chair were at one end of the living room windows, six-foot-high affairs, three or four of them each three feet across that took up the whole front wall of the living room and looked out through the awninged front porch to the main street of the town. Running under the windows was a long, dark radiator—topped with that brown, thin, boardy stuff. It was loose and often fell off when I leaned on it without meaning to. At the other end of it was the TV.

Grandma lived in a different state, and it was hard for me to remember the numbers of my favorite networks. At home we got 2, 4, and 7. At her house, 10 was CBS, and she didn't even get 9 or 13. Then there were all these numbers even higher than 13, and our TV didn't go any higher. Dad went through them all each time we visited and played with different antennas that were on the TV itself. Our antenna was on our roof, and he had only played with it once when he put it up. Of course it was a lot bigger, so that was different, but why didn't Grandma have one that was bigger? I went back to the kitchen to look for a cookie.

Grandma sat rocking and knitting in that chair with her polished black shoes crossed over each other. They tied all the way up to her ankles, like my red ones did, but they had heels on them that were higher than mine, but still not a high heel. And they were thick and looked ugly. Her ankles were wider than the tops of her shoes, and it looked like the laces were tied too tight, pushing those ankles out and over the top. Didn't that hurt? She was fat, but not soft in the middle, because she wore a corset, a nasty thing that left red marks on her back and buttocks. I saw them when she undressed to go to bed with me in the big bed in the front bedroom.

The big bed in the front bedroom had a headboard that was as tall as I was when I stood on the pillows in front of it. There was room on each side of the bed for one person to walk sideways. The dressing table in the corner was too wide to fit, so it stretched catty-corner, one edge touching the molding around the doorframe. There were two feet between the foot of the bed and the door, then a small hall, with the bathroom door facing on the other side. The door to the bathroom opened out into the hallway, because there was no room for it to swing inward.

My mind surged on. Other memories I hadn't looked at since I don't know when flooded in and overwhelmed me. She had been distant and cold. She had a bristly chin. She taught me how to knit but just with scraps of yarn, and she never helped me make any whole piece of clothing—not even a scarf. Once I asked her to help me make a sweater, and she just made it and sent it to me. She never let me wash the dishes, though I wanted badly *to try it the way she did it: immersing her buttery-soft arms in the sudsy warm water as far up as above her elbows. The few times she agreed to hold me, I crawled up on her lap only to find her corset was not as inviting as the touch of her hand. All those bad memories floating to the top made me think she was a different person than the one I had fondly remembered all my adult life. I hadn't liked Grandma either, I was afraid of her, only this was the first time I realized it. Maybe she didn't like me either.*

While I was thus flummoxed, Trudy had moved on. "I didn't like Dad, either," she was saying. "I couldn't wait to get out of there. When you left after high school you left me there all by myself with them. It was awful."

How could I not know this about my sister? I had the barest of clues: when she was divorcing her second husband she had once said, "I didn't really like anybody in the family except you." I never thought twice about that but was glad it was true. And we had had a lot of good times together until this. I knew we were very different, but how had I entirely mistaken who she was? And why was it awful? I couldn't understand then.

—

Guy's ex brought a salad and fruit lunch for us, then said, "Your mom must have been a very good mother for you two to be so devoted like this. What was she like when you were teenagers?"

We talked about our experiences with sex, of course. Mine were all pretty positive, like making out in high school in the hammock in our back yard. Having wet panties when I came in the house, I asked Mom if I was all right. She told me that women needed to get wet in order to enjoy sex, and that I would know who the right man was for me partly by that sign.

Trudy's eyes grew wide. She listened almost hungrily, then said, "She didn't say those things to me. But I didn't ask as many questions. She always seemed open, though. When I was in fourth grade, she made me go to a class for older girls about sex. We watched a movie about girls' bodies. I was too young—there weren't any other girls my age there, they were all older."

"Oh, yeah, I remember that movie—the Walt Disney one all full of glitter and falling in love?"

She nodded solemnly, "Yeah. The one where they show her in the bath, already clean before she steps in!" And she laughed.

My thoughts wandered. Among Mom's things I had found a strange picture of her in a shirtwaist dress by a stream, standing below the camera and holding her arms straight and out and up toward the camera. It's black and white with a dusky quality to the contrast. She looks odd. Dependent, passionate, almost desperate. Not smiling and not seductive. On the back is scrawled "honeymoon," not in her neat hand. It spooked me.

When exhaustion started to set in, I finally left and went shopping. That relaxed me, along with a long shower at friend's house. I chanted sa-ta-na-ma and walked the length of her house and back ten times while waiting my underwear to dry. Then I stopped to pick up Thai and beer for dinner, before returning to The Nest.

Mom had been changed twice with a significant amount of liquid for someone who has not tasted anything wet to speak of for six days. Her breathing changed subtly in ways I can barely discern. Sometimes, when you swabbed her mouth the breathing would get quieter, so perhaps her throat would get dry.

It was so easy to let her go in this place that felt like a home. Even Trudy and I functioned with each other for that week. There wasn't any angry boiling-over in me when I knew my mother was as safe as she could be.

—

It was almost the day that Mom died, might even have been the night before, when Trudy asked me, "What do you think the worst thing is after somebody dies?"

"I don't know."

"But I think about when *you* die. What'll I do when I need your help? I don't think I can do without you."

"When I'm gone, you will still be able to talk to me." My smile was wan, but I could feel my eyes shine. "I talk to Mom even when she isn't there."

"You do?"

"I discovered it one day on a walk with Dog. I was going along thinking about taking a weekend trip to see a friend, and I went off into 'It's too far, I can't afford it.' Visualizing accidents and bad weather and stuff like that. Then suddenly I thought, 'Why am I so fucked up? Who is always telling me *not* to do things?' It was quiet enough for me to hear a voice answer me. It said, 'I didn't want you to get hurt.'

"'Who is this?' I thought, not expecting an answer. But it came immediately: 'Mom.'

"After that, I would just go for a walk and ask questions. Someone always answered, sometimes a good friend or even the dog. Never Dad. Funny . . ."

"I think it was just you he didn't have advice for. No wonder," Trudy said.

The sisters were silent for a moment.

"What'd Mom tell you?" Trudy pushed on.

"Not much. She would always have an answer for why or how, why did I react this way or how she did things. One time I asked her how she put up with Dad and she said, 'I ignored him.' That helped me to ignore Guy when I found myself stuck in spirals about some problem or other we were having. She never told me *what* to do, like if I asked, 'What should I do, Mom?' But if I asked her *how* to do a specific thing, or what she did in the same situation, she always answered right away. Very helpful."

"Do you think you were talking to her, really? Do you think it was ESP?"

"No, not really. I think it was my unconscious. Or maybe *our* unconscious. You know when I was in my twenties I played bridge with a couple of friends, Phoebe and this guy I was seeing—Carl. Do you remember him?"

"Only vaguely."

"Anyway, Phoebe didn't like Carl, and one day when we were alone, I asked her why. She described him and I thought, 'That's not Carl! He's not like that!' But he was like that. He acted like that with her, all arrogant and dismissive. It was the first time I thought about who we are depends on who we are with. So we change. And we behave differently because the people we are with react with us differently. So when I ask myself what Mom would say, the mom I knew answers me. Somewhere deep down I know what she would say. Or I remember, I observed what she did, but it doesn't make it into my conscious mind. It seems to come from somewhere else."

"There is a part of us that no one ever knows—" Trudy responded, "—our real selves—that only we are aware of. And it's a mess! It's all the ways we react to other people, so it's crazy and contradictory and impossible to get a hold of. It's all potential, I think that's why, and who we are appears only when we react to other people. Like scientists can't see chemistry, but they can figure out what a chemical is by the way it reacts with other ones."

"Still, we think of ourselves as consistent and whole." I warmed up to her ideas. "Or at least we want to be that way. And we think of others that way—it's easier to fool ourselves about them, because we only see them when they are with us! So it's just a small slice and it's influenced by us. Like oxygen trying to see how hydrogen reacts to nitrogen, but the oxygen's always there grabbing hydrogen and turning into water. Or sometimes there's enough nitrogen that it slows down the reaction. Whatever—it's confusing to everybody."

"Not only!" Trudy interrupted my professorial self. "I think that's what the Buddhists mean when they say there is no past or future, just the present."

"So the past and future don't exist?"

"Well, when we live in the past or the future, it is our stories we are living in and they don't exist, even though the past and future DO! Especially, our stories about the future (expectations) are dicey. So little of what we envision happens, unless we put energy into it NOW."

"So the past is there?" I pressed.

"You bet. What is past is a trap, unless we are conscious of it NOW. That's what sets us free—like when you told me about the guy at my party who got hit in the eye by a piece of watermelon rind, and lost his eyesight? I felt guilty about him for all those years, but it had a good outcome in a way. Our interpretations of the past are conditioned attempts at recreating situations that DIDN'T WORK to try to make them come out right. That's what leads to obsession."

"So the future doesn't exist?'

"Only in stories."

"Sounds to me like there are no 'real' selves," I giggled. "I told my friend Peter once that I was afraid that I had sold my soul, and he said, 'That's okay, there's more where that one came from.' Maybe that's what the collective unconscious is. It's all those memories and experiences everyone has in all sorts of overlapping combinations. It's all there whenever we do anything. Maybe more concentrated here, more attenuated there. But everybody's got all of it to some degree."

"Well, let's be glad, then, that you aren't about to die, and we can still talk about stuff! Life, it's wonderful, eh?"

"I like it fine."

—

We were all with her when she died. Trudy and Chuck were silent. I had to flee to the bathroom and sob, too embarrassed to sit with them, embarrassed by me.

Others say that you always hear your mother's voice in your head. Mostly, I think they mean you hear critical comments about yourself, the origins of which you are uncertain. I have those, too, but most of them are not critical, and not often in words. I often hear the echoes of the song my mother sang every spring when the sun shone, really shone, and we knew that summer would come again:

> Wake up, wake up you sleepy head
> Get up, get up, get out of bed,
> Cheer up, cheer up the sun is red
> Live, love, laugh and be happy.
> When the red, red robin comes bob, bob, bobbin' along
> What if I were blue, now I'm walking through fields of flowers
> The rain may glisten, but still I listen for hours and hours.
> I'm just a kid again, doin' what I did again,
> Singing a song,
> When the red, red robin comes bob, bob, bobbin' along.

It's not the only song I hear in her voice, but it's the easiest to recognize.

—

"After you've gone and left me cryin'," sang the guitarist on stage at the east end of the famers' market, and I ran into a rock wall, while the others simply walked on. Then it felt too complicated to me to go on; I had lost my balance except when I was still. So instead, I stood and cried for a few seconds in the sunshine, hearing her voice sing me to sleep sailing with a baby across the sea. The grief played itself out by replaying memories—to make them stick better? Perhaps these obsessive thoughts are necessary, not dysfunctional. This is what they mean by processing? By letting go?

I called Mom's old nursing friend O'Dell who had helped us make the decision to move Mom and Dad.

"Your mother," (O'Dell always called her "your mother," never by her first name. Dad called her that too, at least when he talked to me) "used to come over and talk to me. Oh, she was so upset when you moved in with that man out there. But then she did say that she liked him so much, too. But she always said, 'She has to lead her own life.'" I wanted to vomit. How much of her did I *not* know? That she had felt worried and hurt when I did something she saw as dangerous or unintelligent? But I'm as grateful for that as anything she ever did for me: not judging me to my face, not doing anything that showed her so-called negative emotions about me. Why, they let me bring "that man" home and sleep with him in their house! When Mom showed us to the room she said, "Your father is upset about this, so don't say anything to him." At the time I thought, well, they've accepted it. But no, they had only accepted us. Nevertheless, I had wanted Mom to be my girlfriend and she was not.

I'm glad O'Dell told me. I thought Mom never talked about anything to her friends. Of course, she did. She was a human female! It's a relief to me to know it for sure. Only once did she let down her guard with me when she said she didn't want to die.

There's a way that you get older and there's a way that you stay younger—you stay in your generation and your generation hasn't died yet, well maybe some have. But my mom got younger every year until she passed me, we were the same age for a while, and then she got younger than me. Then I took care of her. When I looked in the mirror, I thought, *I couldn't look more like my mother if I were dead.*

I can't remember whom I've called and whom I haven't. Somehow, I am embarrassed to call twice, it seems like asking for pity or something. I didn't need pity.

O'Dell's daughter called. "In the end we miss our parents because they are worth missing," she said.

"Too me," I said, meaning "Me too." Or maybe two me. Or maybe my unconscious said that. Are there two mes? It would be three more years and another dysfunctional family before I could see the answer to that clearly.

Part II

Chapter One   JERMAYNE

Beets and beans and barley grow
Beets and beans and barley grow
You nor I nor anyone knows
How beets and beans and barley grow.
Jermayne singing her favorite song to me in the garden.

I was relieved when Mom died. It was over. I had grieved for Dad for years before he died, and when he finally passed away there wasn't any grief left. Mom knew me right up until she died, so my grief stayed with me for a stretch but wasn't as loud as the songs that are still coming.

    I had expected the closeness Trudy and I had achieved on the balcony would grow, but we had instead fallen back into sporadic contact after she wrapped up the business with Mom's will and distributed the painfully exact, equal-sums of money we were entitled to. I needed to change something, but I wasn't sure what.

    So I stopped going to see Tilda, thinking it wouldn't serve any purpose any more. She'd taught me about cognitive distortions, which we all know about now, but we didn't know about then. You know—all or nothing thinking, mindreading, fortune telling, catastrophizing—that sort of thing. I didn't see ways of applying those categories to the things in my thoughts about Trudy. I thought about her all the time and just couldn't figure her out. I did do some black-and-white thinking about Guy, and sometimes catastrophizing about our marriage. Well, often really, but I don't remember that I recognized it at the time. I just didn't try to resist the thoughts and let them go instead of letting Guy go. I never did let Trudy go; she was there all the time too. She was there with unfinished business.

A half a year passed, and unexpectedly, Trudy invited me to attend the last session of a seminar she was taking about family dynamics and paid my way for the trip to Seattle. I jumped at the chance. Seeing her again with the past in the past relaxed me, and it was possible for me to learn. For instance, she told me that our family had a myth that we were better than other people. I was aware of that, but I hadn't seen it as a myth until then, nor had I considered how destructive it could be. When we got home, we lost the time so hard to find and drifted in parallel again.

Trudy had invited Chuck to come to the seminar, too, but not surprisingly, he declined. He still emailed me once a week or so with political news, and I responded on an equally superficial level. Neither of them seemed to have an impact on my life, though it was painful to think about them. I missed them and missed the self they had known as me. I no longer let myself wonder why they betrayed me, and as I practiced accepting the angry grief, it submerged itself to a depth where I was unaware of it most of the time.

Maybe I could understand what had happened to Trudy and me if I wrote a memoir, organized my occasional diary notes into a coherent story? I tried joining a writing group and taking writing seminars and reading writing blogs online by people who wrote reading blogs. Nothing moved me any closer. Too many pieces were still missing, so for now the occasional diary was reactivated, and I waited for something to shift. I couldn't make the change I needed to happen all by myself.

—

Guy and I plunged into finishing our new house. We were arguing much less fiercely now than we had at the beginning of our marriage, though still arguing, and I accepted the fact that we would never have a marriage like my parents'. Mom once told me that she and Dad had only one agreement about raising children: that they would never disagree in front of them. I don't remember that they ever did. When I started to argue with my first young husband, I half-heartedly tried to resolve it, and finding him unwilling to go to counseling, divorced him. I had an affair or two before marrying Guy twenty years later, and there was plenty of huffing along the way, but when I married Guy I somehow knew there would be no leaving this one, huffs or no huffs. I didn't learn how to take my mother's advice never to argue until we were twenty years into the marriage.

Guy's mother lived in the same town we did, so I had another whole family now—grandchildren, no less. I relaxed into the new grandma-self with a grandpa I could trust who was building something with me, not tearing something down.

But Guy's second son was about to fling monkey wrenches into the family and our marriage.

—

We were still living in town, and Amos was in high school. I didn't know him that well or really at all. One day I was sitting on the front porch steps as he came sauntering along toward me on the sidewalk. I watched his lanky progress, his brown hair and eyes darker than Guy's. He struck me as young and unsure of himself, trying to be sure. As he started up the steps, he smiled at me, and I smelled cigarette smoke.

"Have you been smoking?" I looked him in the eye.

"Yes, but don't tell Guy."

"Don't you think that he'll smell it?" I asked, incredulous. Amos's eyes moved down and sideways simultaneously. "You'd better at least get a stick of gum before you go inside."

He went back around the corner and came through the front door chewing a piece of gum. But, of course, Guy smelled it immediately.

Then there was the time he and a friend had robbed the local dollar store where Amos worked. Eventually, we found out that his friend had socked him in the jaw as he was carrying the day's take to the bank across the street, and then they threw a ski mask into a dumpster nearby.

That night Amos stepped inside the front door of the rental house which let out immediately in the living room. I was sitting on the sofa and looked up. He straightened his shoulders and, taking a deep breath said, "I was robbed!" He scrutinized me carefully, tightening his face. His face was swelling on one side, but he didn't seem to notice.

I thought, *He's lying*.

Guy came down the stairs at that point, and Amos said it again. "I was robbed!"

Guy puckered up his face and narrowed his eyes. He let Amos go on to tell his story, watching him closely all the while. Then he suddenly grabbed him by the collar and threw him against the door. Amos cowered, his skinny shoulders pulled so tightly in toward his chest, that I was surprised he could breathe.

"You were not. You are a liar. I'm going to take you down to the police station in the morning and you are going to tell them exactly what happened."

"Okay," said Amos. "Okay, okay. I'll go in the morning."

"No, I'll *take* you in the morning."

Amos turned slowly toward his bedroom door and—hanging his head—opened it, went inside, and closed it ever so gently.

He served a couple of weeks in juvie.

—

Five months later, Amos skipped down the back steps and into the yard, where I was hanging clothes out to dry in the sunny but damp spring air.

"Maddie's pregnant," he said without a greeting, and waited carefully. I looked up and dropped my arms, still holding onto one of Guy's wet shirts with both hands, clothespins in my mouth.

My first thought was, *why her?* I'd never had children and had regretted those eight years of birth control in my twenties. How could I have been so thoughtless? Then I caught my thought and tossed it out. Of course it was stupid for these two to be pregnant now. Amos was eighteen and Maddie was sixteen. They were both still in high school. I mean, Maddie was in high school. Amos had dropped out.

When I married Amos's father, Guy had been clear with me, "You are not their mother. They have a mother. Just be their friend." I was grateful to comply. At age forty-nine, I took him to mean I didn't have to be a mother or a stepmother or any kind of mother at all. I could just be married to Guy without any strings tying me to his family—except, perhaps, those of my own choosing.

I considered Amos and his happy face for quite a while. Why was he telling me this? What was I supposed to say? He was jumping back and forth between his two feet, still waiting for a reaction. I breathed evenly and took my time. Then I said, "Do you want it?"

Amos stopped bouncing, and he smiled. "Yes. We both do."

I thought I ought to say something else. I said, "Amos, this is a big decision. It will change your whole life. Do you know that?"

"Yes," he said. But he didn't know it.

"It's a hard row to hoe."

"I know," he said, but he was still smiling. "I want to be a dad, like Guy."

It was almost impossible to resist the momentum of the conversation to say, "okay," but I managed it. After all, he hadn't taken my cue about the cigarettes and I didn't want to give him my permission, so I just looked at him and said instead, "Did you tell your father?"

"Oh, yes. Grandma Gurlie is on her way over to talk about it. I have to go back in. I just wanted to tell you." It would be quite a few years before I was comfortable with the kids calling their parents by their first names.

"Thank you." I turned back to the clothesline and held up the shirt. "Good luck," I added to myself, and pinned the shoulders to the line.

Within a day or two an invitation went out to Maddie's mother Marlene, and Marlene's boyfriend Ron, for a picnic at our house, so that we could meet and get to know them. They sat ill-eased on the hard picnic benches and responded to every question put to them. Like having more teenagers to dinner, except better groomed. There was a distinct smell of judgment in the air when they turned down Guy's offer of beer or wine. Enough so, that I felt self-conscious accepting my own glass of

India pale. Enough so, that I couldn't have gotten through the supper without it.

"Shy, just shy," I told a skeptical Guy later that night. "She's a good ten years younger than we are, and he's that much younger than she is. They'll get used to us." We were, after all, the Loud Family and they were the Quiets. Guy just shrugged.

Maddie was living at home with her mother. Marlene would not give permission for her to marry, forcing Maddie and Amos to wait until her eighteenth birthday. They chose that very day for a small ceremony. I snapped our favorite photo of the little threesome looking happy and relaxed, except for the way Jermayne's hair was pulled painfully away from her face in a bun, her shiny hair held in place by force of a dozen small hairclips.

So there wasn't a marriage until after the baby was born. Oh, little Jermayne! The day she was born Guy leaped out of the house to go and meet her. I told him I was too sick to go welcome her into this hard world that day. I lied about that to him, and to myself. Sitting home alone I cried and resisted the thought that I was going to now have to take on the duties of a grandmother, even though I had been able to avoid the duties of a mother.

I couldn't hold out in that place by myself for very long. Being part of my other family was something I had wanted and worked hard for—to be accepted by everyone. I wasn't going to be able to look myself in the face and deny the place I had fought for. I was going to have to learn how to love the dysfunction.

Marlene gave a party not long after the birth, and Guy and I went. I sat in the corner of the small living room, letting everyone else coo and cradle the baby. I felt nauseous, as if she weren't really mine, and the other people had more right to her than I did. These people were not my family. No matter how Trudy and Chuck were acting, I knew that they would be there for me, take me into account. I cared about them. These people were not like that. Guy wasn't even quite there yet for me. There wasn't any foundation to build a family on, just the dream of a family.

Then Amos stood up and took Jermayne gently away from an aunt on the other side of the family and the other side of the room. He walked over, laid the wee girl in my arms and smiled. "Grandma," he said. That's how I got in heels over my head.

—

Amos volunteered for the National Guard and was off overseas. He thought he had a bright future and explained to his antiwar father that he could get his education paid for when he returned.

I got an inkling there was trouble the first time he returned on leave. We took them out for dinner in their hometown an hour and a half away. I was disappointed that they didn't have Jermayne with them.

Maddie squirmed throughout the whole meal, not looking at either Guy or me, and pulling away ever so slightly when Amos tried to put his arm around her. He left his arm on the back of the booth, his fingers working. Nobody breathed. Guy and I did our best to make conversation, but Amos wasn't interested in talking about Iraq, and the only other thing on that menu was obviously taboo. Amos was back in Iraq before we saw him again.

Nevertheless, Maddie turned up shortly after that with Jermayne at the new house, where I was outside in my grubbies enjoying the garden. She'd never been up before without Amos, so I was a bit curious. More curious was that when she got out of the car, she was natty in a short blue dress and heels. She took a small suitcase out of the back.

"Can you watch Jermayne this weekend?" She asked without a smile, one hand shading her eyes.

"Of course! I'm glad you asked. What's up?"

She was opening the car to get Jermayne, her back to me. "I, uh, I'm—a girlfriend invited me for the weekend," she said hurriedly. And turning back and squinting at me she added, "I'll be out of cell range so you can't call me."

Hmmmm. I reached for Jermayne, who grasped Maddie's leg and started to cry. Picking her up and holding her so she faced away from her mother, I nodded to Maddie to leave, and she did, quickly and with no goodbye.

—

Before I lost Jermayne, she and I had lots of good times together: in the garden, cooking and baking, playing with dolls, joking and guessing. One day Jermayne and I got dressed up and went to town, taking the curvy road that passed sometimes along the edge of the lake, other times through the tall, hushed woods. We ourselves had been silent for a while. I was lost in thoughts as usual about my other family, when Jermayne said, "Jay."

"Jay who?" I asked.

She didn't answer for some time. As we came around a curve and into a straight stretch, she said,

"Eye," she said, looking pointedly straight forward, serious.

"I spy?" I asked. "What do you spy?"

Again, a long silence. I didn't say a word, waiting for what would come next.

"See," she said.

Hmmm. "How about O. Are there any Os?"

"No," she grinned as she lowered her eyelids and looked at me out of the corner of her eyes.

"L?"

"Yes!" she flounced happily on the seat, turning sideways toward me with a giggle. Trudy and I had been flouncers when we were little, but never out of happiness. I drove on, while she found stretches of road in the shapes of letters, uproarious until we arrived at our destination.

And then there were the times we tried to help each other through the rough spots. Jermayne loved to bake and this time wanted to crack two eggs into the mixer bowl herself. She struggled with it, but I let her try without interfering, just giving her encouragement when I couldn't give her the feel for what she was trying to do.

"Hit it harder," I advised. She tried, but was still too timid.

"Harder!" Crack! The egg broke and slipped out of her hand onto the carpeted kitchen floor. She started to cry. Dog came to see what the fuss was all about.

"Jermayne, honey, it's okay, we have more eggs."

"But I can't do it right," she stiffened, head thrown back, and made two fists.

At that moment Dog reached the prize and lapped up the broken egg, shell and all. "Dog thinks you did it just perfectly!"

She gave me that smile of hers, that warming, intensely gentle smile of hers, that seemed to come from deeper inside her mouth somewhere, and relaxed a little.

A while later the mail arrived by way of Guy, who had been down to the mailbox a mile and a half away. Jermayne and I were still baking.

"There's a letter here from the Friends of the Library," Guy said, tossing it my way.

"Good!" I said. I had applied for some grant money from a local real estate office to fund a doll tea party that I was putting on at the library with Mom's doll collection. The formal application had to come from the Friends, because they had a non-profit designation, and I wasn't eligible as an individual for a grant. This was pretty quick for a reply, and I felt good.

Until I opened the letter. It was from the Friends, telling me that we had gotten the grant, but that I had no right to use their name in the application and they were turning it down. It was true that the president of the organization had been out of town right before the deadline, and I had asked the library staff member who worked on the tea party with me if it was okay. She had given me the go-ahead.

The letter was so nasty, I started to cry. Jermayne seemed always to know what I was feeling. Even when I wasn't crying, she would say, "What's the matter, Grandma?" as she did now.

"Oh," I said, putting the letter back into its envelope. "It's just a letter from some people. They are mad at me, and the letter's pretty mean."

She climbed down from her stool and came over to stand proudly in front of me, tossing her head of dark, shiny hair.

"You know what my teacher told us to do when someone is mean to you?"

"What?"

"She told us to tell them, 'That was mean! It hurt my feelings. Don't do it again.'"

I went right upstairs and wrote an answering letter as per my instructions, and afterward found myself humming, "Yes sir, that's my baby." Problem solved.

—

That night, Jermayne and I were lying in bed. Trying to go to sleep, or so I thought.

"D'ya know when Gramma Gurlie died?" Jermayne said rolling over into my back, the palm of her small hand testing to see if I was awake. It was only as big as those painted turtles they used to give away as prizes on the Fourth of July in my hometown.

My stepson had wanted to sleep without his vigilant daughter, for once. She clung to him after his divorce, for her dear life it seemed, and sometimes he needed a break from her. I had put my book aside and turned out the light about ten minutes before. Dozing, I heard someone coming up the stairs. Amos appeared, moving from the doorway to my side of the bed, hands chock full of his limp, quiescent five-year-old. He didn't put on the light, but I could see clearly through the old friendly shadows. Amos's moon face had hung forward as he lifted Jermayne over my hip and placed her into the spiral arms of darkness. He didn't say anything. Then he was gone.

"Yes, I remember Gramma Gurlie. I miss her," I said.

"Yeah, well, she went to live in the stars. But she's still AWAKE." She spewed out the last word like a cheerleader yelling "SINK IT!"

Now *I* was awake.

—

Some few days before Guy's mother had died, I had called Marlene to ask her permission to take Jermayne for a visit. Marlene surprised me by allowing it, with very few questions asked. Jermayne loved Gurlie in the way that children love all old people. And just before we left, Jermayne asked if she could sing Gurlie a song. I knew it would be the last time they would see each other.

"I learned it at kindygarten," said Jermayne announced, and then she cleared her throat and began. My heart swam in and out of her voice as she sang the song from Sound of Music.

"Adieu, so long," she sang, her face serious.

"Farewell," she sang.

"Auf Wiedersehen," she sang.

"Au revoir. "Goodnight ... goodnight ... goodnight."

I turned over to face her now. "Okay?" I asked her back. Was she asking me something? I wasn't sure what.

"She sends me dreams."

"She does? Maybe she'd send me some too. What kind of dreams does she send you?"

"Well, they're NOT NIGHTMARES." She almost screamed it, tearing the gloom, which closed over its wounds like water over a drowner. I paused, admiring her fearsome spirit. She rolled away, flopping stiff-backed onto her pillow. Her eyes were wide open.

I took a breath and released it as slowly as I dared. "Do you have nightmares?"

She quickly lowered her eyelids. Her body slumped. "Yeah." Her voice was hoarse and wavering. Then she peeked up at me to see if I would give her something. I wasn't sure exactly what.

"Like what?" I waited.

"My mom shot me." Less fearsome now, more resigned. Her body relaxed.

"I'm sure Gramma Gurlie didn't send you THAT one. Remember how much she loved you?"

"Yeah, I do." After a moment of staring at the ceiling, she went on. "Well, she's in the stars. But she's AWAKE."

—

A memory passed through me. I was only five or so the first time I saw It's a Wonderful Life. The stars talk to each other in one scene; it filled me with cold dread. I couldn't imagine what it would be to be dead and out in the frigid night—and be a star, beautiful, but with no body or eyes. They could talk to each other without mouths or ears? I imagined it must be hell where they were, not heaven. That night I couldn't sleep and crawled out of bed and into my parents' bedroom across the hall. Mom mumbled something and Dad got up and took me back to the bottom bunk of my bunkbed. Trudy was sleeping up top. He told me a story.

"There was a man telling a story about what held up the world. He said it was a turtle. A woman in the audience raised her hand. She asked, 'What holds up the turtle?'

'The turtle is standing on another turtle.'

'And what's that turtle standing on?'

'Why, madam,' said the story teller, 'It's turtles all the way down!'"

For no reason, that made me feel better, and I put the forbidden thumb in my mouth and drifted off.

—

I reached over and put my arms around my granddaughter until she relaxed. "I know," I said finally. That's all she needed. Jermayne fell dead asleep while I stayed awake, at first trying to listen out something that seemed to be speaking to me from the darksome silence, then letting go, comforted by the clear shadows.

Chapter Two

TRUST

No one here can love or understand me
Oh what hard luck stories they all hand me
Pack up all my cares and woe, here I go, winging low
Bye, bye, blackbird
Mort Dixon and Ray Henderson

There is a rainbow taped to the half-wall of the stairs coming up from the basement. It's all wrong—clearly the work of a child—an uneven arc with a dark blue curve down the middle, yellow on both sides of it, and red stripes bleeding from the edges. It has been there now for fifteen years or more, and I tell myself no one notices it, except me. Sometimes I am fearful that my husband or a housecleaner will rip it off, crumple it up and throw it away, but I do not point it out or say anything about it to anyone at all.

I can see the rainbow from where I sit in my chair next to the woodstove, though it angles off into shadow. I look at it every morning while I eat oatmeal and think about the child who made it: my step-granddaughter, sleepy-headed, and sitting in the same chair years ago now, wrapped in a blanket that covered her face, strands of tousled hair stuck to the blanket. Jermayne was probably five or six—at the most, seven years old. It was a Saturday, the Saturday containing the worst hour of my life. More painful than the time I broke my ankle on a four-wheeler. More devastating than the hour my sister told me, "Don't call me. I'll call you." More draining even than the time I drove Jermayne's father to the mental hospital, alone in the car with a man who was unbalanced and whom I feared. This one hour wracked me so; it was even worse than not seeing Jermayne for years on end, and who knows how many more?

—

"Grandma Sarah," Jermayne's call was muffled. I was in the kitchen, and she was hiding under a blanket near the cold woodstove, her shining dark eyes and hair out of sight, with only a few tousled strands making it out of the blanket.

Since Amos had been divorced, he had been scheduled to pick her up from Marlene's house on Fridays and bring her up to ours. When he had not appeared or called her by five o'clock on Friday night, Marlene called me.

"I'll come get her," I said, unfazed by the two-and-a-half hour round trip.

"Okay. But Amos has to realize—"

I listened and agreed to whatever she said, I so wanted her to trust me with Jermayne.

When I was halfway there, Marlene called my cell phone. "He called. He wants to come now. I told him you are on your way."

"I don't want to risk it, Marlene. I'll keep coming. Tell him to meet me back at our house." It was late and I was hungry. "Has she eaten?" It just occurred to me as I write this that Marlene may not have told Amos to meet me back at our house. I have blamed him for years for not coming up that night. Why didn't I call him? I trusted Marlene to tell him, without thinking.

"Oh, yes, we're having pizza now. She's eating with us." She didn't offer to save me a piece, and there was an ever-so-slight emphasis on "us." Or did I imagine that? I hoped she was happy with my decision to keep coming. I couldn't tell.

So Jermayne and I made it back to our place, and went upstairs to bed to read a book together. "Where's Daddy?" she asked.

I said what was true. "I don't know." I wanted to lie and promise her he would come any minute, but I couldn't bring myself to do it. I was afraid he wouldn't show at all.

The next morning I was in the kitchen, still wearing my bathrobe, though the sun was well enough up, and trying to think of something that would grab Jermayne's interest, get her moving out of that chair by the woodstove. My granddaughter had already refused breakfast.

"Want to bake some cookies with me?" No answer.

"A pie?" Normally, Jermayne loved to bake a pie, spilling everything everywhere over the counter and onto the floor, then encouraging the dog to lick it up. But this morning, she was silent.

I walked over to the woodstove corner to see if she had fallen back asleep.

But then the little voice came out of the blanket. "Grandma?"

"Yes?" I said, taking a step closer.

"Grandma, can you make my mind stop bothering me?"

The morning sun swiftly crested the trees outside the window. It was going to be a beautiful day.

"No," I said, taking a step closer and shading my eyes. "But *you* can." Perhaps Jermayne was one of those indigo children I didn't believe in but did believe were a metaphor for how things were changing. Something new was happening. Something better than anything that had happened before. Wasn't it?

"How can I, Grandma Sarah?"

"You know the story we read last night?"

"Yeah?"

"Well, we all like to tell ourselves stories. That's what our minds do best. But sometimes they're not fun. All you have to do is decide you don't want to listen to your mind. It's just a story."

"Okay," she said doubtfully. But she didn't come out from under the blanket.

That was one of the days during the time before things sorted themselves into a kind of peace, like the peace of the lake below my kitchen window that lay still when there wasn't any wind, despite the strong, life-giving currents underneath.

Jermayne's father hadn't been arrested and gone to prison yet, though he had, sometime before, signed the papers giving the other grandmother custody of her. Amos had lost everything when his tour ended. Maddie had stopped communicating with him when he was still overseas, as he complained to Guy in one of the two phone calls he made to us. The other call came during the night his Humvee had been hit by an IED. They knew who had set it off, and he and his buddies wanted to go AWOL and murder the man. Guy had talked him out of it.

Somehow or other, Guy found out or spoke to Maddie, who said that she was going to divorce Amos as soon as he arrived home. Guy advised her to let Amos know, even threatening to tell his son himself, but that didn't happen. The moment Amos touched down in his home state was the moment he found out. Then he lost his home while still living in it. I received shrill phone calls from Amos and Jermayne from their living room while Maddie was in the bedroom with her boyfriend. Of course, during this time, too, both Maddie and Amos were using drugs, or we think they were. Maddie ultimately moved into a house with another single mom, and they sold crack, "Never from the house, though," Amos once assured me. "They always meet their customers away from the house." I looked at him and wondered many things.

Amos moved out too, and got a job working as a National Guard recruiter at a mall. He took up with a series of women with whom he could live while he spent their money. He brought them dutifully home, one by one, showing them to us and gauging our reactions. A brace of single-parented children quick-stepped through our home—focused on forming quick, intense attachments, as we were probably the first adults who had paid any reasonable attention to them.

After the divorce, things changed for the worse for Maddie, who, according to Amos, began dragging Jermayne around, sleeping on the couches of friends. She would bring Jermayne back to Marlene's every morning and drop her off there, where Marlene would bathe and dress her, and take her to school. Maddie finally realized she was not able to care for her daughter and asked Marlene to take custody. Marlene agreed, but demanded that Amos sign his daughter over too. Or maybe it was Marlene's idea.

"Don't do it," I had pleaded with Amos. "You'll never get her back."

"The lawyer says I still can get her back."

"That's not what the paper says, look here at it. It says right here you're giving up all your rights." I flipped to the second page. I held the paper tightly, creasing it under my thumb. Oddly, I didn't feel confident that my "interpretation" of the legal document was grounded in reality, but it was all I had to go on. I wasn't sure what Marlene would do with custody. I imagined never seeing Jermayne again.

Amos turned his face toward the paper but looked past it as if he could see something that took precedence, that was truer than the law. He didn't look anxious or even tired, just done with it. Then he started to cry. "I'm sorry," he said. "I don't want to let her go. I miss her, but this is the only way I can get to see her." I couldn't fathom this young man. No matter how tearful his eyes were, they remained dark and opaque.

"At least give us joint custody!"

"Maddie's already signed them. We have to do something. Marlene's been taking care of her anyway. Maddie wants me to sign. She's not asking for alimony. I'll just have to pay child support. We both will."

"So what! You're divorced now! You don't have to do what she wants."

"I'm paying child support." *Why?* I asked myself. *Does he have to? Even if Marlene has custody?* I sensed that he wanted to, and was glad for that. He would have problems with Marlene, I could feel it, and Jermayne loved her father so much. It would hurt both of them, more than Amos was willing to admit. Surely he must know?

But it was hopeless, and I knew it. What I didn't know was Marlene. Even if I was uneasy with her judgmental ways, at least she was willing to take on Jermayne, who would be better off than she had been with her own mother and father. I considered taking Jermayne myself. I wanted to do it. I'd never had children of my own and had married Guy when his sons were mostly grown. But we lived so far out of town. Not a good place for a lone little girl, and even if she had been my real granddaughter, grandparents had no rights in our state.

After the papers were signed and sealed, I pondered: was Jermayne a step-granddaughter once removed? However, the law that defined our relationship meant little to us. She and I knew what we meant to each other. But I feared it was easy to break a connection like ours without the forces of expectation and custom to buoy us up. I kept hope pinned like a butterfly on the fact that Marlene was still talking to me, sort of.

That summer after the papers were signed, Marlene allowed Amos to bring Jermayne to our house on the mountaintop every other weekend. These were still lovely times: We baked and cooked meals together, painted stones with dayglo colors, then washed them off and painted them again. We packed a small backpack with Cheetos and took them to the fairies who lived across the draw, at the base of the trees marked with the paint the fairies used to draw a circle around their homes. One very hot day we ran giggling through the sprinkler. At night we fell asleep together, reading books and then playing the flashlight game in the dark.

But things got grim with Amos. He couldn't keep a job. He told Marlene he was going out of town, then sat in an ill-furnished apartment drinking and who knows what else, broken-hearted and helpless. Guy offered Amos work around our place, but Amos had accidents with the machinery, then stopped showing up on time. When Guy confronted him, he looked up from under his eyebrows like an eight-year-old and said he was sorry—not arguing, saying whatever it was that Guy asked him to say, incoherent.

—

We were always waiting for Amos to call us, and eventually he started to, at least once a week after a few prodding calls from Guy. But this week Guy's face wrinkled and compressed from top to bottom, his eyes small and lids tight. "Amos hasn't called me back," he reported one day. That was a bad sign. I shared Guy's fears; I didn't have to ask him what they were. Drugs? Selling them? Drinking? Driving? What? *What* meant, "Is he alive?" At least we knew that Jermayne was safe with the other grandparents and Amos still visited her every week and often brought her up to our place for a day or two.

"Let's wait," I said. "He'll want to bring Jermayne up here."

Marlene called me on Friday. "Amos hasn't contacted us about Jermayne this week. Would you like to come for pizza tomorrow, and pick her up?" Of course I accepted. The next morning, Guy had a sinus infection and needed to see the doctor. I was late bringing him home and getting off to Marlene's. I called and left a phone message, "Go ahead and eat pizza without me. I'll be there after six."

When I got there, Ron told me that Amos had called in midafternoon. "He wanted to come pick up Jermayne and take her back to his place. I said, whoa, we already had arrangements with you."

I was puzzled. Why did Amos call Ron and not us? Why so late in the day?

So Jermayne and I got in the car and sang our way back to the top of the mountain and home.

—

Amos eventually appeared late that worst Saturday afternoon, his approach to the house so silent it seemed he had materialized in a moment outside the front door on the uphill side, somehow avoiding the long climb up the hill. He was calm. He wanted to take Jermayne. I felt my insides rise and tumble, afire, pressing on my throat.

"I don't *think* so," I surprised myself. Who is this who has spoken? I wondered whether they would buy it. Amos could just take her and leave. I wouldn't be able to stop him if Guy isn't on my side.

Guy was surprised too. No, shocked. No, outraged. "Why not?"

"Marlene gave me Jermayne to take care of this weekend," I said, unable to look at either one of them. "I'll need her permission to let Amos take her."

"Then I'll take her," Guy says. Does Guy think he has the right to take her? Because he is her grandfather? Because he is my husband? Amos's father? He doesn't have the relationship I have with her. He hasn't put in the hard time trying to communicate with Marlene. Now I am outraged, and feel my stomach fall away. I cast about my mind for a place of power, and finding none, just fling the word "no" out there between us.

Amos is standing in front of me, holding Jermayne on his hip. As soon as I make my announcement, her head falls forward and she starts to pick at the buttons on Amos's shirt. Everybody tensed. My insides are moving, but I am able to sever their connection to the features on my face, which are immobile and in order.

"I'll call Marlene," Amos says, putting Jermayne down. When her feet hit the slate floor, her noodle legs collapse underneath her and she busies herself looking at the floor. Or not looking at us. I pick up her hand.

"I think it would be better if Jermayne and I went and read a book." Amos punches in a number on his cell, then walks out onto the deck.

Jermayne comes sadly with me to the guest room and picks out her favorite story, but she isn't interested.

"Why are you angry?" she wants to know.

"I'm not angry," I lie. "I want you to stay here tonight, and your father wants to take you away. Grandma Marlene let me take you for the weekend, and I want to make sure she knows where you are."

"Why can't I go with Daddy?"

All I could do was shrug and say, "You probably can. Let's just wait and see." That old phrase of Dad's that meant, "No." But I can't take her back into the argument, so I tell her she will have to read a book for a while by herself until we find out. Yuck. I walk back to the woodstove and sit down hard, trying to keep breathing.

Amos is still outside. I get up and go over to where Guy is sitting, head hanging forward, looking out the window. His long legs are stretched out, but his face is disordered.

I say, "You know, I can't let Jermayne go with him unless I talk to her myself."

He explodes. "That's not reasonable. You can't do that. *I* can let her go."

"No, you can't. Marlene entrusted her to me. I hate to say this, but I don't trust him. He's a liar." It is the first time I have said it out loud to him. It hangs in his fallen face, like a bowling ball in a hammock. I am not Amos's mother; am I being cavalier and cruel? Guy turns and walks out on the deck to have a word with Amos.

I have just started up the stairs when Amos finally walks back inside, relaxed and smiling. "She said it's okay. I guess I'm going to take Jermayne home with me."

Gulp. Deep breath. I keep going up the stairs.

"No, Amos. I need to talk to Marlene. Guy told you that." I don't look at him.

Amos comes right up the stairs after me.

"I don't have a problem with your taking Jermayne," I lie again. "But Marlene entrusted her to me for the weekend. I need you to call her and let her know what you are doing. I need to speak with her before you leave. And I need you to call me tomorrow morning, when you take Jermayne back to Marlene's."

Gulp again. I think of the way Jermayne calls me "Gramma Sarah" and how I know who I am when she is in a room with me. If he doesn't do these things, I will be awake all night and unable to function.

If he had shrugged, it would have infuriated me. He didn't. I started to feel some rising steadiness. He stepped back down the stairs and out of the room, and Guy followed him.

When I tried to move my legs, I found I had no control of the muscles, which were slack and began to collapse under me, but I made it back to my chair. I felt grateful that my face was a stone. Once I had the speed of my breaths under control, I tried to deepen them. The muscles in my chest and throat tightened against the effort.

I had to do something, so I went back to the chair and called Marlene. No answer. I left a message. Guy and Amos remained out on the deck for quite some time. I called every fifteen minutes for an hour—though if I hadn't had *any* control, I would have redialed continuously. I did not want Amos to be lying. There would be no way he could talk himself out of it. Guy would be crushed. I practiced hard everything I had learned in meditation class: breathe, don't think, let yourself feel, then let go. But what it felt like was: I wasn't long for this world.

At last, Guy came and stood over me while Amos headed for the guest room and Jermayne. I had fallen in love with a little girl who was in danger. Did I have enough power to save her? I thought that if I sat very still, I could wait out the spell without breaking it, but I wasn't really sure that was true. I couldn't see past my knees and elbows.

Guy leaned down and said, "I have a proposal. I'll drive down behind Amos. We'll go to Marlene's house. If she gives him permission, Jermayne can stay with him. If not, I'll bring her home." Even without a kiss, my prince had broken the spell. Amos reappeared with a smiling daughter in his arms. So I nodded okay, and they all ran down the stairs away from me like a dam breaking. I still couldn't move out of the chair.

After a while I was able to get up and went to the window. Guy's truck and Amos's car were still on the driveway in front of the barn. I saw Amos walking firmly up toward the house. I went and stood at the top of the stairs.

When he came, he came slowly. He reached me at the top of the stairs and somehow managed to look away from me and give me a quick kiss at the same time, like Judas or the Grand Inquisitor. "Thank you," he said, then fled. At first, I told myself the story that he had realized that I was only trying to protect his daughter, and for that he was grateful. Then I told myself the story that he was only being polite so that he could get back into my good graces—that he'd won and realized he could repair bridges for his future use.

—

The worst Saturday was not over yet. Marlene's number rang on my cell. "I'm sorry," she said as if apologizing was one more burden she had to bear. I thought, *who said that line about never having to say you're sorry?* "I was on my way into a meeting when Amos called. I turned my phone off after we hung up, and I just got out of the meeting and got your messages. Yes, I told Amos he could take Jermayne."

Thank God, he wasn't lying about that.

I ran for the door and caught the boys before they left. As I ran down the stairs my mind was still going: *A meeting? At five o'clock on a Saturday night? C'mon.* As I climb back up the stairs a useless song breaks the surface tension: *Laugh and the world laughs with you,* it tells me as I watch it go by and sink into my chair near the fire. My eye catches the rainbow taped to the wall and it reminds me of what a friend once told me: "You know, nobody sees the same rainbow as anybody else. The light that hits the water droplets refracts slightly differently depending on the angle from where you stand. And that's all you see, the refracted light. The light *is* the rainbow."

I was too exhausted now to tell myself another story, but still buzzing enough that I had to do something to slow down. After Guy's happy wave, I gave up the stories for the day and went upstairs to straighten up my office.

I'd learned a trick from my stepson, Kurt. Gawk awkward as a teenager and looking tall and just like his father, he'd disappeared through the swinging door into the kitchen after Guy ordered him to "Get out there NOW and clean it," then stalked off out the back door and into the workshed. Kurt returned moments later.

"Done so soon?" I smiled as I said it.

"It's easy. If you line everything up on the counters so they are square, the kitchen looks clean." He had charm. When you looked at him you could see that Cary Grant had had a gangly stage as a teenager. It was why he could be suave and still do comedy. Just a thin coat of smooth let the knobby knees show through. And sure enough, when I went to look, I saw that the dishes weren't even washed, just stacked in a graduated tower, largest dinner plate on the bottom, cereal bowls from breakfast that morning topping the pile. Guy came back in and indeed did not notice, or if he did, he said nothing.

Chapter Three   NOT OVER YET

In the days and days that led me forward, I struggled. Not with Amos so much—he was an adult, even if doomed to dysfunction; I was not struck to the heart the way that Guy was. I struggled with Marlene who became for me more and more an automaton constructed out of a venomous combination of fear and power. But she at least she was a woman: I was able to negotiate with her for a time. I did everything she asked of me, but it wasn't easy to understand what she wanted. Once Amos told me that she was upset because I didn't wash Jermayne's hair on every night that she stayed with us. Once, on a visit at Marlene's house I was in Jermayne's room with her and we climbed onto the bed to read a story. "Don't sit there," commanded Marlene who had just materialized at the door.

"Why not?" I asked.

"Sit in the living room."

"But Marlene, don't you ever read a book to her at bedtime?"

"No. She has her own bed. She's not allowed on mine and I'm not allowed on hers."

I told myself to keep my eyes on the prize, that it didn't matter what I really thought about Marlene. I could just hide all that for the sake of seeing Jermayne. I played by her rules, and we got up and went to the living room sofa. But I felt bad for Jermayne and imagined her starving for affection.

Marlene would not often talk to me live. We traded phone calls. Once she even told me that she preferred not to speak to me directly: I should just leave messages for her and not answer her return calls, just wait until she left her answer. One day her message said,

> You know we have decided, you know we have decided that—um—we're not going to continue with this—um—every other week—um—every other visit—um—we're looking out for Jermayne's best interest and in looking—um—at some things we've just decided that—um—that's no longer going to work for her. And so she won't be there this weekend and we will be calling Amos and sitting down and talking to him about it and making other arrangements with him to—um—continue seeing Jermayne—um, um—talk to you sometime soon. Bye-bye.

I called her the next morning and spoke to her for a very few minutes. She said that she would not talk about her reasons, that we could visit Jermayne, but only at her house and each visit would have to be scheduled independently.

Guy was furious, could hardly mention her name, much less discuss the situation with me. He couldn't understand why I was willing to swallow anything she dished out. He told me to cut them off. So, I was on my own. I kept driving every other week to the small house where I had first held Jermayne, and even with Marlene watching my every move, it was easy to be with Jermayne. Once she said to me, "Grandma? Did you drive here all the way from your house, just to see me?" I was a goner again.

When Marlene spoke at all she was slow and careful. She plucked her words like money out of a pocket, whose value was determined by other people and completely out of our hands, nonnegotiable. What was she trying to buy from me? I sold her politeness, support and attention. But all Marlene would sell to me was small squares of Jermayne's time, and none of her own trust in me. I tried to make a patchwork quilt of these times with Jermayne. A story of sorts that Jermayne would someday remember as continuous, not broken into bits like the reality. On the weekends I was not allowed to visit, I sent her letters with small things in them: beads, stones, pictures and poems—a tiny, ceramic bluebird with its open beak full of hunger or a song.

One visiting day, I sat parked uphill near an intersection three blocks from Marlene's house, my tires turned against the curb, waiting so that I could be on time to the minute.

A car came into the intersection in front of me from left to right. When it got to the middle is started to speed up. The back window was rolled half-way down, and out of it came a wild scream: "Grandma Sarah!!!!!" Jermayne's tiny face tipped backward, her mouth just at the edge of the glass and wide open, as if she were drowning. She didn't wave, just kept screaming "Grandma Sarah!!!"

I waited an extra minute to give "Grandma" Marlene time to get home and inside her door. Shortly after that, Marlene cut off the visits. I settled into writing to Jermayne every week.

—

Amos was still in the National Guard, and had met a woman a few years older than he was, whom he married. She had a daughter, and Amos spent more time with them than with his own daughter. Marlene was giving him a hard time about seeing Jermayne, trying to make him more responsible, I thought, and I didn't think that was particularly a bad thing, just futile. He began to behave more and more irresponsibly, exasperating everyone and leaving Jermayne to fend for herself.

I enjoyed having another step-step-granddaughter, even though I preferred Jermayne. Linda's daughter was pretty young herself but old enough to have started to notice that she was attractive, using make-up and batting her eyes, more interested in clothing than Jermayne was. She wasn't wrong in doing that—as few young girls are. And she was feeling her oats with me: She didn't want to help with chores while she was visiting, something I insisted on.

One afternoon she was lollygagging around in the house, suffering from early-onset teenage boredom. The sun was shining, the grass was green, all was right. I suggested she help her stepfather stack the split wood in the woodshed. Dissatisfied, she drooped her shoulders and, hanging both arms loosely, tramped out to the dark and disorganized woodshed. I stood on the deck, listening to the birds chirping and gazing at the peonies in full bloom, when she came back out of the woodshed only a minute or two later, and headed towards the house.

"What, done already?" I asked.

"Amos said there wasn't anything to do." I still wasn't used to Guy's family calling parents by their first names.

Doubtful that that could be the case, I marched her back out into the woodshed. Amos was sitting on a stump as if waiting for us.

"What's up? I asked her to help you," I said.

"She didn't tell me that," he said, looking at his feet rather than at me.

I looked at her closely. "You needn't lie to me about it." She only raised her head, tossing her hair away from wide open eyes and stared at Amos. He hung his head lower and lower, not meeting my gaze.

"Did you tell her there was nothing to do?"

Still no answer from either one, so I left.

Later in the afternoon, Amos came looking for me. Thinking back to what he said, his specific words have escaped me, but what they purported was clear. By the time he finished trying to explain himself, or rather to get me off his back, I was convinced there was something between them that he was hiding from me, something more than untoward. And then he said something that made me think he had slept in the same bed as his proto-teen stepdaughter.

I backed him into a corner of the deck and asked him point blank if he was. He didn't answer—just looked at me with dark eyes that were so opaque I thought there might not be a self in there at all. I raised my voice. "You can't do that, Amos. It's not safe for her. It's not safe for you either. You'll get into trouble you won't be able to get out of." He looked away.

He wouldn't talk about it, just becoming sheepier and sheepier until I could have strangled him with my own hands. At length he made it past me back out to the woodshed. Because I may have been a little unsure of what I felt viscerally, I didn't mention it to Guy. Looking back, that seems unlike me, but there is a nag at my conscience that makes me think I let it ride. What good would it do?

Things were out of balance and getting worse. When she was around Amos, she leaned into him and cocked her head against his arm. He watched her carefully and succumbed to all her wishes. My stomach turned; at the same time, I feared her power, it was mixed with a desire to help her avoid her future. She was only ten or eleven, though she looked and preened as if she were older. She may have instinctually understood what she was doing with Amos, but certainly she didn't understand what she was doing to herself.

In those days, Guy tried to help him: paying him to work at our place, paying for a lawyer to try to force Marlene to give him visiting privileges. He often didn't show up, and when Guy confronted him, he apologized, offering inadequate explanations. Guy was clearly maddened but unwilling to call his son a liar. Once, Amos rented a car and then drove it through our steep mountainside woods, banging and gunning the engine. His explanation: "It's all right. The rental place told me since I was a vet, I could do anything I want." Like the government doctors want to help vets by giving them painkillers, I thought.

Another time he somehow broke the door on the tractor with no real explanation of how it had happened. And then he just skipped coming to work for us entirely. When Guy got tough about it, he admitted his error, apologized, and again left it unexplained.

Marlene finally relented and gave Amos a schedule for visits, to be strictly supervised. But Amos started skipping again and lying about where he was, what he was doing. Guy went to see him in his apartment and found him drunk and depressed.

We watched him as he descended into more and more drug use, lying to me and then to his father—skipping work, skipping Jermayne. Skipping further and further in some direction we were unable to follow. At last, Guy was convinced we could not help him. We called a conference on the deck with Amos and Linda. We told Linda to get out of her marriage to him and let him go. We told Amos he had two choices: He could live with and work with us, no pay and no car, and—no drugs. Or he could turn himself into the VA for treatment. He chose the VA. Linda chose not to do anything.

I drove him by myself to the VA hospital an hour and a half away, not knowing who was sitting next to me in the car, nor what he was capable of. We made it, and he checked in for who knew how long.

—

Months later, I was in the parking lot of a furniture store when Linda called. None of us had been able to get much information about Amos from the VA without his written permission.

That day, the wind was stiff and muffled what she was saying, blowing my hair in my eyes until I couldn't see. But my ESP must have been working, because I was able to make out the basic facts. Her daughter had told her that morning that Amos had molested her. Linda had reported it to the police, but was not dealing with it well. She was worried about Amos.

"He's supposed to get out of the mental hospital in a few days," she said. "The police will arrest him when he comes out the door."

"Is she all right?"

"She's okay. I need some help, though."

Flabbergasted, and not really understanding why she called me, I asked, "What does your family say?"

"They never liked Amos. They're glad he will be gone."

"Won't your mother or anybody help you through this?" I hoped.

"No. They are all mad at me for marrying him."

I couldn't take this on after all Amos had done or not done that hurt me and Jermayne. That was hard enough to handle. I wasn't prepared to take on this woman's dysfunction, much as I liked her.

"I have a friend, Natasha—she's a child-advocate for the courts—I think you should talk to her about this. We have to think about your daughter. Is she okay?"

"I guess. She wants to talk to Amos."

"I'm not surprised. You are talking to him, and she's just copying you."

"But I don't want to lose him…"

"Neither does she, apparently. Don't you think it's about time to lose him? For her sake?"

Silence. Then, tentatively, "I guess."

"Will you call Natasha?"

"Not yet."

"May I call her and tell her your story? I think I need her help myself. I don't know what else to tell you."

"Okay, I guess so."

I hung up and called Natasha, an old friend who volunteered with me on a local healthcare board. She was not surprised to hear what had happened—we had discussed my situation with Amos a few times before.

"Remember," she said, "I told you that when there is family dysfunction there are always secrets, and there is always one family member who is mentally ill?" Yes, I remembered that. "We were pretty sure Amos was that person. Now he's outed himself. You have to distance yourself from this. I'll be happy to talk to Linda if she calls, but she has to distance herself too, and it doesn't sound like she wants to do that. That's a common response of mothers to sexual abuse by fathers or boyfriends. They can't see how it will hurt their abused children and are needy for love themselves."

I was relieved to have permission to get out of this position and not take on more responsibility for this increasingly dysfunctional family. I phoned Linda back and told her to call Natasha when she was ready.

She got the same advice I got. But she said she couldn't cut herself off from Amos, and pleaded with me to let her call me. I agreed, but said I couldn't stop her anyway, and added that I would continue to tell her to follow Natasha's advice. She called often for another couple of months, and repeated the litany over and over. By that time Amos had been arrested coming out of the mental hospital and taken to the county jail, and she was visiting him and taking his calls. Her daughter became more and more hysterically attached to Amos, and when Linda finally arranged for divorce proceedings, she almost lost her daughter. The court considered her an unfit mother because she kept contact with Amos. With that pressure, Linda finally capitulated and was allowed to keep her daughter.

Amos was sentenced to twenty years for sexual abuse but not rape, and sent to state prison eight hours away, eligible for parole after eight years. Guy and I did not attend the trial, and I am not certain that anyone was allowed to attend it out of concern for the privacy of her daughter. Except Linda, who testified against him.

Chapter Four — AREN'T WE FUNNY

It had to be you, it had to be you
I wandered around and finally found, that somebody who
Could make me be true
Could make me feel blue
And even be glad just to be sad, thinking of you
Gus Kahn

Now that Dad had been dead for a while, Trudy wasn't so angry when we ran into each other. But as the forgetting set in and the dysfunction ebbed from my good family, it seeped further into Guy's. It had been a year and a half since Amos went to jail. Linda had finally divorced him and moved away with her daughter, and we never saw the two of them again. Guy and I never spoke of the major weather pattern governing our private skies—at least I know it governed mine. Then a phone call, when Guy was mostly quiet on his end. "What time?" and "Where?" was all he said. He turned toward me with the phone still in his hand, and said, "There's going to be sentencing hearing tomorrow. The sentence is being appealed."

The next morning, I got up thinking before I even stood. *We're leaving at eleven. What time is it now?* I checked the clock. *Good, it's before ten. I can take Dog for a run down the road, put the mail in the mailbox, and be back in time to take a shower.*

While I drove and Dog ran, the spaghetti-thoughts about Amos's sentencing hearing slither and snap their way through my thinking place, which extends into the entire world. Those who say that we think inside our heads either have huge heads or very narrow theories. When I think about my stepson, I am in the jail with him, even though I have no idea what the inside of the jail looks like. Even so, my thoughts are anywhere but in my own brain: *Is twenty years a fair sentence in a plea bargain for lewd behavior? He'll come up for parole in eight years, when his ex-stepdaughter will be eighteen. I can understand that reasoning. But Amos won't be able to meet the requirements for parole. How do you know that? You should be more positive. Maybe he will. This state is so hard on sex offenders. Even a sentence for murder comes with a parole of only four years. How do you know that? Guy told me. I don't know it. Guy's usually right about details like that, though. I don't know anything. That's not my job; it's the judge's job. What if the judge asks me what I think? He asked Guy's ex. Did he really ask Amos's mother? I don't know. I'll say, "I have no opinion." That's not true! I do have an opinion. But I don't know anything about sentencing or about the laws. Well, not nothing, but not much. I'll just say, "It's pretty confusing, sir." That's pretty true. Plus, it's not my job. He won't ask me anyway. What if it's a she? I'm just his stepmother, what do I know? Why do I have to go? I don't want to go. Guy wants me to go. No, he doesn't. But he'll like it if I do go. Where's Dog?*

I rolled down the car window. "Dog, good boy, c'mon WOOFIE!" Dog was in the rearview mirror running right behind the exhaust pipe. *How can he breathe?* He looked happy with his tongue flapping out the side of his mouth and his ears turned back and pulled down. He ran easily and hard, with a spark-eye. His body stretched right out on it's own, not holding anything back. *What does he feel like when he's running? It doesn't look like it's an effort for him at all. But he slows down when he goes uphill and pants for a while when he gets home. I would feel bad if it were me. I wish I could run like Dog and not feel bad.*

When we leave, Guy will take the car and meet me at the highway. He will go on after the hearing for a birthday visit to his son. I will drive the truck to the highway and ride with Guy to the hearing, then ride back with Amos's mother. She can drop me at the truck on her way back. *Is it more important for me to go to Amos's hearing or to Al's birthday visit? I don't know. What I do know is I can't do both. By the time the hearing is finished I will be exhausted.* I don't want to ride down with Guy after the hearing either. I fear we will argue about the sentence, no matter how it turns out. He has already let fly some anger at me for communicating with Amos's ex, who stood up in court and told the judge, "I hope you will sentence him as if it were your daughter instead of mine." Guy's ex told Guy that story; he wasn't there. Guy's the dad. He's supposed to get mad at the ex. I'm not the mom. I don't have to get mad at her. I can see why she said what she did. Why doesn't Guy get that?

I looked down at the passenger seat and saw a CD by Ekhart Tolle. I often listened to Tolle while I drive, trying to avoid being in the NOW. *Aren't we funny?*

I leaned down far to the right to look at the clock on my car radio. The light behind the dial was out, so I had to get my eye within an inch or so to read it. *The radio in the old car still has a light, I could put it in this car...* I couldn't stop my thoughts, so I turned the radio on, really turning a knob, not punching a button like we do now. To my delight, the local station was broadcasting an interview with a friend of mine, a massage therapist. She is interviewing two of my friends, an RN and a social worker, who offered classes in meditation. The social worker interrupted the interview to try a three-minute exercise in being present.

I pulled over and did the exercise sitting behind the wheel, while Dog stood patiently by my door, catching his breath while I catch my mind.

By the time I got back up the hill and started up the outside stairs to the house, my thoughts had run away from me again. I am worried that there may not be enough air in the tires for the long trip to the courthouse in the next county and Guy's drive another two hours to the birthday party. *The last time I started the air compressor the hose flew off and hit me in the head.* I ask Guy to help me.

Guy was put out. All I had to do is open the valve and turn it on. *But I can't remember where the switches are. I am too old and don't do it often enough.* Guy started to tell me how to do it, then shrugged and started down to the barn.

On his way down the stairs he said, "It's pretty foggy out, so I'd like to leave a little earlier."

It is ten-fifteen. I still wanted to take a shower and dress. I followed him down the stairs talking to his back.

"No," I said. "We agreed last night that we'd leave at eleven. I told you I had my morning all scheduled up."

When Guy bristled, I felt scratched and poked, rubbed raw, somewhere just off the surface of my skin but not physical like that. Worse.

"I didn't know it would be foggy," he said. There was a pause while I considered this change of circumstance. "You took Dog down to the road and back, you didn't have to do that."

"So what? If I had known you wanted to leave earlier, I wouldn't have taken him for a run." But I might have anyway. I was so tired of Guy agreeing to a time, then changing it in the last hour, or even half hour before we agreed to leave. *I asked him last night if there was anything he wanted me to do. I told him I was going to be ready by eleven.*

"You can see the fog as well as I can."

What's that supposed to mean?! "So what?"

"So you knew we'd need more time as well as I did."

"I—DID—NOT—KNOW—THAT." My body sang. My throat was closing up. *He thinks I'm stupid.* I looked out at the fog. *Or worse. He thinks I'm trying to cross him.*

Dog, who has been lying quietly on his side near the stairs, got up and moved away, keeping very low and with his ears laid flat on his head, to hide himself behind the rocker.

"You won't drive any slower than you usually do anyway." *Why don't I say what I am really thinking? It takes one hour and fifteen minutes to get to the court house. We have allowed two hours just for things like this. Why am I not saying this?*

I said it. He turned with his red face and his mouth straight. "I would too."

As he turns back out the door I said, "Maybe I should go down and turn it on every morning, first thing when I get up. Then I might remember."

Guy didn't say anything. He kept going down to the barn, not looking to the right or to the left, and I got in the car and move it down after him. He showed me how to start the compressor, and I checked and filled the tires.

When I came back up the stairs, Guy was in the kitchen cooking something and looking out the window. "We can take separate cars. Just go ahead and go," I offered. He nods. "Where's the courthouse?"

"It's the same place we went last time."

"I don't remember where it is." I could see he thinks I am either stupid or trying to be difficult. He started to try to tell me, then gave up and turns away.

I said, "Where's your cell phone?" He found it for me. I turned it on and start to look for Amos's Mom's number. "Is it under C or J?" But I'd already found it, I didn't listen to his answer, if he gave one. "I can ride with her."

"That's silly," he said, but his voice is not laughing, it's resigned.

Something happened then. There was some kind of exchange. I can't remember it. It is a blank. But while it was occurring, a part of me broke the surface that is usually submerged but always lurks. I hardly was aware of it, before it screamed "I DON'T EVEN WANT TO GO." *That was the real me,* I think. *That feels good.* And at the same time, I was ashamed for telling the truth.

"Fine," he says. "Don't."

"Why should I want to go? You don't want to go, do you?" He ignored my question. "Why would anybody WANT to go?" I pushed on.

"You told me you wanted to go. Now you say you don't."

I ignored his comment. It was true. I was confused. *I'm only doing this to support you. But I can't say it. He will deny that it will help him. He is right, it will only help him if he thinks I am going in order to support Amos. Life is so complicated.*

That part of me, the real part that I am ashamed of, was still screaming,

I don't have your thoughts. I'm not you. I don't think like you. You can't assume that I do.

"You think I don't try to help you?"

Which left field did that come from? Oh, well. I took a breath then. After a pause I walked over to him at the sink, where he stood with the heel of his hands on the edge of the sink, straight-armed, his left foot slanted back and his right knee bent, head drooping between the shoulders, looking down into the suds.

I said, "I don't think we are really arguing about this. I think we are both scared about Amos."

Guy surprised me by turning toward me, relaxing his arms. He kissed me briefly with his closed-mouth kiss and made a noise that I can't categorize. But I knew he was agreeing with me.

Well, I can keep getting ready. Maybe I'll be a little early.

"If you make me some toast, I can eat it on the way," I said, and he nods.

I felt a little triumphant. We had been married for ten years and had had to fight our way nail and tooth through most of it. We were in our sixties and had started to relent. Perhaps we had learned something. That day, it seemed we had made it through a tough one without too much damage. Perhaps we had learned to love each other a little.

But fate, or whatever that thing is, pushed itself between us again. I couldn't transfer the file onto my portable computer that I needed to take with me so I could work on the drive down. Guy agreed to get it for me and I retreated into the shower. When I emerged, he had on his coat and shoulder bag.

"I'll just go ahead and wait for you at the highway," he said.

"Did you make my toast?"

"No, I was fixing your computer." *SO WHAT!* screams that part of me that felt so real. *So now you're going to go sit and wait for me at the highway instead of helping me get ready.* I didn't have the breath it would take to say it, so I passed. I stopped hurrying and tried to take my time, though my muscles did not relax, and I noticed my chest was just as tight as it was when I had gotten out of bed. *I don't want to hurry. I don't WANT to hurry. I don't want to HURRY.*

—

As I rushed through the tool room, I noticed the small cooler I had filled with frozen meat for his son's birthday dinner, rejuggled my burdens and scooped it up in my right hand. I couldn't close the door behind me, though, so had to dump the load in the back seat, then go back *Oh, damn, Guy's put his suitcase in the backseat on the side closest to me.* I went around the car. The car door is locked. I come back around and unlock it from the driver's side front door, all with my hands full, then back around to the other side, drop the stuff, then back to shut the tool room door. It was 11:05 when I finally turned the ignition key.

I looked up and there it was, the blue, old, battered truck stopped at the top of the rise just below the barn. I fumed. *Why hadn't he just gone? Why hadn't he made me my toast if he was in a such a !@#$%^ hurry. He's probably planning to stop and get a latte when we get to the highway anyway. Why should I have to hurry when he won't?* I pulled up behind the truck as Guy stepped slowly out and walked back. *Is he going to tell me not to come after all?*

As Guy approached the car, Dog appeared from around the side of the barn, his tail echoing a wag. I felt relieved and defensive all at once. But Guy only raised his eyebrows and pulled the corners of his mouth ruefully backwards.

"That was Mike Lawler on the phone." *Who's he? Someone from Guy's office? Does Guy have to work? Maybe we aren't going anywhere. I'm not going by myself, that's for sure.*

"The hearing's continued."

I didn't say anything. I just held onto the steering wheel while a sob rose in my throat, let itself out, and I started to cry. Guy put his hand on my shoulder.

"Aren't we funny?" he chuckled, raising his eyebrows and looking at me tentatively.

Chapter Five

THE STORY OF LOSING JERMAYNE

I'm sorry, playmate
I cannot play with you...
But we'll be jolly friends
Forever more.
Traditional

The continued hearing for Amos's sentence-appeal never continued. Amos signed away all his parental rights to Marlene. Guy and I stopped talking about them: too painful for Guy and too painful for me to watch him lower his eyes and turn away from me without a smile. I kept sending cards to Jermayne, each with a bead or a tiny china bird or something in it to remember me by.

One day I took a hike down to the mailbox, a mile and a half away at the county road. The sunshine was bright and glary, and I was sweaty as I reached into the mailbox for a pile of mostly junk. The letter on top of the pile didn't have a return address on it, an anomaly in the twenty-first-century world of letter bombs and white powder, but I opened it anyway. Typewritten, it said:

> Sarah,
> In response to your last question, the answer is NO. There is nothing you can do to [sic] that will have us agree to a visit.

We do not trust you or your husband. If we can't trust you, how can we trust you with Jermayne? You have not had her best interests in mind the last few years, if ever. You financed Amos's attempt to terminate our guardianship for your own interests. Can you tell us you had no doubts he would be a good father? If you can say that, then you are in deeper denial than we thought. You saw his instability including his drinking and the inability to behave as a responsible adult. Yet you supported him anyway. And, you still support him. We read your husband's letter to the judge regarding Amos's sentence. Unbelievable!

The bond you think Jermayne has with you is really all in your head. It is as if you are obsessed. Do not contact us again.

Thank you.

Marlene and Ron's letter was the first and last written communication I received from them. I remember angrily throwing it away.

Faster than a speeding bullet. More powerful than a locomotive. As clear as Trudy had been with me on our walk beside the lake. Colder than the letter Tilda read from my brother. And, strangely more painful than either of the things my sister and brother had said to me, though it also made me feel as if I didn't know who Marlene was, and she didn't know me.

—

Ten years later, and in the final stages of the Covid pandemic, I was getting nothing done in my unstraightened office. I moved through the Trump-PTSD haze as we all did for a while, not really knowing what just had happened, not knowing, really, what to expect. I randomly threw papers away or dazedly put them back where I had picked them up, when I ran across that letter. I needed to think it through. It struck me differently than it had ten years before, when it had only made me angry and sad.

Marlene was mad at me because Guy had written a letter to the judge asking him to reconsider Amos's twenty-year sentence.

Guy had never visited Jermayne with me, but would only remark, "Why do you let Marlene tell you what to do?" I thought I had communicated with Marlene okay during the time when she allowed me to visit. I had met her standards, driven three-and-a-half hours round trip to spend one hour with Jermayne, consulted Marlene on the worst Saturday of my life, not allowed Amos to leave with Jermayne without her permission. Of course I didn't think he was a good father! I didn't leave him alone with his daughter. Doesn't trust me! I remembered my father once saying to me, "Why do you always try to please everybody?" *You taught me to!* I thought to myself.

It's true Guy and I had paid for a lawyer to restore Amos's visiting rights, as our lawyer had advised us that there was no possibility that he could take custody. To the best of my memory.

And Marlene? Marlene had left Jermayne in the care of Maddie at a time when she knew Maddie was using drugs, if not selling them. Maddie had allowed her lover into the house and left Jermayne and Amos in the living room while they retired to the bedroom. This was good parenting? It took Marlene years to finally commit Maddie to a mental hospital for treatment. How did I know all this? I don't remember.

I felt guilty when I read that letter. Wasn't Marlene doing the best she could? I could see why she thought the way she did, but she was mistaken. Jermayne loved her father, if not me. There is more than plenty of evidence that parents are critical to a child's successful attachment at the age Jermayne had been—Jermayne, who had already lost her mother's attention. Marlene was a trained family counselor; didn't she know that?

At the time I got the letter I had cried like I never did before, all day long. I wept, howling and foolishly hiding so I wouldn't have to talk to Guy. I thought he didn't feel my pain like I did. Like I didn't feel his about Amos. Guy found me and held me, apologizing. "I'm sorry," he said. I remembered what my first mother-in-law said to me when I divorced my first husband. "You can't divorce a mother-in-law, you know," she smiled and held me, the last time I ever saw her. I guessed step-grandchildren were just the same.

I sent Jermayne one last letter, hoping I could tell her one more time that I loved her and nothing would ever change that. It came back quickly, stamped with angry red letters and a finger pointing, so it seemed, right at me: RETURN TO SENDER.

I increased my daily drinking. There wasn't anybody I could turn to. Guy did not want to talk about Jermayne, Amos, or Marlene. My sister and I still weren't speaking. When I talked to professionals, I felt like I was in a movie about somebody else who didn't have as many *details* as I did. The advice they had to give didn't apply to me because it didn't take account of how *normal*, how human, everyone was. They misheard me tell a story that had a plot, and the plot just wasn't there for me. Perhaps I was too hard on Amos, even Marlene. Could she really be as cruel as she seemed? Know not what she did? Nevertheless, I was badly hurt and I blamed Amos for the majority of it.

Then, one day I turned to my friend Natasha again. I wasn't sure why I trusted her so much, but I did. She interrupted my story.

"Did you know that I had a daughter who ran away when she was sixteen? I didn't see her for fourteen years. I didn't know whether she was alive or dead." Natasha speaks slowly, so it took her a long time to get all this out.

I was shocked that I didn't know this. "How did you live with it?"

"I made myself follow two rules," she cautioned. "First, I only thought about her one day a year, on her birthday, and I let myself think about her all day. On every other day of the year, I didn't think about her. Second, when something happens that hurts, cry about it right away and cry until it's gone. Then let it go. That way you don't have to carry it with you."

"And? You said fourteen years." I was afraid to ask whether her daughter was still alive.

"She came back."

"And?"

"She never told me where she had been or why she left."

"And?"

Natasha shrugged. I know we were on the telephone, but I swear that's what happened.

As I let Natasha's advice sink in and take hold, a thought came to me: I didn't trust Marlene, but pretended to. How then could she possibly trust me? So, I wrote her a final letter. I had nothing more to lose. I said everything I really thought about her—that she was cruel, that she was wrong, that she couldn't make Jermayne's love for me go away simply by saying it wasn't so. I don't know whether Marlene read that letter or threw it away, but it didn't come back like the ones I sent to Jermayne.

It didn't matter to me anymore what Marlene thought. She had told me there was no way I could change her. It didn't even matter what I thought—that I wasn't Jermayne's "real" grandmother. What mattered was that I really loved her. Besides, another "worst hour" of my life was behind me, wasn't it? And I had survived it.

—

Guy had told Amos he had to apologize to me, and he wrote me a letter that said, "I'M SORRY," but oddly, he didn't seem to understand what he had done to hurt me. He was always willing to say he was sorry, but he never meant it, or maybe just didn't understand what *sorry* meant. I wrote back to say I hoped we could both learn something from each other. He never wrote me again, nor I him. Maybe it was the people who *didn't* apologize to me that I had to trust—at least I knew that they were being honest.

Years later, Amos came up for parole. I wrote to the parole board explaining that I did not want Amos released as I did not trust him to do what he promised, but that I bowed to their superior experience. They let him out, but my letter caused great consternation to Guy.

When he finally got out, Guy told me he was coming up to retrieve some of the belongings we had saved for him. Guy would not be home that afternoon, and the morning of the visit I found myself in a panic. There were lots of guns around our house, inherited from Guy's father, and I felt I had to get rid of them before Amos came. So I loaded them three or four at a time on the four-wheeler, strapped them down and transported them with great difficulty to an empty and locked shed on a faraway part of the property. It took me all morning. I still can't remember why, but I remember the panic. Amos came and went without bothering me.

Guy became more and more antsy, finally approaching me about having Amos come and live with us until he could get settled. I said he could come—it was Guy's house, too, after all—but that I would leave. We thrashed our way through that with some help. All we needed was a witness to our discussions, our anger, our fear. I had talked a few times to Trudy about Amos and she had given me some good advice, and she also knew Guy. So we asked her to witness. She could hold us to be honest and fair—and compassionate—with each other. She didn't have to say a word. It was hard. We didn't keep silent and it worked, as least insofar as we got through it. My busy mind just watched without comment putting all of its energy into not yelling.

Still, it was a difficult time for Guy, and for me to watch, wanting to help as Amos gradually found a job, a home, a community to his liking. He enrolled at the community college and attended parole counseling and some retreats for wounded warriors provided by the National Guard.

—

But again, Amos was imprisoned on drug charges. It was over for Guy, or at least I was not aware that he was in communication with Amos. It was probably never over for him.

I asked Natasha for help again on this subject, and she reminded me that when there is family dysfunction like this, it is always because someone in the family is mentally ill. That makes sense to me again, and I let Amos go.

Then, Amos was released again on parole, and I vowed to protect myself against him without apology now. In fact, I am not sorry. It isn't me who did anything wrong.

After Guy and I settled in again with ourselves and Amos settled far enough away that he didn't ask to live with us again, I found I could pay attention to my ordinary life. I had almost sixty years of disorder behind me. My mother complained in my baby book that I wouldn't hang up my clothes at age two. Suddenly, I can't stand the messiness of my house. I spend a block of my day straightening it up, not cleaning it, just putting things away, lining the pencils up parallel to the edge of the kitchen desk, tying all the string ends together and rolling them up in a ball, (*where can they all possibly have come from—why do I keep them anymore?*), pushing Guy's work boots up against the wall on the slate of the sunroom/hothouse floor. When I have had enough, I turn to look out at a rainy day and my garden.

At the end of the box where the beans are rotting instead of sprouting, the comfrey is rampant and even beginning to bloom. The tomatoes are bedraggled but alive. I remember last year, when the tomatoes struggled all summer and produced such sour fruit that I had to add honey to the spaghetti sauce I had made with it. I think I should pull this year's tomatoes and plant kale and chard. But who wants a garden without tomatoes?

My glance falls on a maroon, ceramic tile leaning up against the wall behind the sink. With the black silhouettes of a branch reaching across the top and of a small bird sitting on it, down in one corner it reads, "If I keep a green bough in my heart, the singing bird will come." I laugh and catch my breath: *I am made to laugh*, I think. I pick up a trowel and start out to transplant sunflowers along the fence. The rain has sprinkled and passed, and a rainbow shows a pale curve in the east. Nobody sees it but me.

Part III

Chapter One   LUNCH WITH TRUDY

I'll be loving you, always.
Irving Berlin

What with Trudy, Chuck, and Amos in some kind of stasis, I had to get used to the feeling that something was always wrong and accept that my life didn't make sense and that I had no control over it, but I could go on with it and not have to apologize for it. An unsettled feeling settled in my stomach: They say bad things happen in threes, and I had two behind me. What was left?

I'd been thinking about death more and more, ever since I went back to get Dad. It stalked me, always behind my back, it tickled me on the bottoms of my feet and under my armpits, it strangled me to the point of fainting. When I'd eat a new food or take a new pill my first thought would be: *This will kill me.* When I undertook a trip to town, I envisioned the car sliding off the road and turning over. Every time the other grandchildren came to visit, I saw them jumping off the barn roof into the snowdrifts covering the metal fenceposts—impaled! *What a tragedy at such a young age.*

A friend once told me her husband had confessed to something similar. She also reminded me of what she had said years before at the beginning of my Alzheimer adventure: "You will need each other after they die." As long as they had been alive, I knew what I was doing. But now I was so not okay. *Just ignore it,* I thought, the brain winding down, perhaps even in preparation for the end. So, what if I got Alzhammered?

Hadn't I already had it? Wasn't I able to function all right with the people who knew me?

Nonetheless, a fist of fear sat clenched at the bottom of my throat as the sensation of a lump every time I swallowed. I had lost my whole family, both my families, not just Mom and Dad. I might think I had swallowed that, but my throat told me otherwise.

I had Guy and his family, and that was who I was now. I still missed Jermayne and told myself that she would sometime visit us of her own accord a decade from now when she was eighteen and no longer under the control of her other family.

And I could count on Guy. I remembered that just before we were married, I was so scared that once I went to him in tears and confessed, "I don't know if I can promise *'til death do us part*. You know, I was married once before and promised that. Then I had a ceremony once with a fellow I lived with for five years. We promised to try to stay as long as we could. Maybe we should just do that."

Don't worry, he smiled at me. "Just do your best. That's all we can do."

—

My sister called from out of the fallen sky. The blue screen on the cell phone said who she was.

I didn't hesitate. "Hello?"

"Hi." She paused. "I miss you." She paused again as my heart flipped. "Do you want to have lunch?"

I tried not to gush. "Yes." Just the facts ma'am, down to business. We agreed on a time and place.

I arrived a little early; Trudy was right on time. The lunch was simple, and we sat comfortably inside the old grain-elevator-turned-cafe on rickety old wooden chairs.

"It's really good to see you," she said, hurriedly settling her coat on the back of her chair and sitting down across from me. She raised her eyebrows, but with nothing I could call a smile. Perhaps she was nervous too. We exchanged a couple more half comments.

"It must have been hard to be my sister," I tried to open a way, not knowing where it would lead. I imagined us rolling up our sleeves.

"It's okay," she replied, looking across at me with wide-open eyes. "It's just what Mom and Dad taught us to do." She tilted her head, now grayer than it had been the last time I saw her. "It wasn't our fault."

That was it. We spent the rest of the hour relaxing into talk about joyfully mundane and frivolous whatevers, and made plans to see each other and do things together real soon.

After that lunch, we set about really talking to each other—about friends and food and books and what we had done with our lives and what we still had to do. She treated me to concerts, played with our dogs. It was a miracle. Getting to know each other again for the first time in maybe thirteen years, we made a point of seeing each other every week at an exercise class, then talking after she made dinner for us at her house. I would stay the night. We occasionally mentioned the Big Trouble glancingly. We talked a lot about Amos, back in jail on drug charges and breaking parole. No resolution on that score, but I ignored it.

We didn't forget about the pain of that time when we weren't talking to each other. We forgave it and moved on still without talking about it or understanding it. Chuck kept in contact with emails with the usual politics and jokes and his own family, and I presume Trudy got some of these too. I was willing to forget that it wasn't over, or really maybe that was a kind of self-denial. My mother whispered to me again, "Trust in the Lord...." But it made no matter how often I sang "Red, Red Robin." I could only be strong by accepting that we all had Alzheimer's. That worked for me better than forgetting and the silence of not remembering.

Chapter Two OUT OF TIME

Sing me a song of a lass who is gone,
Say, could that lass be I?
Robert Louis Stevenson

I was running out of time. I was in my sixties and did not want to live the rest of my life in the turmoil I had been in since 1999. I needed to find some shade from the daily glittering thoughts about the ruin of both my families. Stop listening when Mom sang her songs? I tried to will it so, and failed.

I reminded myself of how strong I'd been before, when being strong was my only choice: leaving my first husband, quitting my many jobs. With not enough in my pocket, I sang "moving, moving, moving, keep those wagons moving." I decided to look for moments that did not test my strength. I settled down into my life with Guy, hanging onto the other grandchildren, my garden, and my retirement career as a back-of-the-book indexer.

But then my body, which had been quiescent since the lunch with Trudy, began to speak to me. I developed sores on the ends of both my long second toes. I soaked them in Epsom salts, I soaked them in vinegar, I soaked them in the hottest water I could stand—then the coldest. My massage therapist told me to try Listerine. Done. Nothing helped. Finally, one Friday night they were so swollen and red and beginning to bleed along the edges, that Guy told me, "Go see the doctor."

I called my nurse practitioner. She wasn't worried, but I still was. I raced into Emergency Care. The doctor who saw me recommended an echocardiogram. *What?* "Sometimes the heart will throw off blood clots that migrate to the extremities," she explained. I called the NP back. She made that bpbpbpbp sound you make at children when they ask a childish question. "Just wait. I'll get you in to see a heart specialist."

The specialist said no, he wouldn't get an echocardiogram, even if it was himself, but relented enough to schedule a stress test at the hospital. Normal, normal, normal. "If I were you, I'd keep on exercising and run your heart rate right up there."

I wasn't strong enough for this. My heart was leaving me, how can anyone be strong enough for that? I increased my vitamin D dosage to 5,000 units a day and overindulged in vitamin Bs, which I then excreted into our groundwater. I started exercising more. I lost twenty-five pounds. I was eating only food that had no more than one ingredient, and that ingredient was never sugar. I still felt nauseous all the time. I looked farther afield. I got serious about sitting in front of my light box every morning during winter. I took a six-week course in mindfulness meditation and learned that I didn't have to think, and I practiced how not to.

I bought a deck of tarot cards and a bag of runes.

—

In the spring of 2011, I suffered my first and most extreme attack of acid reflux. I had accepted too much work. I am a back-of-the-book indexer. (You know—those things in the backs of books where you look up what page something is on? You need an actual human to write those, and I am one of them.) There were three projects scheduled neatly one week after the next, and when they all appeared on the same day, I did not notify the editors that this would not work for me. I would make it work.

Moreover, every time I booted my portable, Adobe asked me if I wanted to install version 9 of Adobe reader. But I had version 10.1.14. Even my computer was stuck in the past. What was wrong? It should know better. I opened my trusty spreadsheet and budgeted three three-hour work sessions a day, one for each index, extending without weekends into the twilight of the future. My back and neck got so sore that I had to do my working stints standing. I called on and found that my inner Superchild had not grown into Superwoman.

My heart heated up one night so badly that I couldn't sleep. I went to the doctor. He told me to take Omeprazole, a proton pump inhibitor for acid reflux. I did, and it took away the pain, but I wasn't happy when he ruled that I had to take it for the rest of my life. Like other medications I had taken that cause imbalances in the body, this one cures the pain by repressing the normal production of acid in the stomach. So the stomach responds by making more, putting you at a dysfunctional disadvantage. I weaned myself off slowly and went back for more mindful meditation.

Raising my sights all the way to the horizon, I went to see a naturopath. She gave me oils and powders and potions and pills (more vitamin Bs!), told me to keep exercising and to think about my stepson and my issues with not being allowed to see my granddaughter.

So I worked hard on learning to live with unending symptoms and fear-triggers, and even how to relax, especially when I was working, doing what I was supposed to do. But I was running out of time.

—

One Friday in June, Dog slept at my feet while I worked, making smacking noises with his mouth—sounds that reminded me of the smacking of the woodstove logs afire for the last time months ago. It was the week of the solstice, the time of year when everything is still, and the stillness is canny. It is an awareness that the sun is about to stop and turn around and go the other way. Nothing breathes, all rests in eternity for the blink of an eye. At the instant of solstice everything stops, not just the sun. Even the trees and the clouds are not moving, the crickets are quiet, I cannot hear running water.

I looked out my window and see my peonies blooming. They took me back to my mother and her line of peony bushes along the back fence. Now, I have three of them placed at the ends of three garden boxes and facing three different directions of light. They are all happy. One is white and two are red. I caught myself daydreaming in my mother's backyard and, came back into my body, for the first time realized what other flowers my mother grew besides peonies that are in my garden too: pink and yellow rose bushes outside my bedroom window, johnny-jump-ups along the front walk, tulips, daffodils, a sweet cherry tree, ageratums, (in our family called "Major Adams," named by Trudy after the main character in the *Wagon Train* TV show), and of course, the sour-cherry bush. I wondered in what other ways my mother lived in me.

Dad was different in that regard. If he could have had his way, he would not have allowed any plants in the house. They leave rings on the tables, get in the way, like much of our lives got in his way. There were few pictures hanging on our walls growing up. I remember perhaps four or five. After he had driven the nails into the walls, Mom was not allowed to change her mind and move them to a different place. So from the time I was five until I left for college there was a painting of a farm over the fireplace, a replica of Van Gogh's sunflowers in the hall next to the dining room, a pair of young gypsies in two dark frames over an end cabinet next to the couch in the living room. Nor do I remember that our artwork from grade school even made it to the refrigerator, but that couldn't be right.

The nursing home should have been a comfortable place for Dad: There were no carpets to clean or trip over, no irons to check to see if you remembered to turn them off, no plants. Everyone had the same furniture in their rooms, and no, you were not allowed to hang a picture on the wall without special permission. The janitor had to do the honors of the proper hole drilled in the proper wall. And no, you couldn't change your mind or move it once it was hung. But Dad didn't like it there. He didn't *live* there. I thought, *in the nursing homes, life gets in the way and the nurses take it out on you and of you, until you die.*

When I caught myself sailing into the nursing home a decade before, I called myself back to work. I had taken on an emergency index from another indexer who had emailed, "Can you take this one? I won't be done with the one I'm working on for another week. Can we switch?"

I jumped at it.

I'd hardly started the project when Sarah murmured out loud, "But that's me!" Sarah and I were looking down in wonderment at page eight of Kenneth M. Adam's book *Silently Seduced* in my lap that read:

> The following are some common characteristics resulting from the silent seduction of a covertly incestuous relationship. If you find yourself in these descriptions of characteristics, this book is for you.
> 1. Love/Hate Relationships. *Sure, loved and hated all my guys.*
> 2. Emotional Distance from Same-Sex Parent. *Oh, sad. I had been so close to Mom. She was a good mom. But, you know, I really never touched the private part of her. She was opaque to me. She never spoke to me about Dad, except in the most external way. Never criticized him. Never even acknowledged a criticism of him. And fell asleep when I came into conflict with him.*
> 3. Guilt and Confusion over Personal Needs. *That's me. Always has been. What do I want? I don't know.*
> 4. Feelings of Inadequacy. *Me.*
> 5. Multiple Relationships. *Me.*
> 6. Difficulty with Commitment. *ME!*
> 7. Hasty Commitments. *ME!*
> 8. Regret over Past Relationships
> 9. Sexual Dysfunction.
> 10. Compulsion and Addiction. *ME! ME! ME!*

My eyes grew bigger than they could, to take all this in faster than possible.

Hunh. Sarah/I took a sip of forbidden coffee. *Huhn. Eight out of ten. This book is for me?*

I looked up and away, riveted to my next thoughts: *You mean, other people don't live like this? You mean, I don't have to live like this?*

Now a thought grabbed me by the throat. *You mean, I could be HAPPY?*

Sarah's memory threw up a father in a bathtub with a little girl. *It is abuse, sexual abuse, and yet Sarah has never called it that. Now, for the first time, I do call it that.* "It's abuse." I said it out loud.

"You mean—but when we had those discussions about parents taking baths with their children, remember? Around the time, just before Amos was jailed for sexual abuse, you said, 'I took baths with my father. Nothing wrong with that.'" I cross-examined Sarah.

"I thought it was normal!" Sarah thought. "The funny thing is, that memory, it's not like other memories. It's like a still photograph, but it's in 3-D. I'm looking at it from somewhere above the tub and we're not moving. Then we are, but I can't see us. Then, there's a second, separate one. I just have this feeling of slippery, firm and soft, and it's happening to my body, but somehow my tweenie's not attached to my body, or, I'm not attached to it."

As I engaged Sarah further now, she couldn't think fast enough—the memories came rushing at her, each one a story I've heard many times before. Each story with a new meaning now, a new ending—a new, uncertain future. A label where before there was none.

"It's not normal for a man always to have an erection. Until I saw my first man naked, I thought that when little boys grew up, their penises just grew longer and fatter."

"But you saw your brother naked?"

"He was a boy. I never saw him naked after we hit our teens."

"It felt good!"

"What?"

"It felt good. I know, I'm not supposed to say that. But it did."

"Remember that dream I had in college? That my father stood in front of me with a vacuum cleaner attached to his body at his groin, and he put it in my mouth? And what about the one, you know, where my mother is hanging up the wet laundry in the basement of the house where I grew up. She pulls me out of the basket, reaches in and pulls me inside out, then flaps me like a shirt to get the wrinkles out—and hangs me out to dry."

Hangs me out to dry.

Hangs me out to dry

My body is taut and clear and feels something not exactly relief—something more expansive and free. It has been decades that Sarah had wandered, bright and confused, through her life. She'd been anguished, energized, depressed, creative, mystified. Now the pieces fell, fitting next to each other without jamming. I felt her relax, fall apart, and breathe. She started to cry, then it intensifies. It didn't stop for twenty minutes or so. I didn't try to stop her. I didn't say a thing.

By that time, I was taken over by the news, fascinated—like watching the Twin Towers fall over and over again on TV. *Everything exists outside time, forever. I'm taking a bath with my father. We are playing. Only now I recognize it. He isn't playing. He has an erection. I'm looking at it from above. It stands still, like a snapshot in an album.*

I've had this memory all my life. Think about it a couple of times a year. Remember it during a conversation I'd had not many years past about whether taking baths with children was all right and at what age you should stop. I'd contributed to that conversation, "I took baths with my father and it was fine. At some point he suggested we take a bath and I said no and he never asked again." I had that same picture in the bathtub return to me in that conversation, arousal and all, but my brain just didn't take the step of naming it, and so it had no significance. I didn't understand it until that moment before the cold woodstove.

The snapshots kept coming: *I am at the dinner table. My father is at the head of the table. I sit at his right hand. My brother, a lefty, sits to my right, bumping me with his elbow. My sister sits across the table from me, and my mom across from the brother. Dad looks at me and says, "Who wants to take a bath!" smiling, eager. I feel dread like a tidal wave, move me in my chair. Surprised at myself I say, "No. I don't want to." I said no, and he never asked again.*

I am in early adolescence, and my father is on top of me on the living room floor, "squiggling" me. Tickling me, that is. The dread comes. I can't breathe. I say "Stop!" he doesn't stop until I start to cry and go rigid. Finally, he gets up and, looking down at me says, "I'm sorry." I don't understand what has happened. I used to love being squiggled, but suddenly it is dreadful, and I just turn away and flee to my room.

I am a baby. My father is holding me up in the air. I don't have anything under me. I'm afraid and angry and start to cry. He lifts me a little higher and licks me between my legs. That confuses me and scares me even more, and I scream.

Sitting there, eyes numb, bulging and locked to page nine, seeing it but not reading it anymore, I realized that the dread was not normal. The baths were not normal. Now I recognized them for what they are: *Abuse! Abuse! My dad abused me. Abused his daughter.* Loud and clear.

I held my breath for as long as I could, but the body took over and when the breath came back, it came out crying. For who knows how long. However long it was, it felt good.

Suddenly, I was free. Free like I've never felt before. It makes sense, coheres, gives me pause, perspective, and possibilities. What will be will be is no longer something to fear.

That's not the only thing that felt good, as I fell back into and choke as a memory appears that I had never had before. *Dad puts me astride his penis and pulls me back and forth. It feels good.* I remember bits of things I read about sexual abuse: That the victims feel guilty because they enjoyed it. That they think they wanted it. That it is their fault. I don't feel that kind of guilt, I know it was my dad right from the beginning who had initiated it, and that he was wrong. I am not angry. I am astonished and a little sick. What—can this be true? Can this even be possible? How can this be true? Why can this be true?

—

I was drowning in the need to tell someone, *right now*. To get it out of my brain and my chest and into the brains and bodies of others where it will not cause the chaos it causes in me—others who can tell me what to do.

Guy was on a camping trip with some friends and wouldn't be back until the next week, but Trudy was scheduled to come over and spend the night with me at my home on the top of mountain the next day. I didn't want to tell her this on the phone, so I called a friend of mine a couple of thousand miles away and told her.

"Oh, Sarah," she breathed my name as she often did when I told her about some unbelievable challenge or another in my life. "You must see someone who can help you. Do you have a therapist?"

Oh, right. Of course I do.

We had a short conversation, not very much about what was happening to me, and then I called Tilda. Only the machine was there, so no help at all.

Tilda called me right back and we arrange for a meeting on the following Monday.

"Are you all right until then?"

"Yes, I think so. Trudy is coming over tomorrow night, then we're going kayaking on Sunday." It had been two years since Trudy had ended our communication blackout and we had had lunch. In that time, we had built back our sisterly relationship by taking an aerobic class twice-a-week together. Those nights, I would leave the class with her and we'd make dinner at her house, and I'd stay overnight. We were closer than we had been for the previous decade, maybe even for most of our lives. Now, I was grateful that she had come back to me.

"Well, call if you need me before then," said Tilda.

—

Back to my work by the cold woodstove, snapshots subsided and in my right mind, I finished indexing an entire chapter by the time I rose from the chair. It was late, and I was tired. I had no trouble falling asleep.

Chapter Three

TRUDY RETURNS

Through all kinds of weather
What if the sky should fall?
Just as long as we're together
It doesn't matter at all
Harry M. Woods

After a long, wet spring, the rain finally stopped. The next day I was back in the garden, planting carrots (in the same place they grew last year, just to be safe) when Trudy arrived. We were able to sit on the deck for the first time this year. The sun was promising to shine fully on us, instead of slyly looking through the clouds as she had done those last months. I was humming one of my favorite tunes from the sixties. Mom was signalling me what to watch for during the day.

The beer in my hand when Trudy arrived was my second one. We went outside, and I left her watching the lake and the sky to go inside to get her a glass of wine. I sat down facing her on the edge of a wooden deck chair. She crossed her legs and leaned forward with her elbows resting on the arms of her chair, chin thrust forward, both hands around the stem of her glass, and talked eagerly to me about our plans to go kayaking. I waited for my turn to speak, then I said, "I have some big news."

She frowned and tensed, putting the glass down on the iron table nearby. "What?"

I hadn't thought at all about what I would say or how it would affect her, or how she will respond. I just needed to tell. "I had some memories today that I'd never had before. Dad abused me."

There is no pause. "That son-of-a-bitch," she said, spontaneously relaxing back into the chair. She uncrossed her legs and stretched them out to cross them again at the ankles. Her body let go, sank back with abandon, and her arms stretched the length of the long, broad arms of the chair. Her hair loosened itself from a scrunchie and swung free around her ears. Her fat earlobes got fatter; her eyes lost the wrinkles surrounding them. Or so I was struck.

My sister was a budding Buddhist (aren't they all budding?), and on top of that I don't think I'd ever heard her call anyone an SOB, even the CEO of the oil company that spilled all that oil in the Gulf, killing so many fish and birds. She shocked me with the language, but she herself was not shocked.

"I figured out ten years ago that something really bad happened in our childhood. This is it," she said.

Her reaction is fast, but it's not because she hasn't thought about it. I sensed that in the way that her body seemed to suddenly come together, become comfortable, fill up her skin. Like we had been blown apart and now fell back together. What I said perfectly fit her experience of what was real. The pieces of her and the pieces of me fit again, at last.

—

Meanwhile, Guy was due back from his camping trip later that week. That day it felt like I waited a week for him to return. He was riding back with a friend, and the friend's eight-year-old nephew. I knew I would not be able to tell Guy anything until after the visitors were gone. It would require some discussion, some explanation and some holding of me in his safe arms. So when he texted me he was on his way, I texted back: "Have had memories of abuse by my father. I will be weird when you arrive home, but am all right. We'll talk after they leave."

And then ... no answer! It was hours, more hours I spent sweating out the stories tripping over each other: *He is mad. They had an accident.*

He doesn't believe me—oh, now she's really gone off her rocker. He doesn't want me anymore. But at last, he called—worried and warm: "Sorry! We went out of cell phone range just when you texted!" *It would be all right.*

But it wasn't all right when they arrived. We had no opportunity to talk—for days. And it wasn't any better when they left. Panic rose in me, up to my eyeballs. The lump sensation in my throat grew lumpier. I told Guy about what had happened; I saw the compassion in his eyes. He held me. But I didn't cry.

I don't know what would've happened if no one believed me, or even if it took a while for them to believe me. My sister and my husband believed me in an instant. It must've made sense of some their other memories too.

The memory is there and always had been. It is unmistakable what we were doing. Sometimes I entertain the idea that it would be a distortion of something else, perhaps an image that embodied an emotion caused by something else—not factually accurate but emotionally accurate. Perhaps he did something that generated emotions in me like those that come with hidden incest. The book I had indexed said that things like that could happen. I was used to interpreting these sorts of unconscious, ambiguous images in my dreams. But, no. A five-year-old girl would not have those kinds of emotions, except from sexual abuse. A five-year old would not imagine adult arousal, would not have enough knowledge to know what it is. I had had this memory *all* my life. There was no time before it. I had believed into my teens that when boys grew up their penises grew erect as they grew older and remained that way all the time.

But none of that meant everything was hunky-dory. There were more pieces of the puzzle to come that would have to be fitted into the picture. It meant more processing for me and Trudy, and more for me and Guy, who were most likely looking at different memories from mine and fitting them into different pictures. As for the brother, the seed would fall on stony ground.

In one phone call Trudy told me, "You were always the lawyer for us at the dinner table."

"The lawyer?"

"Yes, you protected us."

"From what?"

"I don't know. You always could talk Dad out of whatever he wanted us to do."

—

I had the appointment with Tilda on Monday, and met with her for six weeks. And over those weeks there were more memories that surfaced, memories that had not been with me all my life. And about a week after Guy returned from his camping trip, a paranoic fear clutched at me.

When he disappeared to the barn that day to clean his rifle, there was just one story that could not get itself fast enough nor often enough through my brain: He was going to kill me. It didn't matter why. It was true as far as I was concerned, and I needed to get gone. I shoved a toothbrush in my pocket, but on the way downstairs to the garage, took enough of a breath to realize that this was insanity. I thought to call Tilda.

"What's going on?" I asked, dreading that she would want to take me to the mental hospital in the next city where Tom's father had been so mistreated. I had to know.

"Calm down, everything is all right," she soothed. "Did your father ever threaten you if you told anyone about the abuse? I bet he did. It's not uncommon for abusers to threaten their victims." I still did not see my father exactly as an abuser or myself as a victim, but I had slowed down enough to see that what she said could have happened in other abuse cases. "You've spilled the beans now to Guy, and your little girl is afraid you will be killed for telling."

"I don't remember a threat," I began, "But I believe you. What do I do about Guy?"

"Tell him how you feel. He'll understand. He loves you."

"Oh, right." I breathed.

"And come in tomorrow. Will ten o'clock work?"

"Yes."

Tilda also asked me to write down all my memories and bring them with me to the next session, where she would do rapid eye movement therapy. It seems that talking about the memories somehow defuses them, takes the emotion out of them. It worked for me. It was easier for me to talk about them after these sessions, though I did not notice anything remarkable at the time of the treatment. They became my words, my description of them, but the words were out in the world, rather than in the hysterical feeling in my body where they had lived, gagged, for more than half a century.

That was not a fun evening. I did tell Guy and he did accept that I was fearful, but he did not understand it. I asked him to keep the rifle in the barn, and he refused. He needed it handy in case the coyotes came. "I can't go running down to the barn. There won't be time."

I asked him to do it for me just for a little while, but he would only agree to putting it in his office instead of the bedroom. It would have to do.

I didn't know how to make it do for me. I called Trudy. She said, "Well, if he wants to kill you, he'll do it no matter where a gun is." Always the pragmatist. Somehow what she said made odd sense to me, and though it was not comforting, I no longer wanted to leave home. It was enough to allow me to sleep.

—

I was half-way in on the drive to Tilda's the next day, when another memory struck. This time I was looking from behind my own body, sitting on my haunches, facing him. He was standing, naked from the waist down, and his penis not erect. He gritted his teeth and hissed down at me, "If you tell anyone about this, I'll kill you." My brother? What happened? It seemed as if *I* had done something sexual to him, not vice versa. I stopped the car and cried for many minutes, the same hysterical crying that came along with the other memories.

I have brain lock-up about the memory of my brother. It does not seem important to me now to know whether or not it is true. I don't think about it.

Arriving at Tilda's office. I had three more memories. One was in the bathtub—of course, Tilda already knew about those and didn't ask me much about it.

"What else?"

"We are at the dinner table and Dad leans back when he is finished eating. He asks, 'Who wants to take a bath?' Trudy and Chuck shrink in their chairs, looking down and away. There is a glare of anger coming at me from one o'clock where Mom has her place next to Trudy. Dad looks at me. I say, 'No. I don't want to.'

"That was the end of that. He got up and left. I only have that one memory of his ever asking."

"How old were you?"

"I'm not sure. I have a vague sense I wasn't very grown; Dad was still much bigger than I was, so maybe seven or eight? But we are in the dining room that was finished in a remodel when I was thirteen or fourteen. I don't know."

"What else?"

"Dad used to 'squiggle' us—get on top of us on the living room floor and hold our hands over our heads while he tickled our ribs. This one time, I panicked. I started to cry. I just wanted him to get off me, and he did, but it seemed like a long, long time before he did.

"'What's wrong?' he called after me as I fled. I didn't answer. I didn't know what was wrong. Squiggling was something I really liked. I just felt I was in danger. I wanted out."

"That was the only time you remember that happening?"

"Yes."

"What else?"

I looked up from the notes in my lap. This was a hard one, the one I had on the drive in about Chuck. When I reported it to Tilda, she pointed out that I may have displaced the memory onto my brother, because it was so dangerous to believe that my father would kill me.

The six or seven memories that surfaced during those six weeks in 2011 were all accompanied by hysterical crying which I could not control. Oh, I tried out other thoughts about what may have happened with my father. But they came unbidden, out-of-the-blue ones, catching me off-guard and making no sense, crying out of my body and not out of my ruminations—for me those were all touchstones of the veracity of the memory. I put them all aside and waited for Tilda to help me interpret.

—

At the next session I had another memory to tell. One afternoon I was helping Guy to stack some firewood under the deck. I started to stack it and had finished with a dozen or so pieces when he told me to stack them somewhere else. It was the wrong thing to say. We argued. I did not want to redo the work. He gave a good reason why we should do it his way. I recognized that my fury was out of proportion to the situation, and this time walked away to slow my breathing. This was quite a change of character for me. From the early years of our marriage, I had rather run away to a friend's house to spend the night, or more often just light into him.

When I came back and started to move my pile, Guy approached me and tried to hug me. But that other person hiding behind my heart stepped out, and I bent at the waist, straight-arming him with both hands out in front of me, holding him at bay with my hands in the middle of his chest, hanging my head. "Don't touch me," I said, "You are right. But I don't want you to touch me."

Confused, I excused myself and went to the other side of the house and lay back in a deck chair with a beer to chill. As I lay there a memory surfaced. I am in the shower with my father, in my body, my eyes level with his erect penis. He wants me to suck on it; I don't want to. He lifts me straight and pushes me gently against the back wall of the shower. "Why not?" He asks. "Don't you love me? I love you." He leans toward my genitals with his tongue. I bend at the waist, straight arming him with both hands out in front of me, head down.

My whole body begins to cry.

After I calmed down, I explained the memory to Guy and he listened carefully. "You know," I surmised. "He taught me what love is. He taught me that love is doing whatever the other person wants you to do, even if you don't want to do it."

"I see that. That is sick." He paused, but did not take his eyes off mine. "You don't have to do whatever I want."

"I *know* that. The problem is now to *feel* that way too. It is impossible for me not to feel it. Whenever you ask me to do something, I feel like if I don't do it, I don't love you."

He had to think about that. "And I don't love *you*."

"Yes," I hung my head. "And you don't love me."

—

Dad smiles. He is so good-looking. I sit facing him in the bathtub and he says, "If you tell anyone about this, I will have to kill ya."

It's creepy. He says it like he loves me, like he wouldn't like to have to do it, but he would be forced to if I do not obey. If I tell. It's what anyone in his position would do. His eyes twinkle, and he keeps on smiling—or perhaps this last, worst, memory turns into a still. Little Sarah in the tub feels nothing.

And I feel all those years all that fear sitting imprisoned and rotting my brain, unrecognized. I feel it escape now, tangle up my breath before it leaves my body—now, when I am sixty-one years old—and finally howl it out.

Chapter Four

THE LAUGH THAT LAUGHED ITSELF

You made me love you
I didn't want to do it, I didn't want to do it...
And all the time you knew it...
James V. Monaco and Joseph McCarthy

The pieces kept falling like Tetris blocks, and as they appeared I turned them around to fill up all the holes. Memories, not whole thoughts, would pop into my head: Dad erasing the days he didn't exercise. Mom's giving me her wedding ring. Things with a kaleidoscope of meanings that were hard to explain even to myself. I had begun the conversation with Trudy that is still ongoing ten years later, though more scattered than it was those first few months.

I apologized to Trudy in an email, because I chickened out about doing it in person. She wrote me,

> If we can avoid blaming ourselves, we don't have to blame others. Even if you feel like you "should" have behaved differently, even if you enjoyed parts of it—you were set up to be the "3rd" partner—IT WAS NOT YOUR FAULT! We have been pretty good sisters, despite all this shit, and life has not been so easy, but it was still okay. Now it can get even better.

New, important things were going on with me: I understood I made mistakes from not listening because I am bullheaded. Today, I am thinking that this nuclear family stuff has to come to an end, a failed experiment in evolutionary terms. In my body, I'm feeling like I did after my divorce from my first husband: If I dream, I'm tired during the day. But if I don't dream, I feel like I'm crying all the time—eyes feel raw, stomach aching, and chest empty, empty, empty. I am not having crying fits like last week.

I invited Trudy to go to my next meeting with Tilda, writing, "I miss you. I want us to be real sisters."

—

It was time to begin it with my brother. I was afraid of what he would say. I didn't want to surprise him by barging in with an email while he was concentrating on his work or thinking about his own kids. A phone call would be worse. Trudy and I decided she would give him a warning that an email was coming and to be ready and quiet to receive it, and I could send an email the day following.

> Dear Chuck,
> Last week I started having flashbacks of sexual abuse by Dad and was wondering whether you have any inklings about it. There is no question for me that it happened, though I don't have a good grasp of the extent of it. It certainly makes sense of some of the problems that have existed between you and me and between Trudy and me, and I'm hopeful that as this unfolds, we will have a smoother path ahead. It has already lightened up my marriage.
>
> For example, I need to apologize to you both for my role in screwing everything up. I love you both and have missed you most of my life.
> Sarah

He didn't answer for days. I wondered what he was thinking, but I don't remember being worried about it. At some point he finally emailed and suggested he call me, and we scheduled it.

—

He started off talking about things that were going on with his family and in his life. I listened and acknowledged, back in my old anxious self, needing him to come to the point—*right now*. He went on for twenty minutes before he came around to the subject of the call.

He said that he didn't have reason to believe that what I remembered had happened, but that he would go to see a psychotherapist if I thought it would help me. I said it was just information that he might like to have in trying to understand our family dynamics, that I thought he might want to go to work out some of his own stuff. I had seen him lose his temper badly a couple of times when he was tired or the kids were too noisy. It reminded me of the way Dad would suddenly lose his temper and we would be surprised.

But I didn't know that Chuck going to a therapist would help me. Anyway, my understanding is that therapy is valuable only if you want to go for yourself or to work out a relationship. He said he saw that we had wounded each other but that he preferred to let wounds heal and scar over, not dig around in them causing more pain. I don't know if I laughed at this, but I thought—well, *my wounds haven't scarred over for fifty years, why would I expect that to happen now?*

Then there was a noticeable pause in the conversation, and I waited to see what he would say next.

"I'd like to ask you one thing, then." he said.

"What's that?"

"Don't tell my kids." Now it was my brother who wanted to go back to the way we were in the fifties.

I don't think I even answered. I didn't say anything, committing the worst sin our family had proven capable of. More silence.

I found myself again in the dumbfounding cloud that had stifled me on the day in the car with Dad and hotdogs. "Who's Chuck?" Chuck didn't recognize me either.

Another thought struck. Perhaps Chuck had continued the family tradition. I have not thought about that again, but it did strike. And, if so, of course I was exactly the wrong person to ask about that secret thought. Or was I? I knew I was exactly the person who was too scared to talk about it to him now.

Finally, I said, "Well, I don't know what I will do. If they don't bring it up, maybe I won't. But if they ask me directly, I won't lie."

Having little to add after that, we said our goodbyes and disconnected.

After recounting the phone call to Trudy later, she laughed. "Don't worry," she said. "I'll tell them."

—

Tilda's eyes went wide. "How did you know?" she whispered.

Trudy had come with me to the psychotherapy session, and had just finished saying, "Sarah was the favorite. I never thought about it until Chuck said it when he visited Dad in the nursing home. He was right, she *was*."

"How did you know?" Tilda had only begun to shift her eyes from Trudy to me when a laugh, gruff as a smoker's but starting deeper in my chest, shot out of me, like somebody else was hidden inside my whole body, taking up all the space up to just an inch inside my skin, and I had only that surface inch to live in. It took me a moment to understand, but I couldn't say it. I had dissolved almost completely into laughter and had to wait until I could get some breath.

"He treated us all equally in every way . . . but one," I said, still not finding breath for the "A-bomb."

It was true: he'd paid for us all to go to the best schools, encouraged us to. Let us all drive as soon as we were eligible. Gave us all health care—clothing and toys and games and trips and an education. Yes, perhaps Chuck felt that he let me do things sooner than he was allowed to do them. I certainly felt that way about Trudy. (She went to the beach after her Senior Prom, spending the night there. I had to come home and wait until morning for my date to pick me up and take us to the lake.) But it was normal for parents to be stricter with their first born and relax with experience. In Dad's will he said to sell everything and split the money three ways. In one later conversation Trudy looked away from me and said wistfully, "Mom made you heart-shaped birthday cakes. I always wanted her to make one for *me*." My heart wilted. For her, this was at least as traumatic as whatever trauma I repressed. This was how she knew, and she lived with it all through her childhood and into her adult life.

It was unnerving that Tilda even asked us the question, after I had already broken the silence and told her. We were there to talk about the abuse and work our way through it! Wasn't it obvious? Didn't she believe me? What did she expect me to say? He gave me a bigger allowance? But perhaps she was maintaining some kind of psychotherapeutic neutrality, waiting to see if I would uncover some other cause for the memories.

I was the favorite. *That ain't just whistlin' Dixie*, as Mom would say. Now I sounded like a born-again something, like the girl I scoffed at in college who became a Christian because, when she decided to believe in the Christian God, it enabled her to leave her past and her home, and go out and make something of her life.

As the puzzle of my life took shape, my conscious memories started to come and fill up the spaces between the newly revealed unconscious ones that I had repressed: Dad taking photos, tape recording dinner conversations, radio shows. Trudy arguing as a child that "it isn't true if it isn't in the files." The papers we found of his that comprise all the bank statements from the time he opened his first bank account at thirteen until Mom took over writing checks in the late nineties. The chart he kept of his exercises that omitted the days when he didn't do them.

There were other times in my life when I had been sexually assaulted by strangers. But only one experience felt like what was happening to me now, and it was not assault. After I graduated from college, I was having lunch with an erstwhile professor, when he admitted to me that he had fallen in love with me when I was his student. I was flattered and even felt some attraction toward him, but it made me feel squeamish. I got up from my chair and left without comment. But I dreamed I longed for him for years.

Tilda took in all these memories and validated them and my interpretation of them. But she also gave me a warning: "You may want to be careful whom you tell about this," she said, and at first, I thought she was warning me that someone might hurt me if I told. But it wasn't that.

"Some people won't hear you, often because they've had some kind of trauma they haven't dealt with, themselves. They showed us a movie once in grad school in a course on abuse—I'll never forget it. There were three sisters who were all abused by their father, and they decided to confront their mom. Well, they were all sitting there waiting for a response while she was pouring out tea for them, and she didn't respond. She didn't seem to notice what they said at all and just started to talk about other things. It was uncanny."

And sure enough, I was unnerved when some very close friends whom I told about it looked me straight in the eye and went about our conversation as if I hadn't spoken at all. But then I stumbled across something Vaclav Havel said: "Hope is not the conviction that something will turn out well, but the certainty that something makes sense regardless of how it turns out."

—

I dreamed that Trudy was on Mom and Dad's bed and there were some of Mom's dolls on it. She jumped off and asked Mom, "Do I have to take a bath with Dad?"

I wondered why I didn't ask Mom that? But I wouldn't have been so direct. I would have asked, "Is it all right if I take a bath with Dad?" That was a big difference between me and Trudy—she asked if she had to follow the rules, I asked whether what Dad wanted to do was within the rules. Trudy trusted her own judgment; I trusted Mom's. Mom, happy to let everyone do whatever they wanted to do if she could, probably would've answered Trudy's question: "No," and mine, "Yes."

There were other dreams, dreams unmistakably about abuse, which I have a hard time sharing. In one of the milder ones, which was a recurring dream every week or so for decades, there is hair in my throat, making it difficult to swallow and even breathe. I reach deep down and rip it out by its roots. It is very satisfying to do this: like pulling tough weeds out of the garden. But there the satisfaction is fleeting; there is always more hair and it gets harder and harder to pull it out.

In the almost fifteen years since I had these memories, the dreams have never recurred.

—

I read a lot of books and articles about sexual abuse and incest. Some of them said the memories of abuse weren't true, were induced by psychologists in naive children and women. Some of them described the victims as wallowing in their victim-ness and using it as an excuse for their own failings.

It was a surprise to me how many were written by famous women: Mary Tyler Moore; Esther Williams; Marilyn Van Derbur, the Miss America from Colorado whom I'd seen win on TV the year I was seven. I had a college prof whose brother was the psychologist who had counseled Van Derbur. The psychologist said about my case that it sounded very mild, probably only happened once or a few times. Granted, Van Derbur was raped by her father almost every night when she was in high school and suffered major depression and dysfunction in her later life. I had to agree that was much worse. But mild? Like I broke my ankle once, and it wasn't as bad as breaking my neck.

—

One night, Guy settles down with me to watch *Made in Dagenham* a 2010 film about women who went on strike in an auto factory in England for equal pay. We reach a scene near the end of the movie, where the heroine, Rita, is arguing with her husband Eddie, who also works at the plant and has been laid off because the strike has shut down the factory.

The husbands are not being supportive of the women's strike, and Rita doesn't like it. Eddie calls what he is fighting for "rights" and what she wants "privileges."

My gorge rose and I got up and walked away at a clip with my head down as low as it can go, sobbing. Guy caught up with me and turned me around into his chest, hugging me. "That's it, isn't it," he whispered. "That's the heart of it."

The anger twisted and it is sadness it wrung out of itself. It was far more anger than I've had or would ever have.

Abuse is a situation where what is true and what can be talked about are two different things. If that's so, how do we know what is really happening? We must talk about it. I was so traumatized by the threat my father made that I became unsure about what was safe to talk about. I even was pushed so far as to question what I knew to be true, and, unable to change my judgment about it, forgot it.

I couldn't trust my own mind. If that's so, how do I know that my dad abused me? I laugh. The very fact that it is so difficult to talk about is undeniable evidence. The silence that strangles all of us is the force of it. It's too hard to believe. It was the silence that was the worse abuse, because if I had talked about it, maybe my life would have turned out better. Maybe not, though: what if I had told my mother, and my dad went to jail when I was five, and she became a single mother and had to earn a living, and I didn't go to college. Or, what if she just sang "Que sera, sera"? I sink into a swamp. That way lies madness.

In an unbalanced dance, a sort of new learning to walk, I tried getting angry without thinking about it, just reacting. I wrote dismissive emails to my bank, to the people who sent me spam, to my state senator. Most of them didn't answer, but the senator straightened me out pretty fast, if not about the issue, then about jumping the gun and making snap judgments.

I tried again, but never generated any anger at my father, just more sadness.

It happened such a long time ago, it shouldn't matter anymore. But it did, and I wondered how and why? Then I stopped wondering and started to listen.

Chapter Five

LUNCH WITH NATASHA

The experience of ugliness gives the opposite feeling, insecurity—a feeling close to that of fear, horror and anxiety.
R.W. Pickford

Trudy looked sideways across the cafe table at me, her body still turned toward Natasha, and leaning forward, planted her left elbow, the arm tensed in front of her on the table like a battlement. "You couldn't hear what the doctors were saying," she said to me. (Did she say "couldn't"? Or "didn't"? I can't recall.) I took it as an accusation.

Her comment came out of nowhere, and my heart was gripped by one fist of anger, my brain by another of fear. I just nodded stupidly while the thoughts raged, struggling against the iron skin that pinned me back inside myself. Forcing myself to take a breath, I moved my chair back and said, "I suppose, but they didn't hear me either." Trudy turned away to address Natasha, smiling but looking ugly to me nevertheless. My vision tunneled, and I stopped hearing what they were saying.

You didn't hear me, either. You didn't know any of it. You weren't there. You didn't talk to me at all. I may have made things worse for Dad in some ways, but in others I made them better. You looked the other way. I'm not the only one who believes these things: the entire Green House project is based on the same kind of perceptions I had of how patients are treated in traditional Alzheimer's settings. The fact is that you didn't care how Dad was treated.

But... maybe I was the one who couldn't hear the doctors. Was that what Dr. Thomas (himself a doctor) was trying to tell me at the Green House retreat? Same as Trudy not hearing me because the doctors spoke more clearly to her than I did. She didn't have the same feelings I did for Dad. In fact, she had the opposite feelings, so what I was saying didn't make sense to her.

Of course I heard them. They were wrong. I was right about the visiting. I was right about his allergy to Zantac. I was right about the Risperdal. I was right about the physical therapy. I was right about the urine infections. They were wrong: they thought that I was abusing him when I took him to the TV room. They were right about some things: most families wanted them to hide the bodies behind the blue sign neon sign: Alzheimer's. Then the families didn't have to do anything, just pay the fees and shut up.

I said none of this to Trudy, not when Dad was in WholeCare, nor in front of Natasha. It was too dangerous. No telling what would happen. Better to be silent and run home to Guy, who would agree with me.

But I stayed and let the anger run out. As I woke up to the lunch conversation, Trudy was listening to Natasha tell stories about some of the families she worked with in child protective services. How an eight-year-old boy had sat at the family Thanksgiving table and with great calm told the family how he would kill his father and not have to face any legal consequences because he was too young.

Natasha's eyes widen when we tell her about our plan to contact a radio show to do a story about us. Her reaction pulls me up enough to feel the danger in the plan. When Trudy says she would only do it if she were anonymous, it gives me pause. Do I want to do it at all if it is anonymous? It seems a reversion to our old ways: from not speaking to each other, to burying a bleeding hatchet. I have to talk about this. But of course, one of us cannot remain anonymous while another is not.

Natasha is now talking about her liberation in her marriage. "I'd had seven children. It was different then. I was taught as a child, "If you close the bedroom door, someone else will open theirs. So, I never closed it. He was autocratic. He made the decisions. And then he had an affair."

"It happened at a professional conference, and he said, 'You wouldn't come with me to the conference.' As if it was my fault! I chewed on that for a while. Then I closed my bedroom door."

Natasha was calm and with us in the present. She was looking at us, not staring into a space over our heads. She wasn't reliving the experience, just describing it. "And when I was ready to talk, I said, 'Here is what I believe. I believe that you needed to have other sexual experiences, and that you did not want to put our marriage at risk, so you did it far away from home with someone who doesn't mean anything to you. You need to recognize that and go on.'"

I assumed the bedroom door was open, though it was unclear to me whether all the children were already with them when it happened. She didn't tell us anything more. Hard to ask. Was she sorry? Did she still love him in the same way after?

After Trudy excused herself and left, Natasha and I were silent for a moment. Then, she said, "You and your sister reacted very differently. That's a fact."

Duh, I thought—then, *what a funny thing to say*. I asked her what she meant.

"I was shocked that Trudy had a clear enough sense of your father to push him way." She raised her hands and pushed at the air above her head. "I tried to push my father away, but there was nothing there," then put her arms down on the table and leaned forward on them.

That was a show stopper for me. I had spent the worst part of a decade, unable to see my dad from my sister's perspective and unaware of her own perspective. I now run across almost indecipherable notes, inside a book I had been reading at the time of the Big Trouble. My perspective then was "She's so ugly." I feel a pang of shame. It was Trudy who opened the door slammed shut between us, not me. It was she who was willing to forget and forgive, not me.

Natasha was still watching me closely for an answer. I wondered if I was the sister who was mentally ill.

"'It's all very confusing,' said Alice,' I answered," and she smiled, a wan little smile.

I often hear Jermayne's voice singing our favorite song to me the spring before the fog closed around her, the one about how the garden grows. The spiders are fat this spring because it is wetter than usual. The rain is cold, but it is needed to make things grow as much as the sunshine, which is plentiful enough between the bursts of rain. There is so much green in the grass it doesn't fit between the edges of the leaves and crosses over—with the abandon of crayon colors made by a small, tight fist—until you can't see the lines that make the edges anymore, though the shape and attitude of the individual leaf is still there.

One spring morning, I am saying goodbye to Trudy at her front door, when she cocks her head. "Are you sorry?" she asks.

"Sorry for what?"

"Are you sorry you took care of him?"

I don't react. I can't make sense of Trudy's question, as if she thinks me a new person now that I have remembered and labelled the memories. Of course I am not sorry; it changed everything, but it didn't change me. I don't think Trudy is asking for an apology I can't mean.

When I was younger than Jermaine, I sat on the floor of a car behind the driver's seat. I could reach the cigarette lighter at the rear of the front seat console and was burning designs with it into the vinyl back of the seat. I am still not sorry for that, even though my father asked me for an apology. I wasn't sorry, but I said I was, just like my brother did once. After he said he was sorry he added, "Mom told me I had to apologize."

When Dad said he was sorry for squiggling me, did he mean it? I don't think he knew what he was sorry for. Just that it felt like I was reacting to him in a way that he ought to be sorry for. He stopped, that was what was important, sorry or not.

When I hear Mom's voice saying she's sorry, it's more like, "Oh, honey, I'm sorry you have to go through that. It must be awful." Not apologizing for anything she has done, but just for how the garden grows.

Am I sorry? That's not a question for me. It's a question for Trudy.

Does she want me to be sorry? I wanted for a long time for her to be sorry for the way she treated me. For so long I wanted Trudy to feel guilty and to admit that she was wrong when she abandoned me and judged me. At first, I couldn't forgive her if she didn't ask me to forgive her first.

But my sorry question wasn't a question for her, and it's not a question for me anymore either. When I did forgive her, my own pain at the way she treated me left. No, that's not right. I didn't have to forgive her, I had to accept her. When I could stop judging her, there was no need for forgiveness, it just evaporated in the sun of our freedom to be who we are for each other. It happened to me, but not because I tried. It happened all of itself because it had to, and I was coincidentally there when it rained down. It was forgiveness that forgave itself and I wasn't struggling anymore.

Was I sorry that I wanted to see Dad every day and make sure he wasn't hurt, give him something to do and touch his hand, hug him? No, that was all enjoyable for me. It was why I wasn't a saint. It was why Trudy didn't want to do it; it hurt her to see me take pleasure in what was happening between me and Dad *again*. That's my current fancy.

I hesitate too long, and she says, very gently, "The care was very human. I understand it would feel good." Then the elephant standing there rammed into me. The question for me was, "Was he sorry?"

"No, I loved him," I hear myself say to Trudy, finally, ignoring the elephant tracks on my face. "It felt good when he was still alive and before the memories. I didn't feel like a saint, but I was happy knowing that I could make Dad's last days less boring, less lonely, less useless and isolated. I felt like a good daughter, paying him back for raising me." As Trudy and I saw each other more often and got to know each other again, we forgot about the sorry question.

"No, I loved him," I hear myself repeating on my way home. But she is asking about now, too, isn't she? Even *after* the memories surfaced. I do feel good about it. I'm still not angry with Dad; he still seems, as I feel around in my dark mind for some concept, to have some dignity left to him. I loved him. He gave me life and then he abused me—and worse, he made nonsense of a fundamental part of my identity that lasted for six decades. He did something wrong and he knew it.

I recall the part of Van Derbur's book when she confronted her dad as an adult. There was a gun in the scene, but nobody used it. I couldn't make sense of it—she seemed to love her father.

Do I still love him now? I don't know. Does it matter?

—

Soon after the lunch, we had a dinner party.

Our neighbor Henry was standing with Trudy and me in the hubbub in my kitchen, getting ready for a neighborhood dinner. As I handed him a glass of the white wine from the bottle he brought with him, Trudy said something about my abuse memories.

"What's going on?" asked Henry, and I give him the short story, from the longer story always running and changing in my head.

"Doesn't sound so bad," he said as Trudy walks away.

"I don't know who am I now."

"What do you mean?"

"What I can bring and what I have to leave behind."

He took a quick sip. "Why not bring everything?" He laughed raising his glass. "Salut." At the same instant Sarah stepped back into me and we are laughing, too, now in one three-dimensional body.

I scrambled into bed after the party, leaving the dishes unstacked in the sink and on the counters. I needed to write. I wasn't done with the love question. And as I write, my past ran away down a mountain in a cloud burst, deepening crevices, cutting new rivulets, speeding irresistibly in all directions, where the turns and twists are lit brightly for a moment by lightning, then blurred and lost in the rain and thunder of fear and cacophony, until the very past disappears. My Self wanders farther and farther away, never looking back, shaking my head. This is just what happened. I can't imagine that it might have been different in even a small way, nor what would have come of it if it had been. Now Dad is just the man who begot me, cared for me, supported me—loved me, even—and even abused me. I am past it far enough that I can see he was a human being, and that it is not my fault that I love who I thought he was. He didn't entirely break. And certainly, I have not broken at all from the memories but have become more whole—and my younger self has become more whole too. It was a lucky fate that set me free: Trudy was always my real sister. I just didn't recognize it.

Trudy says, "At least we didn't have children and pass on his genes." When it's my turn to walk through the valley of the shadow of death, I will go with *The Origin of Species* in my pocket, and leave my mother's Bible behind, though I'm sure it served her well.

Chapter Six

PSYCHOTHERAPY

The narrative construction of a personal past relies on an interaction between the hippocampus and self-referential processes in the medial prefrontal cortex (mPFC). This process is facilitated by (moderately) emotional events due to inputs from the amygdala. In contrast, in the case of extremely negative (conflictual or traumatic) experiences, the amygdala inhibits declarative memory formation by the hippocampus and an integration of these memories with the self-image.
National Library of Science

"I have done that." says my Memory.'" I could not have done that," says my Pride, and remains inexorable. Finally, my Memory yields.
Friedrich Nietzsche

Tilda used her various techniques to try and help understand me better. Once, when we were deep into it, she asked me a question. I can't remember what it was, only how I responded.

"You want to make me say that!" I was near tears.

She turned so pale, I immediately tried to pretend I hadn't said it, and she went along.

I try to remember what the question was, but nothing ever comes.

I used a prompt I found on a writing site to write a dream about something or other. In the story dream I am my mother, and I am (my mother is) dead. Nobody will talk to me/my mother. It's too weird. *I* can talk to anyone I want to, anytime. And nobody can see me, of course, or even hear me. When I tell them something, they just have a thought. It feels like I am a ghost. I *am* a ghost! (in the dream).

I'm sitting on a high stool in my daughter's kitchen, watching her (Sarah, in the dream) move back and forth between the cutting board and the stove. She is sooooo graceful, slicing the carrots, then sweeping them with the knife towards her cupped hand, bending forward slightly to catch them. In one dancing step she turns and drops them in the stir fry. When I was alive and with her, I loved how graceful she was. Now I can watch her for hours on end.

Sarah picks up a cucumber, and keeping it in her hand, slices toward her thumb.

"Don't do that, you'll cut yourself," I tell her. She sighs and puts the cuke down on the cutting board, imprisoning it with her left-hand fingers and slicing it properly with her right. That's how I know she hears me. I sit down and fold my arms. "Better." I tell her. She doesn't hear that.

She says, "Oh, for heaven's sake." It must be her father talking to her at the same time. She sounds just like him.

The dream switches to Sarah's therapist's office. I ask her why she can't keep a clean house, when her therapist breaks in. "Whose voice is it in your head that says those things?"

Sarah shakes her head. "Why, nobody's voice, I guess, just mine." Then later we start mulling over her divorce, and I said, "Don't be so stupid," or something like that. And she asks, right out loud, "Who's saying that?"

"Your mother, of course," I answer.

And she thinks, *My mother, of course. Oh. I get it.*

I'm not sure what she gets, exactly, because that's all she said. It's easier talking to children. They never stop to think.

—

There are so many people talking to me. My father and mother of course. A lot of them are not even dead. My sister, brother, several friends, and even high-school and grammar-school classmates. And teachers. And TV commercials and the internet. Maybe if I ask, I can find out who is really doing the talking. I try it a few times and it works. I hear all of them telling me things to think. And even still alive as alive can be, I talk to people and they think the thoughts I tell them.

But Jermayne never answers my call, not even in my dreams.

Chapter Seven — ALL THAT GLITTERS

What we consider real is also imagined;
every life lived is also an inner life, a life created.
Margaret Atwood

As Guy pounds up the stairs, Annie the cat trots up right behind him. He leans down to pat the top of her head, and as he does, the cat stretches up, turning her head this way and that to feel the caress, maybe even to return it—who knows? The sun is streaming through the door to Guy's office, just at the top of the stairs. As my husband's gold hand touches the radiant fur, I think: *This is why I love to be alive. This is beauty. This is why I don't want to die.* I close my eyes and recite the old Navajo prayer:

> Walk in Beauty.
> In Beauty may you walk.
> All day long may you walk.
> Through the returning seasons may you walk.
> On the trail marked with pollen may you walk.
> With grasshoppers about your feet may you walk.
> With dew about your feet may you walk.
> With Beauty may you walk.
> In old age wandering on a trail of Beauty, lively, may you walk.

In old age wandering on a trail of Beauty, living again,
may you walk.
It is finished in Beauty.

Sure, my muscles ache. I bruise and tire more easily, my formerly reliable memory is slowly moldering away. Sometimes I allow myself to float in the dark waters of the horror of death for a moment and then swiftly swim away. Still, I am happier than I had ever been in my life, more accepting of Guy's weaknesses and grateful for his strengths: a devotion to work, his forthrightness, acceptance, and a sound night's sleep. After a tumultuous decade, I am too downright worn out to eke out any spare energy for trauma. I can instead sit in an easy chair by the fire and look over the rainbow that hangs by the stair.

But not for long. Today I have a mission. After Dad and Mom died, I volunteered to work for the County Board of Guardian, where I was assigned an elder in assisted living to look after. I like being around demented people, and sometimes I feel more like myself with them than with undemented ones. On the drive into town, I am still thinking about seasons and pollen and grasshoppers and dew and wandering on a trail of Beauty. But by the time I reach my destination, my thoughts have taken a familiar and darker turn. I dreamed of being a mom, but my dream did not come true. My marriage relieved that ache a bit—but then there was the disaster of Guy's son in prison, the resulting loss of contact with my granddaughter. Well, that's as it is, I thought, never quite able to get to the new-age asylum "It's all good." This story had certainly not finished in Beauty. But maybe it wasn't entirely over yet.

I pull back the door handle and step out of the driver's seat with my left foot. As I slide from beneath the wheel, my right hip screams. "Ouch." I say it out loud and make a mental note to move the seat back before getting out of the car next time. But I know I won't do it. I'm in too much of a hurry.

The doors of the assisted living where Betty lives are heavy, thick glass. I push them open and step directly into a living room, archetypal with TV set turned on and nobody watching. I have been Betty's guardian for a year, visiting her once a week for an hour or so, taking her to doctors' appointments. She is demented. I don't really know who Betty is—she is so far gone, and I have little information about her family or her life.

Most of the time I am with her she spews out what the literature calls "word salad." But it isn't really salad. The sentences all have nouns and verbs in them. There is order, an underlying sense of things happening, of people, horses, conflict. Humor, if not exactly jokes. At any rate, she makes me laugh. I enjoy listening to her, and after months of it I detect something there, some kind of communication happening, if only a connection established by one person talking and another one focused on listening to her. The intention is clearly still in her and, as long as she holds my attention, she is successful.

I have been on a vacation for two weeks and now I am visiting her on my regular day. Even though Betty's memory is supposed to be stuck in 1950 inside a wood-frame house with a husband, two small children, and a dog or two—she looks at me and immediately says, "It's about time." Betty knows who I am. Accidental?

Sometimes we go for coffee and pound cake at a local coffee shop. We have a wonderful time, Betty insisting between each bit of cake that I should have some, too, but eating the whole piece herself. Once, when we got back to the assisted living, she grabbed my arm and turned me toward her. "If I have to tell anybody anything," she beamed, "I'll sure tell them. You're the one." And she glittered as she kissed me. Word salad?

Come for the weekly visit, I look around for Betty. Here comes Frankie down the hall, shuffling her feet in bedroom slippers. "Hi, Frankie!" I call. She looks up and smiles at me—so warm, that smile. Even with deteriorating teeth, her face is more attractive than those of the busy aides, frowning while they work at setting tables for lunch. Frankie no longer sports make up, and her clothes are loose and worn. Even the shoes on her feet are not shoes. They are bedroom slippers with hard soles that she wears everywhere, even outside on our walks together.

"Hi," she says, and I can tell she doesn't know who I am.

"Want to go for a walk with me and Betty?"

"Well, maybe. But I'll have to change my shoes." She turns back towards her room. Frankie doesn't have any other shoes, but she will discover that again soon enough, or forget what she's looking for. I follow her into her room.

On the same dresser in the same position as the one in Betty's room, stands her wedding picture, an 8 x 10 sepia print that is hand colored. She is Life-Magazine beautiful, and her dark-haired, military husband stuns me for a moment. "Wow, Frankie, you are so beautiful!" I am careful to keep the verb in the present tense. Frankie blushes and gazes at her husband. "He looks like a kind man, too," I add.

"Yes, he was nice," she answers, keeping her gaze fixed on the photograph. "He died a while ago. I miss him," she finishes, stating a fact. There is no longing in her eye and no regret.

Not finding any shoes, Frankie gives up looking and hustles me back and out the door to her room. I stride away from her down the hall. Before our walk I need to go over some accounts with the director. When I come out of the director's office Betty and Frankie stand arm and arm gazing at the mass-produced painting on the wall of the hallway, just where I left them, mesmerized. I am mesmerized, too. Isn't it the same one that hung in Classic Knolls those many years ago?

"Hello." They don't hear me, or don't respond.

I reach out to touch Betty. "Hello, Betty."

"Oh," she jumps turning to look at me and then turns back to the painting. "Look at that, would you? It's so pretty." Betty uses only four adjectives: nice, little, clean, and pretty. And two adverbs: *so* and *very*. "It's very nice." I cock my head and try to look at it a different way. The artist was skilled in rendering a child's face, but it looks dead to me. The child's straw hat is trimmed with dried flowers. The only other living thing in the painting is the dog who stands straight next to the little girl, not wriggling, mouth closed, not even at dog attention. The painting leaves some doubt whether the dog is even breathing. I also doubt that Betty is being polite, so I shrug. *Eye of the beholder and all that*, I think, lost on her trail of beauty.

Let's get out this stuffy building," I say to Betty. "Want to come with us, Frankie?"

Frankie looks down at what she is wearing, her longish, light-brown hair falling forward around her face. It is still shiny and straight, though streaked with gray. Her hands are open toward me at her side, as she examines the worn, red, polyester trousers and faded cable-knit cardigan. She looks up.

"I guess I can. Is it cold?"

"Oh, no, it's a bright, beautiful day out. You might even be too hot in that sweater."

She pulls it closer around her chest and steps toward me. Betty had taken my hand as soon as I said, "Let's...." Her trigger finger tickles my palm.

We make our way to the glass front doors and push outside onto the macadam drive. I am still trying to forget about time, to come into the moment with these two women who have thirty years each on me and who knows what else. They have surprised me before.

I look up at the newly built housing development to our right, the evergreen trees across the road and the dimensional blue sky above, behind, and even below them. There is no wind. We will go to the cemetery, just a block or so away across the side road that leads down to the river. It is summer, and the cemetery is filled with hydrangeas and oversized bouquets of flowers on the graves themselves. I head to the right, slow down a bit more and let go of the two women's hands.

Frankie and Betty do not usually walk as quickly as I do, but soon they are out in front of me. I lag along feeling the sun's shine on my skin. They head along the cracked sidewalk, Frankie a few steps ahead of Betty. Then I see that the road had been recently repaved and a large drainage ditch dug along each side of it. The ditch is so deep that we can no longer cross anywhere we want to but will have to go a block farther on or farther back on this side to reach a bit of walkway crossing a culvert in the ditch.

"Where are we going?" asks Frankie without turning around.

"To the cemetery," I call. "Look how beautiful it is."

"We don't want to go to the cemetery," Frankie grouses, watching her feet and lengthening her stride. "We'll be living there soon enough. I don't want to go there any sooner."

"Oh, come on," I plead, putting a smile into my voice, though her answer has chilled me. "Just look at the flowers. Everything in there isn't dead, you know. You'll live in my memories too. Do you like hydrangeas?"

"Well, OK," she says, and turns off the sidewalk to cross the road. But the gully is in her way. She stops at the edge of it, looking at the ground in front of her feet. "Hey, Betty, c'mere a minute," she says in a hushed voice, holding her left hand out behind her and feeling for Betty's hand.

Betty hurries as best she can—that is, she presses her lips together and lowers her head like a bull, but, still careful lest she lose her balance, she doesn't move any faster than before. After a few wobbly steps she takes Frankie's hand and comes abreast. Betty, too, stares straight down.

"Oh, it's beautiful," she breathes. "Look."

"Yeah," breathes Frankie back. "I never saw anything so beautiful."

Now I am interested and speed my steps to where they stand. Catching up to them, I look down at the gravel, searching the ground in front of their feet for a dandelion or a lady bug.

"Do you think we could take one home with us?" asks Betty, turning her face up and back towards me. It shines.

"Sure," I say, still unsure of what I am allowing.

"Me, too?" says Frankie, leaning down.

"Sure."

Betty picks up a piece of the gravel, then carefully puts it down and choses another. "I just don't know which one," she says, screwing up her eyes to examine the rock more closely. "They're all so pretty."

I take a reeling breath.

"Why not take them both?" I say, finally getting it. I continue to look and look at the piece in her hand. Its shape resembles that of a piece in a jigsaw puzzle, and I briefly consider whether you could assemble all the gravel in the ditch into a coherent picture.

"Oh, no, I wouldn't do that," says Betty. "I only need one." And she puts the small, irregular, gray and dirty piece of stone in her left hand, under the trigger finger.

After Frankie decides on hers, I take their hands and guide them back toward the crosswalk and the graveyard across the road. I look at the hydrangeas. I feel Betty's hand inside of mine clenched around the rock. Then I take a closer look at these strangers I'm holding hands with.

I don't know who they are, but they're cute.

Author's Note

Memories, then, are peculiar experience—near symbols of the self that both reveal and conceal goals, purposes, desires, and images of the self in the past.
Martin A. Conway

At the very end of writing this "novoir"—a process taking almost twenty-five years—I decided to check the notes I had kept concurrent with the experiences. If it was to be a memoir and not a novel, I wanted it more than anything to be true. And a lot in my notes and the nursing notes verified that it was as I remembered it: For instance, the nurses did not give Dad enough water to prevent urinary infections.

But many things in the notes are missing from the book. Trudy had been doing way more with Mom than I thought. She took Mom on weekend trips and to hear her play music. (I even took Mom to Trudy's concert and was there!) She arranged to send Mom off to visit Chuck. We all walked together to raise money for Alzheimer's research. There is a photo of the three of us celebrating Mom's 80th birthday. Trudy and I put on a Thanksgiving dinner at Mom's assisted living, and she found places to move Mom and Dad when that was necessary. Trudy also did all their financial paperwork and investing, including me in the process. I had forgotten these memories when I first wrote—but I remembered them when I found them in my notes.

Things I wrote in the notes are often warped: The nurses were not selfish and mean; the institutional economic and legal structure simply limited their interactions. And neither were Trudy and Chuck. "It's just what Mom and Dad taught us to do." I was stunned to find that many of my *interpretations* in the notes of who my siblings were and why they acted as they did were *more* warped than what I was writing in the book.

My sister is right to call this my story and not hers. But without her dogged honesty, compassion, and love, the memories that are key to the story may never have surfaced. She is the hero.

November 2024

Acknowledgments: Dona Nobis Pacem

Peering through these shimmering memories, I see that others present with me saw and heard differently. I humbly ask all who read this book to respect the freedom of people to express themselves or not, unprompted, as they have mine.

The Guides: Trudy, Guy, Chuck, Tilda, Tara Brach, Georg Wilhelm Friedrich Hegel, Sigmund Freud, Charles Darwin, Marilyn Van Derbur, and those who do not remain silent.

The Midwives: Christine Martinez, Melissa, Susan, Brenda, Jason Black, Marty Andrucki, Paul Cohen, Paul Rapp, Dory Mayo, Colin Rolfe.

www.ingramcontent.com/pod-product-compliance
Lightning Source LLC
Chambersburg PA
CBHW020326170426
43200CB00006B/290